Jewish Responsibility Towards the Nations
Today and in the Messianic Era

Lighting Up The Nations

RIVKAH LAMBERT ADLER, Ph.D.

Lighting Up The Nations: Jewish Responsibility Towards the Nations Today and in the Messianic Era

Special discounts are available for synagogues, churches, book clubs, corporations, associations, resellers, trade bookstores, and wholesalers. For details contact the publisher at the above address.

Dr. Rivkah Lambert Adler and some of the people mentioned in this book are available to speak at your synagogue, church, fundraiser or special event.

Layout by Alberto Bastasa (abetbing17@gmail.com)
Cover design by Rochel Weiman (kavconnect@gmail.com)
Cover photo by Devra Ariel

ISBN: 978-0-9993789-7-7 (Paperback)

This publication is designed to provide accurate and authoritative information in regard to the subject matter covered. It is sold with the understanding that the authors or the publisher are not engaged in rendering any type of professional services. If assistance is required, the services of a competent professional should be sought. Effort has been made to verify accurate Internet addresses. The authors and the publisher assume no responsibility for Internet address errors.

1. Judaism 2. Torah. 3. Israel 4. Current Issues
I. Adler, Dr. Rivkah Lambert
II. Lighting Up The Nations: Jewish Responsibility Towards the Nations Today and in the Messianic Era

Also From Rivkah Lambert Adler:

Ten From The Nations:
Torah Awakening Among Non-Jews.

100 Days of Thanking Hashem:
A Jewish Gratitude Journal.

Contents

Advance Praise..6

Dedication 13

Acknowledgements 15

Epigraph...17

Publisher's Foreword
Gidon Ariel 19

Editor's Introduction
Dr. Rivkah Lambert Adler..24

Torah Awakening Among Non-Jews
Dr. Rivkah Lambert Adler..32

IN OUR DAYS 39

The Fourth Revolution in Torah Learning
Rabbi Yitzchak Ginsburgh...40

Kingdom of Priests
David Curwin...48

The Oral Torah Dilemma
Dr. Rivkah Lambert Adler..65

Vital Jewish Values for the Nations
Rabbi Elan Adler 69

The Land of Israel Fellowship (A Case Study)
Dr. Rivkah Lambert Adler..78

On Gentiles Studying Kabbalah and Chassidut
Rabbi Amichai Cohen...82

China Discovers Talmud and Kabbalah (A Case Study)
Rabbi Dr. Yakov Nagen..93

Sheva Mitzvot Bnei Noach and The Jews
Rabbi Yitzchak Michaelson 98

My Lesson in Unconditional Love (A Case Study)
By Dr. Jair Jehuda.. 105

IN THE MESSIANIC ERA 117

Universal Recognition of the God of Israel in the Messianic Era
Dr. Rivkah Lambert Adler.. 118

Redemptive Servitude: A Commentary on Isaiah 49:23
Rebbetzin Fraidie Levine 131

Rachel Weeps for Her Children: The Return of the Ten Tribes
AnaRina Bat Tzion Kreisman... 138

Ger Toshav - What Jews Need To Know
Rabbi David Katz... 151

The Third Temple and The Nations
Rabbi Avraham Greenbaum 156

Editor's Conclusion
Dr. Rivkah Lambert Adler.. 166

Request For Reviews 168

ADDENDUM 169

WHO IS THAT GOY? Who may study Torah? Keep Shabbat?
Rabbi Avraham Greenbaum 171

Appendix A: Midrashic Sources On The
Unification of Judah and Israel
Prepared by AnaRina Bat Tzion Kreisman................................... 261

Appendix B: The Seven Noahide Laws
Chabad.org.. 263

Glossary 264

Bibliography 271

Advance Praise for
Lighting Up The Nations

For thousands of years, the Jewish people have been forced into a defensive posture vis-a-vis the nations of the world. Tevye's rabbi's famous quote from *Fiddler on the Roof* summed it up: "May God bless and keep the Czar... far away from us!"

Now that the visions of the Prophets are miraculously manifesting before our eyes and the Jewish people are being ingathered from the exile, our fundamental posture is radically changing. Our fear of the nations is being transformed to blessing and the darkness of the exile is being transformed to light. In *Lighting Up The Nations*, Rivkah Lambert Adler taps into this transformative energy and makes it understandable to theologian and layperson alike.

- Rabbi Ari Abramowitz
The Land of Israel Fellowship (*thelandofisrael.com*)

It is *dvar pashut* (a simple and obvious thing) that it is a central pillar of the meaning of what *Am Yisrael* is - that we are here to share the wisdom of the Torah with all the Nations of the world, and that as we proceed, deeper and deeper, further and further to geula, that will become more and more manifest. Rebbetzin Rivkah's decades of deep devotion to Am Yisrael and geula is truly inspiring.

- Rabbi Shimon Apisdorf
Award-winning author of Jewish books

As the Jewish people are returning to the Land of Israel in an ancient promise coming true in our time, there is a shift happening from the particular Jewish story towards the universal Biblical ideal - in which the Torah has a message for all humankind. Rivkah Lambert Adler is touching on that redemptive chord, which is vibrating, but is not yet being heard by most. This book will help you hear the song of global redemption.

- Rabbi Yishai Fleisher, International Spokesperson for the Jewish Community of Hebron and media personality (*yishaifleisher.com*)

Rachel is weeping for her children, but Redemption is coming! We can sense it. As a non-Jew, I am grateful for people like Dr. Rivkah Lambert Adler who are bringing awareness and building bridges between the Jewish people and those thirsty ones who wish to drink from Judah's well of knowledge regarding Torah. While this book was primarily written for a Jewish audience, mature, Torah-aware (non-Jewish) believers in Hashem will gain a deeper understanding of the Jewish heart and mind as they read *Lighting Up The Nations*. Understandably, it will take a great deal of patient willingness to build trust and understanding between Jews and the nations, but those brave Jewish souls who are willing to step out are prophetically fulfilling their role as a Light to the Nations. These are exciting times, and I want to personally thank those Jewish lights who recognize the souls within those of us who deeply desire the restoration of all of Israel.

- Chasity Galyon, MS Ed. and Seeker of Truth from Knoxville, TN

The Torah tells us that we are here not only to elevate our souls, but to transform the physical world into a Divine garden where God's essence is fully revealed. At that time, the sages say, all of humanity will seek to learn Torah and all will serve God as one.

Throughout the centuries of exile, the Jewish people risked their lives to keep the Torah. It was impossible to imagine that millions of non-Jews would someday start seeking the Torah's wisdom with a passionate hunger and thirst.

And yet, that day has arrived. Sincere, humble souls from among the nations are seeking a deeper truth and a new relationship with God that only the Torah can provide.

According to many of the greatest rabbis of our generation, including the Lubavitcher Rebbe, a fundamental part of the Jewish mission in these times of redemption is to teach the peoples of the world Torah-true wisdom, helping them to take their place in creating an inhabitable world which ultimately will be *filled with the knowledge of God like water covers the ocean bed* (Habakkuk 2:14).

Such a foundational change does not come easily to most of us. We, as Jews, need to more deeply understand and internalize our new role. *Lighting Up The Nations* is an important step in helping us do exactly that.

- **Shifra Chana Hendrie**,
Founder and CEO of The Gate of Unity
(*gateofunity.com*)

Any Jew who loves Judaism and loves humanity will naturally want to share Jewish wisdom with people outside the Jewish nation. How can we not, when that wisdom could revolutionize others' lives and at the same time increase respect for Torah? In *Lighting Up The Nations*, Dr. Rivkah Lambert Adler makes the case that if non-Jews are thirsting for truth, God wants us to be the wellspring they come to.

- **Gila Manolson**,
Author and international speaker
(*gilamanolson.com*)

In her fascinating and important book, Dr. Rivkah Lambert Adler outlines why our biblical mandate of Isaiah 60:3 to be a light unto the nations has unprecedented relevance and urgency in our generation. *Lighting Up The Nations* should be required reading by all Jews to appreciate the spiritual opportunities we have to finally fulfill our historic destiny.

- **Rabbi Tuly Weisz**, Founder of Israel365
(*Israel365.com and theisraelbible.com*)

I have known Rivkah Lambert Adler for many years, and she has always impressed me with her geulah consciousness, and especially her willingness to do her part to help make it happen. When it comes to redemption, there are many roles to play, and she seems to have found hers by sharing the wisdom of the Torah with those beyond the Jewish people who appreciate its centrality in human history and a perfected world, something that is certain to happen in future times. This recent work of hers is an important step in that direction.

- **Rabbi Pinchas Winston**, Author of more than 100 books on Torah philosophy (*thirtysix.org*)

Praise for
Ten From The Nations:
Torah Awakening
Among Non-Jews

Couldn't put this book down! I enjoyed reading how other non-Jews came to love the Torah and how similar some of their experiences were to mine. But, more than that, I cried when I read how my Jewish brethren are beginning to notice something big is starting to happen world-wide and many are open to it. This book is uplifting, encouraging, and validating. Rivkah has done a wonderful work and is very courageous to bridge a 2000 year divide. – **B. Smith**

[T]he stories from these brave witnesses are crucial to understanding that Divine restoration is underway and that the people of God should arise and prepare for the next steps. The discerning reader will be provoked to much prayer for wisdom and discernment as to how to respond to this evidence. I salute Dr. Adler for her courage! – **Cathy Helms**

This is a wonderful book of individual stories of people from many walks of life coming to similar conclusions independently of one another. It's well written and desperately needed today... Thank you Rivkah Lambert Adler for being so brave and willing to engage in dialogue with those that love the God of Abraham, Isaac, and Jacob just as much as you do. I hope it will be used as an instrument for peace among all of Israel. I can also see that as fast as people are changing and returning to a love of Torah, Truth, a True understanding of the God of Israel, and the People of Israel this book will be a history book in no time at all. Their stories are just a drop in the bucket of countless others. It's so nice to have them written down giving legitimacy to so many people who thought they were the only ones. YOU'RE NOT!!! Must read folks!!! – **Jeremy Landauer**

Dr. Rivkah Lambert Adler has courageously dared to become the lightning rod around which an AMAZING conversation is taking place. Over the last 30 to 40 years a quiet revolution has begun within both Christendom and Judaism that is beginning to be felt very publicly and Adler's important work, *Ten From the Nations*, begins to chart the breadth, width and depth of this revolution.

Like an iceberg, with 90% of its mass hidden under the waters, a Torah Awakening has been happening across the globe. Christians are quietly waking, as if from deep slumber, to the continued relevance of the Torah, the five books of Moses and the contained Instructions in Righteousness. Both Jews and Christians are seeing this growing, even accelerating, shift and grappling with its significance... I encourage reading and wrestling with the contents of this book! - **Pete Rambo**

This Book was Wonderful, Timely and Challenging. I read all of it in about 4-5 hours, which was amazing because I cried through several pages. I could identify with the Journey of many coming from a Christian background. The struggles and blessings many have found in Keeping the Torah. Just to have our Jewish brethren take a closer look at us and wonder why or how this came to be thrills my soul... I appreciate the tremendous Chutzpah of Dr. Rivkah Lambert-Adler in compiling the individual contributions and opinions. The fact that these Two groups can find Holy Ground in the Torah is nothing less than Miraculous. The Jews have been at this for thousands of years and we have much to learn from them, having just rediscovered this treasure ourselves. - **Mary Stowell**

Dedication

For all the non-Jews whose souls are thirsty for Torah.

I honor your journey.

Acknowledgements

This is my opportunity to publicly thank:

The Master of the Universe, who keeps nudging me along this road.

Rabbi Elan Adler, Rabbi Amichai Cohen, David Curwin, Rabbi Avraham Greenbaum, Dr. Jair Jehuda, Rabbi David Katz, AnaRina Bat Tzion Kreisman, Rebbetzin Fraidie Levine, Rabbi Yitzchak Michaelson and Rabbi Dr. Yakov Nagen, the book's contributors, who shared their wisdom and their passion in order to help awaken the rest of the Jewish people.

Gidon Ariel who originally inspired me to begin working with the Nations in 2014 and who envisioned a place for this book at Root Source Press.

Rochel Weiman who believed in the book so much, she volunteered to design the cover with her whole heart. Her design alludes to God's blessing to Abraham: *"And I will multiply your seed like the stars of the heavens."* (Genesis 26:4)

Devra Ariel for the gorgeous cover photo of the dawn breaking.

Omar Gill for the original, professional design of the taxonomy that was adapted for use in this book.

Eliyahu Berkowitz, Chasity Galyon, Dina Yehuda, Veronica Johnson, Piper Kelly, Gila Manolson and **Reuven Prager** for reading and correcting many errors that my eyes missed.

Shifra Chana Hendrie who has been doing this work for much longer than I have and who first brought me to meet Rabbi Yitzchak Ginsburgh to discuss our shared commitment to teaching the universal wisdom of Torah to those non-Jews who want to learn from us.

Acknowledgements

Rabbi Yitzchak Ginsburgh who confirmed for me that this work with the Nations is my shlichut.

AnaRina Bat Tzion Kreisman whose vision for the future relationship between Jews and the Nations most closely matches my own.

Rabbi Pesach Wolicki for showing me the Rambam's teshuva and **Steven Rohde Gotlib** for helping me find it online.

Donna Jollay, Al McCarn, Bob O'Dell and Levi Schwiethale who advised me about some of the book's more sensitive content.

*"I am the Lord; I called you with righteousness and I will
strengthen your hand; and I formed you, and I made
you for a people's covenant, for a light to Nations."*

Yeshayahu 42:6

*"And Nations shall go by your light and kings
by the brilliance of your shine."*

Yeshayahu 60:3

*And the foreigners who join with the Lord to serve Him and
to love the name of the Lord, to be His servants, everyone who
observes the Sabbath from profaning it and who holds fast
to My covenant. I will bring them to My holy mount, and I
will cause them to rejoice in My house of prayer, their burnt
offerings and their sacrifices shall be acceptable upon My altar,
for My house shall be called a house of prayer for all peoples.
So says the Lord God, Who gathers in the dispersed of Israel, I
will yet gather others to him, together with his gathered ones.*

Yeshayahu 56:6-8

"In the Time of the Messiah, when all Nations will, in a clear voice, call on G-d's name, all will believe in G-d."

- Rabbi Gedaliah Fleer *Rabbi Nachman's Fire:*
An Introduction to Breslover Chassidus.

The only way the Temple will ever be a house of prayer for all the Nations of the world, as we pray, is if they learn to see God through the eyes of Torah.

And no one can teach that to the world
except the Jewish people.

– Rabbi Pinchas Winston *Living Higher: On*
A More Miraculous Level of Reality.

"To the Children of Israel, He gave the Land of Israel, and the mission to teach the rest of mankind about the Supreme authority of the One and Only King of the Universe."

- Tzvi Fishman. *The Book of Hirsh: A novel.*

Publisher's Foreword

IDEAS WHOSE TIME HAS COME

As with her previous book *Ten From The Nations*, Dr. Rivkah Lambert Adler has provided us with a groundbreaking study of a phenomenon that barely existed centuries or even decades ago.

The present volume, *Lighting Up The Nations*, brings together Torah-observant Jews who work in the field of teaching Torah to non-Jews, each one presenting a defense of this activity from a traditional Torah and halachic perspective.

As a Torah-observant Jew myself, I certainly welcome these articles, and I am confident they will bring more Torah teachers from the position that teaching non-Jews Torah is forbidden or barely allowed to the realization that it should be encouraged and is even an obligation.

As the co-founder and director of Root Source (root-source. com), having taught Torah to Christians for over a decade and enabled tens of thousands of non-Jewish students to learn via over 1,000 Torah lessons recorded by a dozen Orthodox teachers (including Adler), I have come to certain conclusions and perspectives that I think are worthwhile considering, even if I do not footnote them with rabbinic sources.

1. The era that we are living in today, with the existence and centrality of the State of Israel, has paradigm-shifting ramifications not only for Torah-observant Jews, but for many Bible-believing Christians all over the world. While the image of *the wandering Jew, Synagoga and Ecclesia*,[1]

---

[1] *Ecclesia and Synagoga* are medieval, anti-Semitic statues of two women, representing Christianity and Judaism. Ecclesia, rep-

replacement theology[2], and other such Jew- and Judaism-cancelling concepts and ideologies may have been rampant (if not always front and center) for Christians throughout history, the new image of a strong Jew, "a free nation in our Homeland," is now an irreversible reality and forces them to reconsider their relationship with the concept of Jews.

2. The Internet and social media have changed the rules of the game. There is no way to prevent anyone with a modicum of interest from accessing Torah in the widest sense of the word. To pretend that this is not reality, and continue to restrict teaching Torah by Orthodox teachers, only leaves the field open to non-Orthodox Jews and non-Jews. While debating such people might gain a few likes, it is more effective to compete for thirsty students' attention on the front end and respectfully offer more authentic Torah teachings.

3. The Christians that I have encountered span a spectrum of positions toward Jews, Judaism and Torah. Some still see Jews as no more than targets for the Gospel, some want to learn Jewish wisdom in order to apply it to their faith and understanding of Jesus, some want to abandon what they have concluded are outdated and even false or immoral Christian theologies, whether to convert fully to Judaism or find another spot on this complex journey.[3] To envision all Christians as monolithic is anachronistic (if it ever was acceptable).

---

resenting the Christian church, is portrayed as proud and noble and Synagoga, representing Judaism, is portrayed as defeated. The Ecclesia and Synagoga motif is common in European cathedrals.

[2] Christian doctrine that asserts that Christianity replaced God's covenant with the Jewish people.

[3] See Adler's taxonomy in the section "Torah Awakening Among Non-Jews"

4. It is important to distinguish between lay Christians, even Evangelical Christians, and Evangelists. Evangelists are professional missionaries. For our purposes, I am only dealing with missionaries to Jews, though the vast majority of missionaries do not deal with Jews and have never even ever met one. Professional missionaries usually answer to a boss or a funder and may have a "sales" quota. The great majority of "religious" Christians spend about as much time and effort trying to get Jews (or anyone) to consider accepting the Christian faith as most Jews, even Orthodox Jews, spend trying to get other Jews to upgrade their Jewish faith.

5. The most important goal that all people should set for themselves is relationship. Without a relationship, any effort to achieve something else will be much harder, if successful at all. But a relationship with someone else can and should be a worthy thing to strive for in and of itself. As Rav Tzvi Yehudah Kook famously taught, the sage Hillel in Pirkei Avot taught "love others *and* draw them close to the Torah" *not in order to* draw them close. In other words, relationships have value and should not be undertaken exclusively for the purpose of drawing people close to Torah. To me, this means we should strive to reverse the millennia of animosity between Jews and Christians and just try to "play nice together."

I have many other lessons learned, and most certainly will have more as the years go by. I encourage you, perhaps challenge you, to read this book and discover if any of your paradigms have shifted.

Gidon Ariel
CEO, Root Source
Maale Hever, Menachem Av 5771
gidon@root-source.com

INTRODUCTION

Editor's Introduction

DR. RIVKAH LAMBERT ADLER

<u>Whose Torah Is It Anyway?</u>

One of the first verses that a Jewish child learns is *Torah tzivah lanu Moshe morasha Kehillat Yaakov* - the Torah that Moses commanded us is the heritage of the congregation of Yaakov (Deuteronomy 33:4)

Before the Torah is read publicly in synagogue, one of the blessings recited thanks God "who has chosen us from among all the Nations and given us the Torah."

In our daily morning prayers, we bless God for commanding us to immerse ourselves in Torah study. We ask God to sweeten the words of Torah in our mouths and in the mouths of the entire Jewish people. We thank God for choosing us from all the Nations and giving us the Torah.

In this context, it would be easy to assume that Torah was intended to be the exclusive property of the Jewish people.

Therefore, it's not a surprise that I used to believe that the Torah belonged only to the Jewish people - that it was given to us by God as our inheritance. It's only later that I came to understand that, while it contains Divine guidance that only applies to the Jewish people, **the Torah also has universal wisdom that can benefit every human being on earth.**

Predictably, I resisted the perspective that the Torah was meant to be shared with non-Jews. I'm quite certain I'm not the only Jew who was initially uncomfortable with the idea of the Torah having any relevance to the rest of the world.

Since the advent of Christianity, it has been neither safe nor smart for the Jewish people to attempt to share the universal wisdom of the Torah with the rest of the world. We have been too busy protecting ourselves from being kicked out of our homes or from being forcibly converted or even killed.

Today I understand that it has always been the responsibility of the Jewish people to guard and protect the Torah, and to learn its wisdom in great depth, *until such time* as the rest of the world was ready to hear the messages God embedded in the Torah for them.

In his classic work *The Nineteen Letters*, Rabbi Shimshon Raphael Hirsch wrote that, "Israel was charged with the mission of being the guardian of Torah **until all mankind will want it and be able to maintain it.**"

I believe, with the non-Jewish awakening to Torah happening in our day, we are living in such a time.

If the idea that Jews have a God-given responsibility to share the universal wisdom of Torah with the rest of the world is new to you, there's a good chance that the perspectives shared in this book will make you uncomfortable, at least initially. Nevertheless, I urge you to read on, because the story ends with all of humanity accepting the dominion of the God of Israel.

Being A Light To The Nations

I also used to believe that being a Light to the Nations meant that the Jewish people was supposed to live together in Israel and to create a perfect society here. In my previous understanding, I thought we would be so admired by the rest of the world that they would naturally want to emulate us.

Today, I believe that being a Light to the Nations is a much more active role, requiring us to build relationships with the non-Jewish world and share the light of the Torah with them (if they are open to receive the light that God hid in the Torah.)

I often explain that I picture a bridge between the Jewish and the non-Jewish world. I like to imagine that I am standing at the foot of the bridge on the Jewish side. If someone is walking in the direction of the Jewish people, in the direction of Israel, in the direction of the Torah, I am there to welcome them. But I will not cross the bridge and yank them over to the Jewish side. The impetus has to come from them.

To a large extent, this book is a natural outgrowth of my first book. When I published *Ten From The Nations: Torah Awakening Among Non-Jews* (available on Amazon) in 2017, I had two goals. One was to assure current and former Christians who were feeling drawn to Torah that they were not alone, but rather part of a larger movement that God appears to be orchestrating. This was crucially important because many of them do not have the benefit of being in a like-minded community

My second goal was to introduce the Torah-aware non-Jew to the rest of the Jewish community, which I did by letting them tell the stories of their spiritual journeys.

Non-Jews Studying Torah?

In December 2018, I took a screenshot of a rather obtuse comment made by a Jewish woman on Facebook. She wrote, *"Not sure wtf (sic) christians have to do with the geula."*

In part, it is in response to that uninformed and crassly-worded comment that *Lighting Up The Nations* was created. This book, although it will likely also be of interest to Torah-aware non-Jews, is primarily directed to the Jewish reader, in order to help us better understand what the proper relationship is between the Jewish people, the Torah and the rest of the Nations.

Indeed, the more I met Torah-aware non-Jews, the clearer it became to me that I was being guided to facilitate their learning of authentic Torah. In the introduction to *Ten From The Nations,* I wrote: "I believe that, by virtue of being a Light to the Nations, Jewish people who are able to teach should be teaching. Hashem sends us our students. The Jewish people's relationship to the

Torah is over 3,300 years old. The people awakening to Torah need rabbis and Jewish educators willing to teach them."

For many, this is a controversial position, since it appears to be in direct conflict with a well-known teaching in the Talmud (Sanhedrin 59a) on this topic. *"Rabbi Yochanan said: "A non-Jew who engages in Torah study is liable to receive the death penalty, as it is stated: 'Moshe commanded us the Torah, inheritance of the congregation of Ya'akov'—it is an inheritance for us, but not for them."*

As with the rest of the Talmud, simply taking this statement at face value is misleading. While I elected not to include a halachic analysis of the issue here, on a personal level, I did seek out rabbinic guidance in order to better understand what I was and was not permitted to teach. This is when I came upon the work of Rabbi Yitzchak Ginsburgh.

In 2017, Rabbi Ginsburgh published "The Fourth Revolution: Torah Study for Gentiles"[4]. In this article, while acknowledging the *Sheva Mitzvot Bnei Noach* (Seven Noahide Laws in Appendix B) as "the most fundamental human obligations," he argues that this level is necessary but not sufficient for the non-Jew who is seeking truth. Rabbi Ginsburgh claims that, "They must study Torah in a way that reveals its depth and its profound relevance to their own lives."

Speaking to the Jew, he adds that, "Teaching Torah means sharing with the Nations of the world some of the infinite wisdom and beauty that it contains," and reassures the Jew that, doing so is not a contradiction to our mission of being the Chosen People. "On the contrary, the nation that has the Torah in its possession is the one who can share its light and goodness with all peoples, 'to illuminate the Nations' (Isaiah 49:6). Teaching the Torah to non-Jews augments the Jewish people's status as 'a nation of priests and a holy nation.' (Exodus 19:6)."

---

[4] The full text of the article appears below, in its own chapter.

Rabbi Pinchas Winston elaborates on how this responsibility fell to the Jewish people in the first place.

"Meanwhile, there are a lot of agnostics and atheists out there. Or there are believers, but in the wrong version of God. There are so many spiritual approaches today, but how many of them miss the mark, either partially or completely?

"Who can blame them? The one nation [the Jewish people – Ed.] whose mission it is to fix all that isn't interested or has little or no credibility. Their main resource, Torah, is not respected among masses of their *own* people, so how could it be among masses of *other* peoples? Consequently, and dangerously, the secret to life remains, for so many, a 'secret.'

"It might have all been different had *Eisav* (Esau) not sold his birthright to *Ya'akov* (Jacob). Until that time, Eisav had been the destined leader of the nation, responsible for carrying out the intended mission of the descendants of *Avraham* (Abraham) and *Yitzchak* (Isaac). He was the first born, and the right of the first-born belonged to him. Ya'akov would have always been a teacher, but it would have been Eisav's job to take his message, the message of Torah, to the rest of the world.

"But he did sell his birthright to Ya'akov, and with it, the blessings necessary to live up to his future mission. And though Eisav has tried from time-to-time to take it back from Ya'akov, he has not been able to. He can't, and Ya'akov can't give it back to him even if he wants to. He and his descendants are here to teach the world truth, period."

There is an eye-opening halachic response from the Rambam about this issue. The Rambam *poskened* (gave a ruling in Jewish law) that it is permissible to teach Torah to Christians and not to Muslims. Why? Because even though Christianity is *avoda zara* (idolatry), Christians have the same Bible and the same reverence for it that we do. If we teach them our perspective, *it might bring them closer*. For Muslims, although they are monotheists, there are vast differences in our perspectives and our texts. If we teach them something that they don't agree with, it might cause them to hate us more.[5]

In 2012, Rabbi Dr. Shlomo Brody penned an Ask The Rabbi column for *The Jerusalem Post* titled "May a Jew teach Torah to a gentile?[6] In his column, Brody cited the halachic opinions of multiple rabbis through the centuries.

Of special relevance is the opinion of Rabbi Yehiel Weinberg who passed away in 1966. About his position, Brody wrote, "Particularly notable was Rabbi Yehiel Weinberg, who himself taught at a pre-World War II German university. He contended that the proscription only banned gentile study intended to form competing religious ideals and rituals. **It remained perfectly permissible, however, to teach even an exclusively non-Jewish audience if the goal was simply to spread Jewish wisdom."**

A Warning For Readers

As with *Ten From The Nations*, this volume highlights a controversial topic – the responsibility the Jewish people have to be a Light to the Nations. The primary audience for this work is the Jewish people. If you are a Jew and this is the first time you're hearing these ideas, they may cause you discomfort. I get it. I completely understand the proprietary sense Jews have about the Torah.

It takes time to integrate a different paradigm.

I know in advance that this book will also attract a certain percentage of readers who are not Jewish but who occupy the liminal space between Judaism and other faith traditions. Those readers in particular should be aware that this volume contains

---

5   The full text of the teshuva is here: https://www.hebrewbooks.org/
    pdfpager.aspx?req=1730&st=&pgnum=299

6   https://www.jpost.com/magazine/judaism/
    ask-the-rabbi-may-a-jew-teach-torah-to-a-gentile

some sensitive material and proposed Messianic era scenarios that may not sit comfortably with them.

Editing Decisions

With multiple contributors, there are various spellings of transliterated Hebrew words. I did not change them. So, for example, you may see variations like halacha and halakhah, both references to the system of Jewish law.

This work contains a lot of Hebrew words and concepts. When contributors didn't include an explanation of Hebrew words they used in their text, I italicized the word and added a translation in parentheses the first time the word appears.

In order to make the meaning of the Hebrew words as accessible as possible, there is also a glossary at the end of the book. If the Hebrew word only appears one time in the text, it may not also appear in the glossary. Sometimes the glossary has a bit of an expanded definition. A good basic glossary of Jewish terms is available online at jewfaq.org/glossary.htm.

Regarding biblical quotes that are included in the book's essays, in all cases, the translations and verses appear as the contributor submitted them. If you want to look them up in your Bible, it's important to note that there are some differences in the numbering of chapter and verse between Jewish and Christian Bibles.

Final Thoughts

When *Ten From The Nations* was first published in 2017, reader responses fell into two main categories. The vast majority of readers applauded the book's publication, recognizing that it was the first book of its kind to tell the story of Torah-aware non-Jews. Many Jews were fascinated, learning for the first time about non-Jews who did things like study the weekly Torah portion and bake *challah* (braided Shabbat bread).

I also received exceedingly harsh criticism from a small but vocal group of Jews. I was recklessly accused of, among other things, cooperating with Christian missionaries to the detriment of the Jewish people and of selling my soul to rake in Christian money. I recognize that the publication of this book might subject me to more criticism.

The foundational idea presented in this book - that the Jewish people have a biblical mandate to share the universal wisdom of Torah with the rest of the world - is likely to further agitate those who vigilantly guard the border between the Jewish people and the Nations.

To my critics and supporters alike, I boldly assert my belief that the Jewish people understanding and acting upon this biblical mandate is part of the process of redemption.

Rivkah Lambert Adler
Av 5781 (August 2021)
Efrat, Israel
rivkah@kotevet.com

Torah Awakening Among Non-Jews

DR. RIVKAH LAMBERT ADLER

So said the Lord of Hosts: In those days, when ten men of all the languages of the Nations shall take hold of the corner of the garment of a Jewish man, saying, "Let us go with you, for we have heard that God is with you." (Zechariah 8:23)

"A huge paradigm shift is happening. All over the world, current and former Christians are becoming aware of Torah. They are learning about and implementing what most of the world thinks of as Jewish practices, including celebrating Shabbat and the Biblical holidays. They are refraining from eating pork and shellfish. They are studying Torah and seeing the Land of Israel, and especially the return of the Jewish people to the Land of Israel, in a new light. They are building positive relationships with the Jewish people." - From the Editor's Introduction to *Ten From The Nations*

I have spent the past seven years learning about, documenting and working with the phenomenon I call Torah-aware non-Jews. Sometimes, for those coming from a Christian background, their initial motivation is based on their significant spiritual relationship with the personality they call Jesus or Yeshua, which they claim is Jesus' Hebrew name. At this early stage, some Christians acknowledge that the Jewishness of Jesus/Yeshua has implications for their lives. They begin to study Torah and to adopt certain practices in order to live more like Jesus/Yeshua himself lived.

When I read this passage in Sara Yocheved Rigler's book *I've Been Here Before: When Souls of the Holocaust Return*[7], I realized that there is yet another possible explanation for the souls who are inexplicably drawn to Torah:

"The Holocaust, however, created an emergency situation. According to the revered Klausenberger Rebbe, Rav Yekusiel Yehuda Halberstam, who himself was a Holocaust survivor and lost his wife and eleven children, after the Holocaust, millions of souls had to come back, but there weren't enough Jewish mothers to receive them. So they went to non-Jewish mothers." (p. 198)

This explanation, based on the concept of reincarnation, likely explains at least a percentage of those souls who were born as non-Jews but who are driven by an insatiable hunger and thirst for Torah.

A Proposed Taxonomy

In order to better understand the Torah awakening journey of individuals coming from Christian backgrounds, I created a proposed taxonomy of the steps I have observed over the past seven years. In creating this proposed taxonomy, I added some important caveats which bear repeating:

1) These positions are not necessarily mutually exclusive.
2) This process is not linear. Not everyone passes through each position.
3) Some people will skip some positions entirely.
4) Some will find themselves represented by multiple positions at the same time.
5) Some journeys end at a given position and sometimes individuals double back.
6) Only *a very few* will ultimately convert.

---

[7] Rigler, Sara Yocheved. *I've Been Here Before: When Souls of the Holocaust Return*, Mekor Press. 2021.

A PROPOSED TAXONOMY OF THE TORAH AWAKENING JOURNEY OF CHRISTIANS

I am a Christian and I attend Sunday church. I believe that all the promises God made to Israel now apply to the church and that Christians are the New Israel, replacing Jews as the people of God. It is necessary to bring Jews to belief in Jesus.

Jesus did not celebrate Christmas or Easter and, in fact, these holidays have pagan roots. I wish to live more as Jesus lived, so I celebrate the Biblical Feasts and Shabbat.

I believe that the return of the Jews to Israel and the establishment of the State of Israel in 1948 demonstrate that God's Biblical promises to Israel are being fulfilled in our day. I am a Christian and I stand with Israel.

I recognize that Jesus was Jewish, so to understand his life and his teachings, I need to better understand Hebrew scripture.

I joined a messianic congregation.

I no longer refer to him as Jesus, but by his Hebrew name, which is Yeshua. I now refer to God the father as Abba or as Hashem.

I study the weekly Torah portion and other Jewish texts I study Hebrew. I visit Israel regularly. I have friends who are Orthodox Jews.

I left Sunday church.

I believe that I am descended from the Ten Lost Tribes and that is why I am so drawn to Torah and to Israel. I identify as an Ephraimite from the House of Israel and I wish to be reunited with the House of Judah while retaining my relationship with Yeshua.
(NOTE: This stage is only experienced by a subgroup of Torah pursuant Christians)

I experienced a Torah awakening in the past and I have returned to traditional Christianity.

I experienced a Torah awakening in the past and I have left faith entirely.

Created by Dr. Rivkah Lambert Adler, August 2020

IMPORTANT TO NOTE
These positions are not necessarily mutually exclusive.
This process is not linear. Not everyone passes through each position.
Some people will skip some positions entirely.
Some will find themselves represented by multiple positions at the same time.
Some journeys end at a given position and sometimes individuals double back.
Only *a very few* will ultimately convert.

I no longer believe that Yeshua is divine, but I do believe that he is Messiah/Moshiach ben Yosef and will come back as Moshiach ben David.

I no longer believe that Yeshua is the messiah for whom the Jews have been waiting, but he is still my rabbi. He is the one who brought me to Torah.

I have renounced all belief in Yeshua but I am very spiritually lonely. I no longer identify as Christian. I am not Jewish. I don't know what my path is.

I identify as a Noahide, anxious to keep the Torah laws for non-Jews.

I identify as a Ger Toshav and await the re-establishment of the Sanhedrin so I can be officially recognized.

I am in the process of converting to Judaism.

I am a Jew.

Cultural Appropriation or Baby Steps?

Most often, a Torah awakening journey is undertaken by people who don't know any actual Jews, and certainly not any Torah-observant Jews. Without Torah Jews to guide them, they get some things wrong. The clearest example of this is snap-on *tzitzit* (ritual fringes attached to four-cornered garments).

Disregarding the clear Biblical requirement for a four-cornered garment, it is not uncommon to see non-Jewish men wearing decidedly unkosher fringes attached to a piece of leather that they snap onto their belt loops. You can see samples of these being sold at numbers1538.com, a website that refers to the exact verse where the mitzvah of tzitzit are first mentioned.

> *Speak to the children of Israel and you shall say to them that they shall make for themselves fringes on the corners of their garments, throughout their generations, and they shall affix a thread of sky blue [wool] on the fringe of each corner.* - Bamidbar (Numbers) 15:38

There is also a *tallit katan* (four-cornered garment worn under a shirt to which tzitzit are attached) imprinted with the words "Numbers 15:38" being marketed to Torah-aware non-Jews.

I have seen other examples of misuse or assigning Christological significance to Jewish ritual items, such as a *mezuzah* (a small *scroll with two biblical passages written on it)* case with both a *menorah* (seven-branched lamp that is a symbol of the Holy Temple) and the Christian Ichthus (cross and fish) symbol affixed with a red pushpin or the *shammash* (helper) candle of a Chanukah *menorah* (nine-branched lamp) or the *zeroa* (shankbone) at a *Pesach* (Passover) seder or challah said to represent Jesus.

A knowledgeable Jew will likely have one of two reactions upon observing Jewish ritual items used in Christological ways. Most will find it an abhorrent practice of cultural appropriation, transforming something holy into something profane.

The second, less common and more generous reaction, is to understand that we are in the midst of a transition, and as with all processes of transition, it isn't always smooth and easy.

Decades ago, when I was in the process of becoming Torah-observant, I was still eating decidedly non-kosher fast food burgers while wearing a *sheitel* (wig). I would keep the first day of a *chag* (Jewish festival) and go to work on the second day. In short, I was in process. Without understanding my journey, a Torah-observant Jew could have noted my actions in those days and rightfully called me a hypocrite or a deceiver, trying to pass as Torah-observant while openly breaking many of *Hashem's* (God's) commandments.

When I see Christians who are misusing Torah or Jewish ritual, I tend to recall the earliest days of my own *teshuva* (repentance) process when I still had a long way to go, but I was at least on the right road.

The Role for Jews

Like it or not, this curiosity about Torah coming from non-Jews is a real phenomenon, and it is growing. As I argued in the introduction to *Ten From The Nations: Torah Awakening Among Non-Jews*, it is also part of the process of *geula* (redemption).

Having published the first book describing the Torah awakening phenomenon of current and former Christians, the need for a follow-up became clear. The book you're reading now is another part of the story. It's all about the Jewish mandate to respond to the growing curiosity about the Torah that is coming from the non-Jewish world.

While the primary audience for this book is Jews, those non-Jews who have an attraction to Torah, to the Land of Israel, to the Jewish people and to the God of Abraham, Isaac and Jacob will also benefit from reading this modest work.

IN OUR DAYS

The Fourth Revolution in Torah Learning

RABBI YITZCHAK GINSBURGH

Who is the Torah intended for? For Torah scholars? For men? For women? For Jews? Perhaps even for non-Jews? As conservative and stringent as the Torah is, it surprises us with ground-breaking innovations and revolutions

One of Maimonides' principles of faith states, "This Torah will not be replaced and there will be no other Torah from the Creator, blessed be His Name." Torah study is the most all-inclusive commandment; therefore, we would expect that this precept—that the Torah not change in any way—be especially upheld in regard to the laws governing Torah study. Surprisingly though, we find that throughout history, these laws, more than any others, have undergone some of the greatest changes. Each change has brought with it a revolution that has dramatically broadened the range of Torah scholars.

In this week's Torah reading, *Parashat Yitro*, God presents the Jewish people with His Torah. In celebration of that fact, let's look at three major revolutions that have occurred throughout the generations in the realm of Torah study. Towards the end of this article, we will present our own belief that we are on the verge of a fourth revolution, and it is the responsibility of our generation to usher it in properly.

The First Revolution: Transcribing the Oral Torah

Initially, there was a clear distinction between the Written Torah and the Oral Torah. The sages ruled that, "Things that are passed down verbally, you are not permitted to put in writing." The Oral

Torah was destined to remain the living, effervescent Torah of the study halls. Only the books of the Bible (the Pentateuch, Prophets and the Writings) could be transcribed. The laws and interpretations of the Torah, the sermons and the regulations instituted by the sages were all intended to be passed down by word of mouth alone.

But, after the destruction of the Second Temple, the exile from the land of Israel threatened to last a long time. Rabbi Yehudah Hannasi (also known as Rabeinnu Hakadosh, or simply "Rebbi") foresaw that the trials and tribulations of the exile were liable to erase the Oral Torah from the Jewish mind, God forbid. The Oral Torah was in dire jeopardy. To preserve it, Rebbi took the bold and crucial preemptive step of transcribing the final version of the Mishnah, "So that the Torah should not be forgotten from the Jewish people." Rebbi explained that he had taken his license from the verse, "A time to act for God [by their] transgressing Your Torah" (Psalms 119:126). The sages explained this radical step, stating that the prohibition of writing the Torah must be breached, because it is a time to act for the sake of the Torah. In other words, sometimes, in order to strengthen Torah's foundation, a certain aspect must be annulled (*Menachot* 99b).

It seems clear that had Rabbi Yehudah Hanassi found an alternative, one that would preserve the Oral Torah without the need to transgress the prohibition of transcribing it, he would have favored it. Clearly, this was his last resort. Yet, considering the outcome from a deeper perspective, it becomes clear that his revolutionary act brought about only positive developments. As such, we see retroactively how the process was directed by Divine Providence. For centuries, the Oral Torah had remained inside the study halls and it was strictly forbidden to limit it by confining it to the written word. But, in the time of Rabbi Yehudah Hanasi, it reached a stage of maturity that allowed it to continue thriving even in its written form.

The revolution that Rabbi Yehudah Hanasi began resulted in the growth of the Torah library, consisting of tens of thousands of volumes, which today have mostly been transferred to huge computer databases. The Torah library that began with the Mishnah continues to expand today. The figure of the Jewish scholar, proficient in hundreds and thousands of books covering all areas of Torah, was forged by this revolution.

The Second Revolution: "His Torah is his Trade"

"Rabbi Tzadok says…, Anyone who benefits from words of Torah, removes his life from the world" (*Avot* 4:5). This is the source of the prohibition against being paid for learning Torah. To this prohibition, Maimonides devoted one of the most acrimonious statements in his *Mishneh Torah*. He wrote, "Anyone who sets his heart on learning Torah and does not work at a trade, but survives on charity, he has surely desecrated God's Name, humiliated the Torah, extinguished the light of the religion, caused evil to himself and removed his life from the World to Come" (*Hilchot Talmud Torah* 3:10). Maimonides continues by proving that the sages of the Mishnah and the Talmud worked for their living and refused to benefit from the Torah.

Rabbi Yosef Caro, the author of the *Shulchan Aruch*, ruled against Maimonides' strict ruling. He ruled that it is permissible to study Torah and live from donations, as many young Torah scholars do today. He acquits all those who reject Maimonides' ruling with the same principle that the sages condoned the transcription of the Oral Torah into writing, "It is a time to act for God [by their] transgressing Your Torah." Rabbi Yosef Caro explains, "Had the livelihoods of the scholars and the teachers not been available, they could not have labored in the Torah as they should and the Torah would have been forgotten, God forbid." Once again, breaching the original law that prohibited Torah study as a means to making a living was an essential step that allowed the Torah to be conserved.

In this case too, the original superficial necessity paved the way to realizing a deeper, more positive objective. If Torah study is the ultimate goal, it should be permissible to receive financial support in pursuing it. This ensures that the Torah continues to flourish among the Jewish people. Like the first revolution, the second one also forged a new role in Jewish life: the role and figure of a teacher whose official, full-time job is the learning and dissemination of Torah. This figure is usually identified as the rabbi of a congregation, or a Torah scholar who puts his life and soul into Torah learning. It was this transition that institutionalized the tradition of modern *semichah* (rabbinical ordination) that began during the era of the *Rishonim*, spanning the eleventh to the fifteenth centuries CE.

The Third Revolution: Torah Study for Women

Maimonides begins his Laws of Torah study with the phrase, "Women are exempt from Torah study, as it says, 'You shall teach them to your sons [and not to your daughters].'" In its original sense, the *mitzvah* of Torah study is exclusively for men. Maimonides summarizes the law, "A woman who studies Torah receives a reward for doing so… yet, even though she receives a reward, the sages commanded that one should not teach his daughter Torah, because most women are not oriented towards study. Rather, they reduce the Torah teachings to meaningless issues, in keeping with their meager intellect" (*Hilchot Talmud Torah* 1:13).

Throughout history, most Jewish women received no formal Jewish education. The cheiders, schools and yeshivas were only for men, while girls were educated at home. The many wise women who were Torah scholars throughout history stand as an exception to this rule.

In recent generations, together with other signs of emancipation, the gates of higher secular education were opened to women. In light of this, many great rabbis, such as Rabbi Yisrael Meir of Radin (known as the *Chofetz Chayim*), came to the conclusion that Torah homeschooling for girls would no longer suffice. It was incumbent on the community to establish Torah educational institutions for girls (such as the Beit Yakov schools for girls that were founded by the renowned Sarah Schnirer). Here too, the ruling was based on the verse, "It is a time to act for God [by their] transgressing Your Torah." If women do not learn Torah and their entire education is secular, they might leave the way of Torah observance and be lost to religious society, God forbid.

The Lubavitcher Rebbe, Rabbi Menachem Mendel Schneersohn, went even further. He claimed that in our generation, Maimonides' statement that "most women are not oriented towards study," is no longer applicable. Women have developed and advanced, and are no longer likely to reduce the Torah teachings to something meaningless. Quite the opposite. In addition to his own insights into modern society, the Lubavitcher Rebbe referred us to the teachings of the great Kabbalist, Rabbi Isaac Luria. The latter, in his seminal works on Kabbalah, describes the imminent rise of the *sefirah* of kingdom, reflecting the positive developmental process that is currently occurring in the feminine dimensions of reality.

Here too, that which transpired as a result of a superficial requirement is now revealed as part of a most desirable development.

The Fourth Revolution: Torah Study for Gentiles

The first three revolutions in Torah study shifted the boundaries of Torah learning within the Jewish people alone. The Torah was given to us alone, as the verse states, "Moses commanded us the Torah, an inheritance for the congregation of Jacob." Moreover, the sages stated, "It is forbidden to transmit the words of Torah to a non-Jew" (*Chagigah* 13a). The law even states, "A non-Jew who studies Torah is liable to die [by the hand of God]" (Maimonides, *Hilchot Melachim* 10:9).

Yet, regarding this restriction—limiting Torah study to Jews alone—a wonderful change can be expected. We are all familiar with the words of the prophet Isaiah: "And many Nations will go and they will say, 'Let us ascend the mountain of God to the Temple of the God of Jacob and He will teach us of His ways, and we will follow His path,' for from Zion shall the Torah emerge [to non-Jews] and the word of God from Jerusalem" (Isaiah

2:3). Jeremiah also prophesied, "To you will come Nations from the extremes of the earth and they will say, 'Only falsity did our forefathers teach us.'" (Jeremiah 16:19). The prophet Zephaniah heralded an era when, "...I will convert the peoples to a pure language so that all of them call the name of God, to worship Him with one accord" (Zephaniah 3:9).

A non-Jew is commanded to study and observe the seven Noahide commandments, as the Talmud states explicitly, "Even a non-Jew who deals with the Torah [studying things that pertain to the seven *mitzvot*] is like a High Priest" (*Baba Kama* 38a). It is the task of the Jewish people to teach and disseminate the Torah of the Noahides to all of mankind, as Maimonides and others explain (see *Hilchot Melachim* 8:10; *Tosfot Yom-Tov, Avot* 3:14). The Lubavitcher Rebbe stressed that in our generation, the world is ready and it is time for us to put this into practice.

In practice, the Noahide laws are the most fundamental human obligations. But, keeping the seven Noahide mitzvot does not suffice. This level of Torah study alone cannot fully realize the idea of *tikkun olam*. It is difficult to imagine how to implement more than this without advance preparation. Maimonides states that the other monotheistic religions pave the way to the final redemption. But, the Nations of the world can only recognize the Torah as the source of all the sparks of truth that their religions contain if they are exposed to the entire Torah in all its glory. They must study Torah in a way that reveals its depth and its profound relevance to their own lives.

In order to realize this vision, a fourth revolution must be added to the chain of revolutions in Torah study. We are being called upon to begin offering Torah to the non-Jews, without limiting them to studying only the seven Noahide laws alone. They need to be exposed to the entire expanse of Torah teachings. This should begin with the wealth of spiritual and psychological ideas that are available through the Torah's inner dimension— Kabbalah and Chassidut— without skipping over the laws relevant to all of mankind that exist in the revealed dimensions of Torah (including the seven Noahide laws).

The intention in teaching non-Jews Torah is not to preach conversion. If a non-Jew wishes to convert to Judaism, he or she may do so, but this must be from their own free choice, without coercion. Teaching Torah means sharing with the Nations of the world some of the infinite wisdom and beauty that it contains. At most, this might be an incentive for conversion, but it cannot be considered coercion. Nor will this impair the special mission of the Chosen People. On the contrary, the nation that has the Torah in its possession is the one who can share its light and goodness with all peoples, "to illuminate the Nations" (Isaiah 49:6). Teaching the Torah to non-Jews augments the Jewish people's status as "a nation of priests and a holy nation" (Exodus 19:6).

The Fourth Revolution – Good News for Jews too

We have seen how each of the first three revolutions prevented the Torah from being forgotten from the Jewish people. It would seem that the only ones who will benefit from the fourth revolution are not Jewish. What benefit can it be to the Jewish people?

Teaching Torah to non-Jews is a great challenge to any individual who takes it upon himself. But, encountering people who are far removed from Torah will bring him into contact with questions and new perspectives that will rejuvenate his relationship with the Torah and infuse it with new motivation. We can already see this happen with people involved in Jewish outreach, in Chabad houses and the like.

But, teaching the Torah to non-Jews offers far greater value to the Jewish people. It is no secret that modern Judaism is suffering from a deep crisis. Many individuals (and even groups) have distanced themselves from Torah study and even from their Jewish identity. One outstanding reason for this crisis is because they identify with universalism. In contrast, Judaism functions as a national religion that apparently has nothing to offer the rest of humanity. Perceiving Judaism through the prism of teaching the Torah to non-Jews will open the minds and hearts of many distant Jews to see the Torah in a new light.

The time has come "to act for God [by their] transgressing Your Torah." With God's help, the fourth revolution will heal the crisis of our people and all humanity, bringing true peace and light to the world.

From a farbrengen at David's Tomb, 24th Tevet 5755

Available online at https://www.inner.org/chassidut/ the-fourth-revolution-in-torah-learning

Kingdom of Priests –
Missed Opportunities

DAVID CURWIN

For the first 11 chapters of Genesis, God directed His attention to all of humanity. After the Tower of Babel episode, where mankind was divided into nations and languages, He took a different path. By choosing Abraham, His focus and message were addressed to one nation in particular, the nation that would be known as Israel. However, **from the very beginning, it is clear that God wanted this nation to bring benefit to all the nations of the world.** As God mentioned in his opening words to Abraham, *"All the families of the earth will be blessed through you."* (Genesis 12:3).

After several generations, Abraham's descendants became a nation of their own. After their miraculous redemption from slavery in Egypt, God gave them the Torah at Sinai, a covenant between Israel and the Almighty. Just before the Torah was given, there are a few verses that serve as a preface, indicating the nature of the covenant:

> *Now then, if you will obey Me faithfully and keep My covenant, you shall be My treasured possession among all the peoples. Indeed, all the earth is Mine, but you shall be to Me a kingdom of priests and a holy nation…* (Exodus 19:5-6)

In these verses, **God made it clear that He is still the God of "all the peoples," but Israel is to have a special role.** One of those roles is to be a "kingdom of priests." The meaning of that phrase is explained by the medieval Jewish commentator, Rabbi

Obadiah Sforno (1475-1550). In his commentary on Exodus 19:6, he wrote:

> *With this you will be the treasure of them all, by being a kingdom of priests, to explain and to teach the entire human race to "invoke the name of God and serve Him with one accord"* (Zephaniah 3:9)[8]. *This is how it will be for Israel in the distant future, as it says, "and you will be proclaimed priests of the Lord."* (Isaiah 61:6), *and as it says, "the Torah will come forth from Zion."* (Isaiah 2:3)

As Sforno points out, Israel's mission was to serve as priests to all the nations of the world, to teach them to call in the name of God together. And with his last quote from Isaiah, he indicates that the point of the Temple in Jerusalem was to be the source of that message for the rest of the world.

This was a very lofty mission, and had it been fulfilled, humanity could have repaired its fissures. As we can see, that goal has not been achieved. In this essay, I will show several examples where Abraham's family, and the nation of Israel, missed the opportunity to act as a "kingdom of priests," and by doing so postponed the blessing that all of humanity was promised.

Abraham

While Genesis does not explain why God chose Abraham for this mission, from his latter behavior it does appear he was an ideal choice. Shortly after arriving in the land of Canaan, Abraham built an altar and *"invoked the LORD by name"* (Genesis 12:8) – the goal for all of humanity, as described by the prophet Zephaniah.

---

[8]   The first half of the verse in Zephaniah, "For then I will make the peoples pure of speech" hints to a reversal of the punishment of the builders of the Tower of Babel, who could no longer speak one language, leading to the division of humanity.

Later, we see how Abraham interacted with leaders of the nations in Canaan. After helping them secure victory over an invading army, he is greeted by two local kings:

> When he returned from defeating Chedorlaomer and the kings with him, the king of Sodom came out to meet him in the Valley of Shaveh, which is the Valley of the King.
>
> And King Melchizedek of Salem brought out bread and wine; he was a priest of God Most High. He blessed him, saying, "Blessed be Abram of God Most High, Creator of heaven and earth. And blessed be God Most High, Who has delivered your foes into your hand." And [Abram] gave him a tenth of everything.
>
> Then the king of Sodom said to Abram, "Give me the persons, and take the possessions for yourself." But Abram said to the king of Sodom, "I swear to the LORD, God Most High, Creator of heaven and earth: I will not take so much as a thread or a sandal strap of what is yours; you shall not say, 'It is I who made Abram rich.'" (Genesis 14:17-23)

In this story, Abraham educated both leaders, and fulfilled his mission to teach the nations about God[9]. Through his behavior, he encouraged the righteous king Melchizedek to acknowledge God and bless Him. And to the wicked king of Sodom, Abraham insisted that it was God, not any human king, who made him rich. All the benefits that Abraham would receive were to further God's mission, not for his personal profit.

---

[9]　There is, however, room to suggest that Abraham could have even a more positive influence on the king of Sodom. In the Talmud (Nedarim 32a), Rabbi Yohanan claims that Abraham should have used that encounter to encourage the inhabitants of Sodom to follow God as well. R. Yohanan goes so far as to say that the enslavement of Israel in Egypt was a punishment for this missed opportunity. Perhaps had Abraham made that effort, the destruction of Sodom could have been avoided as well.

Abraham's response to these kings was noble. However, it stands in contrast to his behavior two chapters earlier. In that episode (Genesis 12:10-20), Abraham and his family emigrated to Egypt due to a famine in Canaan. When they arrived, Abraham was concerned that the Egyptians would kill him, in order to take his wife Sarah. He requested that she pose as his sister, both to save his life, and so they would *"treat [him] well."* (Genesis 12:13). Sarah was taken into the palace, and in compensation, they *"treated Abram well because of her, and [Abram] thus acquired sheep, cattle, donkeys, male and female slaves, she-donkeys, and camels."* (12:16)[10].

In Canaan, Abraham made clear to all that it was God who provided him with success, and he would not let it even appear as if he would personally benefit from being on God's mission. In Egypt, he made no such statements or demands. And while it was important for him to make that impression among the kings of Canaan, this was a missed opportunity with Pharaoh. Egypt was the center of civilization in that age, and as such it was essential that they too learn that blessing comes from God. It would fall to Abraham's descendants to teach Egypt that lesson.

---

[10] There is some debate among the medieval commentaries as to the meaning of Abraham's goal that the Egyptians would "treat [him] well." Radak (on Genesis 12:13) writes that he was not interested in financial benefit, but only hoped that the Egyptians would let him live, for it is inconceivable that Abraham would allow his wife to be taken from him for that reason (see also Abarbanel, Genesis 12, 13th question.) But Rashi disagrees with this premise, explaining the phrase as "give me gifts." And as we've seen from the end of the story, in Genesis 12:16, the same phrase "treated well" is used in reference to the gifts Abraham received. Therefore it appears that despite the implied criticism of Abraham's behavior, Rashi's explanation is closer to the plain meaning of the text.

Joseph

Four generations later, Abraham's great-grandson Joseph would return to Egypt. When Pharaoh had a perplexing dream, he called upon Joseph to interpret it for him. Joseph had experience explaining dreams in the past and went on to provide the solution that Pharaoh was looking for. But instead of claiming credit for himself (which would have been especially useful in promoting his reputation), he attributed the knowledge to God[11]:

> "God has told Pharaoh what He is about to do" (Genesis 41:25)

> "God has revealed to Pharaoh what He is about to do." (Genesis 41:28)

In response, Pharaoh also recognizes that God is the source of Joseph's knowledge:

> "Since God has made all this known to you, there is none so discerning and wise as you" (Genesis 41:39)

On the face of it, Joseph here has rectified Abraham's omission: he introduced God into Egypt, and as a result, Pharaoh himself acknowledged God. However, the English translation obscures a significant point. When Joseph is talking about God (and when Pharaoh responds), he always uses the name *Elohim*. While this is a divine name in Hebrew, it has a specific connotation: it refers to a universal God, a "supreme being," but not one specifically associated with Israel.

There is another name of God with that association: the ineffable Tetragrammaton, typically rendered in spoken Hebrew as *Hashem* (*the* Name). Throughout the Bible, both names are used to refer to God. But while all people were familiar with the name (or at least the concept of) *Elohim*, the name *Hashem*

---

[11] In an earlier episode, Joseph had made the same claim to his cell-mates, who also wanted their dreams explained: "*Surely God can interpret! Tell me [your dreams].*" (Genesis 40:8)

was reserved for use by Abraham and his descendants[12]. And in fact, when Abraham responded to the king of Sodom, he used the name *Hashem* when he said, *"I swear to the LORD"* (Genesis 14:22). It was not sufficient for the nations to know *Elohim*. They needed to know *Hashem* as well, since it was through Israel that God's plan to redeem the world would proceed.

Now perhaps it could be argued that when Joseph first encountered Pharaoh, he was not in a position to describe God in anything but the most universal terms. He was a former slave and prisoner, and was addressing the monarch, sovereign of Egypt. But Joseph's situation changed in the years to come. He was appointed vizier and directed all policy in Egypt. He was second only to Pharaoh himself. When the people of Egypt came to him for food during the famine, he used the opportunity to consolidate power, and subjugate the masses. Certainly at that time he could have used the name *Hashem* instead of *Elohim*, thereby fulfilling Abraham's mission, to *"invoke the Lord [Hashem] by name."*[13] By that point, everyone knew he was a Hebrew, and Pharaoh had met Joseph's father, Jacob. He was

---

[12] While the name *Hashem* is found in stories prior to Abraham, it is usually used when God is directly interacting with humans on a personal level, as opposed to the more general or universal sense that *Elohim* implies. Additionally, *Hashem* and *Elohim* are often used together, as in the phrase, "I am *Hashem*, your *Elohim*." In these cases, it is clear that *Hashem* is a proper noun, used to provide the identity of *Elohim*.

[13] See Ramban's commentary on Genesis 12:2 where he writes that God told Abraham *"to leave these places [Ur and Haran] as well and to fulfill his original intention that his worship be dedicated to Him alone and that he call upon people [for the worship of] the Name of the Eternal in the Chosen Land."* Abraham taught the people in Mesopotamia to know the name of God, he continued to do so in the land of Canaan (see Ramban on Genesis 12:8), and now the mission was to do the same in Egypt – if not by Abraham, then by his descendants.

not concerned about introducing a foreign heritage. Why not mention the "proper name" of God?

But there is no evidence that Joseph ever did use the name *Hashem* when interacting with Egypt. *Hashem* had been with Joseph in Egypt (Genesis 39:2-5,21), but Joseph did not bring *Hashem* to the Egyptians. That opportunity was squandered. And after Joseph died, the fortunes of Israel were reversed. From an elite in Egypt, they became a despised caste, forced into slavery. Their conditions deteriorated so badly that God needed to intervene. He appointed Moses as His prophet, and in their initial conversation, Moses was concerned about how to introduce God to the people of Israel. He asked, *"When I come to the Israelites and say to them, 'The God of your fathers has sent me to you,' and they ask me, 'What is His name?' what shall I say to them?"* (Exodus 3:13). God told Moses that he should use the name *Hashem* (3:15).

However, it was not enough that Israel should once again be familiar with the name *Hashem* and what it meant. Pharaoh and the Egyptians needed to learn it as well. Following God's command, Moses went to Pharaoh and addressed him: *"Thus says* Hashem, *the God of Israel: Let My people go that they may celebrate a festival for Me in the wilderness."* But Pharaoh refused to listen: *"Who is* Hashem *that I should heed Him and let Israel go? I do not know* Hashem, *nor will I let Israel go."* (Exodus 5:1-2)

Without the distinction between *Hashem* and *Elohim*, the significance of that conversation could be misunderstood. Pharaoh did not say he was unfamiliar with the concept of God. We see that Pharaoh's magicians referred to the plague of lice as *"the finger of God [Elohim]"* (8:15), and after suffering from the lice, Pharaoh told Moses to *"Go and sacrifice to your Elohim within the land."* *Elohim* was familiar, as it was in the time of Joseph. But they did not yet recognize *Hashem*[14], and this was,

---

[14] This is the opinion of Ibn Ezra in his commentary on Exodus 5:2-3, where he writes that Pharaoh asked Moses, "Who is this *Hashem*

according to God, one of the objectives of the plagues and the Exodus:

"And the Egyptians shall know that I am Hashem, when I stretch out My hand over Egypt and bring out the Israelites from their midst." (Exodus 7:5)[15]

God has linked the release of Israel from slavery with Egypt knowing *Hashem*. And if those two are linked, we can conclude that had Egypt already known *Hashem*, there would be no need to redeem Israel from bondage. In fact, had Egypt known *Hashem*, that is, known that God was not only the Almighty Creator of the world, but was interested in the advancement of humanity via a particular people – Israel – they would never have enslaved them in the first place. They would have recognized that their concerns over the loyalty of the stranger (*"Let us deal shrewdly with them, so that they may not increase; otherwise in the event of war they may join our enemies in fighting against us"* - Exodus 1:10) was not a legitimate excuse for oppression and cruelty.

Therefore, looking back to Joseph, we can see that had he taken the opportunity to introduce knowledge of *Hashem* to Egypt, God's goals could have been accomplished centuries earlier, without the abusive oppression of Israel and the devastating punishment of Egypt[16].

---

who is *Elohim*?" and Moses responded that *"Hashem* is the God of the Hebrews."

[15] See Exodus 7:17, 10:2, 14:4 and 14:8 for similar phrases.

[16] A parallel to this criticism of Joseph can be found by looking at Genesis 47, where Joseph enslaves the Egyptian people. This policy both set up the infrastructure for future enslavements and encouraged the resentment of Israel for their special treatment by Joseph. That combination paved the way for the subjugation of Israel after Joseph's death.

Solomon

After leaving Egypt, receiving the Torah, and entering the Land of Israel, it took several centuries before the conquest of the land was completed, and Israel could transform from a confederation of tribes to a united nation. King David secured the military victories necessary for this transition, and during the reign of his son, Solomon, the nation experienced peace and prosperity like never before.

Since these political and military goals had been accomplished, Solomon could now turn to a new effort: building a permanent Temple for service to God. Ever since the days of Moses, God had been served in the Tabernacle, a portable structure that had resided in several locations during that time. Solomon's Temple in Jerusalem, however, was an impressive edifice that took years to build, and was considered a fitting abode for God's presence.

During the dedication of the Temple, King Solomon gave a long speech, where he recounted the history of Israel and explained the purposes of the Temple he had built (I Kings 8:15-61). In addition to describing the function of the Temple for the nation of Israel, Solomon also noted that it would be a house of prayer for all peoples:

> Or if a foreigner who is not of Your people Israel comes from a distant land for the sake of Your name — for they shall hear about Your great name and Your mighty hand and Your outstretched arm—when he comes to pray toward this House, oh, hear in Your heavenly abode and grant all that the foreigner asks You for. Thus all the peoples of the earth will know Your name and revere You, as does Your people Israel; and they will recognize that Your name is attached to this House that I have built. (I Kings 8:41-43)

He defined the purpose of all his effort "to the end that all the peoples of the earth may know that the LORD alone is God, there is no other." (8:60).

With these words, Solomon echoed Abraham's mission, as assigned to the people of Israel. When the people of the world heard about God's name, and His miracles, they would pray towards the Temple and know God's name, and that *Hashem* alone is God. God's vision for humanity could be accomplished by collective effort, not by the violence associated with the Exodus. This Temple could be the reverse of the Tower of Babel: the people of the world would gather around a magnificent building to serve God instead of to abandon Him.

However, this utopia never came to be. After Solomon's death, the nation divided into rival kingdoms, and idolatry was practiced once again. The Temple certainly never fulfilled Solomon's aspirations for the people of Israel. And several centuries later, it was burned to the ground by the Babylonians.

Why would God let this happen to His home on earth? Many reasons can be given for the rapid decline of the situation, from the oppressive tactics taken during the building of the Temple, to the permissive attitude toward the idolatry of Solomon's many wives, to the mistaken idea that any building could be permanent if God did not support the people building it. But for our purposes, we shall focus on how **the Temple never fulfilled its function of causing all peoples to know God's name and revere Him.**

Unlike the sacrifices that Israel brought in the Temple, which continued until its destruction, we do not see that the nations of the world ever viewed the Temple as inspiration to worship God. There may be one exception to that claim, however. This was during the visit of the Queen of Sheba:

> *The queen of Sheba heard of Solomon's fame, through the name of the LORD, and she came to test him with hard questions. […] When she came to Solomon, she asked him all that she had in mind. Solomon had answers for all her questions; there was nothing that the king did not know, [nothing] to which he could not give her an answer. When the queen of Sheba observed all of Solomon's wisdom, and*

> *the palace he had built, the fare of his table, the seating of his courtiers, the service and attire of his attendants, and his wine service, and the burnt offerings that he offered at the House of the LORD, she was left breathless. She said to the king, "The report I heard in my own land about you and your wisdom was true. But I did not believe the reports until I came and saw with my own eyes that not even the half had been told me; your wisdom and wealth surpass the reports that I heard. How fortunate are your men and how fortunate are these your courtiers, who are always in attendance on you and can hear your wisdom! Praised be the LORD your God, who delighted in you and set you on the throne of Israel. It is because of the LORD's everlasting love for Israel that He made you king to administer justice and righteousness."* (I Kings 10:1-9)

At first glance, this seems like a successful visit. The queen is impressed by Solomon and the Temple, and praises God in response. Is this not a fulfilment of the mission to be a kingdom of priests?

However, a closer read reveals some cracks in that façade. While there is mention of "the name of the LORD," it is brought up as how the Queen heard about Solomon's fame. The Queen was indeed impressed with the Temple, but the multiple uses of "he" and "him" (referring to Solomon), indicate that she was mostly in awe of Solomon's wisdom and wealth. And even when she praised God, it was for how He had made Solomon king. It was as if God was serving Solomon, instead of Solomon serving God.

We actually find an alternate scenario for their encounter in the book of Psalms. In Psalm 72, David composed a prayer for his son Solomon, who would succeed him as king[17].

---

[17] Although this is psalm 72 out of 150, it concludes with the phrase *"The prayers of David the son of Jesse are ended"* (Psalm 72:20), indicating that chronologically, this was the last of David's psalms.

In this psalm, David predicts that foreign rulers will visit Solomon, and even mentions the monarch of Sheba: *"Let kings of Tarshish and the islands pay tribute, kings of Sheba and Seba offer gifts."* (Psalms 72:10)

He goes even further, and prays that this will apply to all nations, *"Let all kings bow to him, and all nations serve him."* (Psalms 72:11). But the next verses explain why the world's leaders will acknowledge and serve him: *"For he saves the needy who cry out, the lowly who have no helper. He cares about the poor and the needy; He brings the needy deliverance."* (Psalms 72:12-13)

As David stated in the opening of the psalm, these are the conditions for a worthy king:

"That he may judge Your people rightly; Your lowly ones, justly" (Psalms 72:2); *"Let him champion the lowly among the people, deliver the needy folk, and crush those who wrong them."* (Psalms72:4)

Ruling with righteousness, reflecting God's obsession with justice, should be what impresses the nations of the world. If his throne is established on justice, then *"all nations will bless themselves through him"* (Psalms 72:17), a direct parallel with God's initial promise to Abraham: *"all the families of the earth shall bless themselves through you."* (Genesis 12:3)

David laid out for Solomon the path to fulfill the mission of Abraham. Had he followed it, the nations of the world would recognize God, follow His just ways, and all of humanity would be blessed. Instead, when the Queen of Sheba visited, there was no presentation of a just society[18]. There was only focus on Solomon's wisdom – a gift he had received from God to

---

[18] The one mention of justice in her visit, when she told Solomon that God *"made you king to administer justice and righteousness"* (I Kings 10:9) does not directly say that he was administering justice, only that to act justly was why he was appointed king.

enact justice (I Kings 3:11-12). An opportunity was missed, and it never repeated itself.

The First Temple did not serve its purpose, and so eventually it would fall. Would things be different in the second Temple?

Zerubbabel

After the destruction of the First Temple, the Jews were exiled in Babylon for seventy years. During that time, the Persian empire defeated the Babylonians, and then Cyrus, the Persian emperor, allowed the Jews to return to their homeland and rebuild the temple.

> In the first year of King Cyrus of Persia, when the word of the LORD spoken by Jeremiah was fulfilled, the LORD roused the spirit of King Cyrus of Persia to issue a proclamation throughout his realm by word of mouth and in writing as follows: "Thus said King Cyrus of Persia: The LORD God of Heaven has given me all the kingdoms of the earth and has charged me with building Him a house in Jerusalem, which is in Judah. Anyone of you of all His people—may his God be with him, and let him go up to Jerusalem that is in Judah and build the House of the LORD God of Israel, the God that is in Jerusalem." (Ezra 1:1-3)

This had been earlier predicted by the prophet Isaiah, in the second half of his book:

> [I] am the same who says of Cyrus, "He is My shepherd; He shall fulfill all My purposes! He shall say of Jerusalem, 'She shall be rebuilt,' And to the Temple: 'You shall be founded again.'" (Isaiah 44:28)

> Thus said the LORD to Cyrus, His anointed one [...] For the sake of My servant Jacob, Israel My chosen one, I call you by name (Isaiah 45:1,4)

It was I who roused him for victory and who level all roads for him. He shall rebuild My city and let My exiled people go (Isaiah 45:13)

But Isaiah did not only predict that the Jews would return to their land and rebuild the Temple. He also foresaw that this new Temple would be a home to all people:

Let not the foreigner say, Who has attached himself to the LORD, 'The LORD will keep me apart from His people' [...] As for the foreigners who attach themselves to the LORD, to minister to Him, and to love the name of the LORD, to be His servants— All who keep the sabbath and do not profane it, and who hold fast to My covenant— I will bring them to My sacred mount And let them rejoice in My house of prayer. Their burnt offerings and sacrifices shall be welcome on My altar; For My House shall be called a house of prayer for all peoples. (Isaiah 56:3,6-7)

In the past, the foreigners had felt excluded from the service of God. In this new Temple, they would be welcome, for it would be a house of prayer for all peoples, just as Solomon had aspired in his time. Once again, this seemed like a prime opportunity for a fulfillment of Abraham's mission. **By allowing all people to participate in the service of God, the Jews could become a kingdom of priests.**

But unfortunately, this is not how events transpired. When the Jews started rebuilding the Temple, they were approached by former adversaries[19]:

When the adversaries of Judah and Benjamin heard that the returned exiles were building a temple to the LORD God of Israel, they approached Zerubbabel and the chiefs of the clans and said to them, 'Let us build with you, since we too worship your God, having offered sacrifices to

---

[19] Thank you to Rabbi David Fohrman for pointing out to me the importance of these verses in Ezra.

Him since the time of King Esarhaddon of Assyria, who
brought us here.' Zerubbabel, Jeshua, and the rest of the
chiefs of the clans of Israel answered them, 'It is not for
you and us to build a House to our God, but we alone
will build it to the LORD God of Israel, in accord with the
charge that the king, King Cyrus of Persia, laid upon us.'
(Ezra 4:1-3)

Zerubbabel, the Jewish governor, declined the offer of help from
these non-Jews. Despite the precedent of non-Jews helping to
build the first Temple[20], he told them that building the house of
God "is not for you" and that they alone would take on this task.
How distant was this response from the vision of Isaiah!

The reaction to this short-sighted approach came quickly:

Thereupon the people of the land undermined the resolve
of the people of Judah, and made them afraid to build.
They bribed ministers in order to thwart their plans all
the years of King Cyrus of Persia and until the reign of
King Darius of Persia. And in the reign of Ahasuerus, at
the start of his reign, they drew up an accusation against
the inhabitants of Judah and Jerusalem. (Ezra 4:4-6)

The possibility of a speedy construction of the Temple was
no longer viable, the other exiles were much more hesitant to
return to the land, and Jews would have continued tension with
their neighbors in the years to come[21]. Perhaps for this reason
Zerubbabel, a descendant of David, never merited to become
a king like his ancestors, and the Jews would not restore their
monarchy, but rather remain subjects of Persia.

---

[20] Chronicles II 2:2-15. It is significant for our discussion, that in
response to King Solomon's request for help, Huram, king of Tyre
replied, *"Blessed is the LORD, God of Israel, who made the heavens*
and the earth." (2:11)

[21] The mention of the accusation during the time of the Persian
emperor Ahasuerus may correspond with Haman's decrees against
the Jews in the book of Esther.

The Second Temple would stand for centuries, like the first, but it too would fall, this time to the Romans[22]. **It never fulfilled its destiny of being a house to all nations. Isaiah's prophecy would be postponed to future times.**

Conclusion

Throughout this essay, we have seen several opportunities for the realization of Abraham's mission, and each time the opportunity slipped away. Israel was assigned the task of being a kingdom of priests, but preferred to look inward, to what would benefit themselves, instead of outward, to what would bring blessing to all of humanity.

Concern about keeping Israel unique, following its own laws, and remaining distinct from the rest of the world is not only understandable, but a requirement of the very divine covenant they agreed to when assigned their mission. However, when that sense of particularism descends into parochialism, their entire mission is at risk.

Two thousand years after the Roman defeat of Israel, the Jewish people once again are on the world stage, as an independent nation in their own land. The State of Israel has diplomatic relations with the vast majority of the countries of the world. Pre-COVID, tourists visited Israel in record numbers, and Israelis traveled all over the world for business and pleasure. Israel and Israelis are featured in the news, in the arts and sciences and in commercial industry worldwide. It is fair to say that Jews have never experienced such exposure to the world in their history.

If there was ever a time to perform their role as a kingdom of priests, of showing the world how to recognize God through ethical behavior and the pursuit of justice, now would be

---

[22] It is noteworthy that according to Jewish tradition, one of the causes of the destruction of the second Temple was the refusal of the Sages to accept the sacrifice in the Temple sent by the Roman emperor (Babylonian Talmud, Gittin 56a).

it. We have seen what has happened in the past when those opportunities were missed. Will this be the occasion that Israel looks outward, lives up to its destiny, and brings the blessing that the world so desperately needs?

David Curwin is a writer living in Efrat, Israel. He has been writing about the origin of Hebrew words and phrases, and their connection to other languages, on his website Balashon.com since 2006. He has also published widely on topics relating to Bible and Jewish philosophy.

The Oral Torah Dilemma

DR. RIVKAH LAMBERT ADLER

To a Torah Jew, it is axiomatic that the Oral Torah was given by God to Moses on Mt. Sinai along with the Written Torah. I refer to this belief as the second largest theological divide between Judaism and Christianity and one that every Jewish teacher who undertakes teaching Torah to current or former Christians will face.

A person coming from a Christian background will invariably have been taught, or will have concluded, that the Oral Torah is nothing but "traditions of men" and therefore consider it easily dismissible or worse, teeming with evil and witchcraft. There is a deeply-held aversion to Talmud among Christians and that applies to kabbalah as well.

This is a significant theological difference that must be addressed directly. A Christian will never properly understand the Bible from a Jewish perspective if they are missing this understanding. Since current and former Christians have great reverence for the Bible, it's been my experience that the best way to prove the God-given validity of (and necessity for) the Oral Torah is to use the Bible itself.

Quite simply, there are too many laws and concepts in Hebrew scripture that are vague and cannot be understood without the Oral Torah. A few examples should suffice to make the point.

The Bible instructs how to count the beginning of the year.

This month shall be to you the head of the months; to you it shall be the first of the months of the year. (Exodus 12:2)

To which calendar is this referring? Is it referring to solar months or lunar months? To the Egyptian calendar, since the Children of Israel were living in Egypt at the time? To the Chaldean calendar of Abraham's birthplace? Without the Oral Torah that provides more information, there is no way to properly understand this verse and therefore no way to set up a calendar according to God's command.

Another example: There is the blue dye known as techelet. Techelet dye is used in the commandment of tzitzit, as it says:

> *Speak to the children of Israel and you shall say to them that they shall make for themselves fringes on the corners of their garments, throughout their generations, and they shall affix a thread of sky blue [techelet] wool on the fringe of each corner.* (Exodus 15:38)

Neither the source of this special blue dye nor how to produce it is defined in the Bible. For this, we need the Oral Torah. Without the Oral Torah we also lack details about how to make the fringes. How many strings constitute a fringe? How long should they be? We are told one of the threads should be blue, but what color should the rest of them be? Do all the fringes need to be wool or only the blue thread? The Bible offers no specific instructions.

Another example: Moses commands that "no man leave his place" on Shabbat.

> *See that the Lord has given you the Sabbath. Therefore, on the sixth day, He gives you bread for two days. Let each man remain in his place; let no man leave his place on the seventh day.* (Exodus 16:29)

How are we to understand how to fulfill this requirement without more information? What constitutes his place? Does this mean he can't leave the room he was in when Shabbat began? Or his home? Can he leave his property to visit a neighbor on Shabbat? Can he venture out of his neighborhood? Out of his city? The clarification is found in the Oral Torah, not in the Bible.

Another example: God instructs that the Shabbat should be sanctified and that no labor should be performed on it.

Remember the Sabbath day to sanctify it. Six days may you work and perform all your labor, but the seventh day is a Sabbath to the Lord, your God; you shall perform no labor, neither you, your son, your daughter, your manservant, your maidservant, your beast, nor your stranger who is in your cities. (Exodus 20:8-10)

What's missing from the Bible is any explanation of what constitutes forbidden labor. What work is permitted and what work is forbidden on the Sabbath? For this, we need the Oral Torah.

Later, in the Book of Jeremiah, God reminds the people that they should observe the Sabbath "as I commanded your forefathers."

*Neither shall you take a burden out of your houses on the Sabbath day nor shall you perform any labor, and you shall hallow the Sabbath day **as I commanded your forefathers**.* (Jeremiah 17:22)

But where are the details of what exactly God commanded our forefathers to be found? They do not appear in the Bible itself. The specific laws that God Himself said He commanded are found in the Oral Torah.

One final example:

*If the place the Lord, your God, chooses to put His Name there, will be distant from you, you may slaughter of your cattle and of your sheep, which the Lord has given you, **as I have commanded you**, and you may eat in your cities, according to every desire of your soul.* (Deuteronomy 12:21)

This verse from Deuteronomy refers to the laws of kosher slaughter that the Jewish people have been given, but the laws themselves do not appear anywhere in the Bible. Again, the specific laws that God Himself said He commanded are not found in the Bible. They are in the Oral Torah.

This, then, is the Jewish perspective that must be communicated to the non-Jewish student. The complete, authentic transmission from God to Moses contained a written component that we call the Bible and an oral tradition that accompanied and elucidated it. They were given at the same time on Mt Sinai and without the Oral Torah (which was eventually also written down), many of the commandments God issues in the Bible simply cannot be understood, let alone fulfilled.

Vital Jewish Values
for the Nations

RABBI ELAN ADLER

During my years in the active rabbinate, in Stamford, Connecticut and Baltimore, Maryland, I felt it a great privilege to speak at interfaith occasions. Sometimes I was a guest speaker at a dinner or similar function, most often being invited to offer the benediction or invocation at a Martin Luther King Jr. breakfast or *Yom HaShoah* (Holocaust Remembrance Day) commemoration at Social Security or the US Department of Health and Human Services. As a president of the Baltimore Board of Rabbis, there were many invitations to address interfaith groups of all ages, including political events on a local and national level.

As an Orthodox rabbi, one of my greatest joys at these events was the honor of representing a rich tradition of teachers and messages, of scholarship and wisdom, of intimacy with God. And I knew in my heart that when standing in front of an audience that represented the widest face of God, I was doing holy work. I was there to remind people that, although we have different faiths and beliefs, we share a commonality of goals and dreams for ourselves, our families, our communities and the world.

I represented God and the Torah. I was there to be a Light unto the Nations. There was no interest on my part to be a 7 watt night light; it was either a 2000 watt beam or I would feel that I failed in my mission, namely, to share the idea that while God and the Torah may not obligate everyone equally, they unequivocally speak to everyone.

This is our responsibility as Jews. It hit me years ago that this duty to share the universal messages of the Torah is hinted at in words no less holy and sacred than those of the Rosh Hashanah *Amida* (the central prayer in Jewish liturgy, also known as the Shemonah Esrei). *"Instill Your awe on all you have created... let all Your handiwork revere You...speedily reign over all your creations..."* And in the Aleinu prayer: *"May all the inhabitants of the world recognize You and bow down to You...may they accept the yoke of Your kingship...on that day Hashem will be king over all the earth, He will be one and His name will be One."*

How will the Nations arrive at this level of allegiance and obedience to the Master of the Universe? Who is going to teach them, inspire them and motivate them to learn and comprehend the universal messages in the Torah that are meant for all of God's creations? They won't arrive at *Hashem Echad U'shemo Echad* (God is One and His Name is One) blindly. **We are the Lights for the Nations.** As I see it, the following are some of the most important universal Torah values intended to guide all of humanity.

SHABBAT

As God told the Jewish people, He has a treasure which He would like to share with them, and it is called Shabbat. At the most, Shabbat is a day spent in *oneg*, the pleasure of a day of rest, and *kavod*, giving honor to God the Creator. It is a day of *zachor*, to remember throughout the week that Shabbat is coming and a reminder to prepare for this holy day, and of *shamor*, being careful to not violate the restrictions that are in place to help guarantee a *Shabbat Kodesh* (a holy Sabbath). At the very least, for the Nations, it is a day to take off from work if possible, and reflect, redirect energies, rejuvenate and get in touch with the soul and spiritual part of life. Clearly, the Nations are not required to follow the laws, and there is debate as to whether gentiles may keep all the laws of Shabbat. There can be little debate, however, about the physical, emotional and spiritual benefits of taking a Shabbat, even if not making a Shabbat.

CONSCIOUS EATING

In the Torah portion of *Shemini* (Leviticus 9:1–11:47), God teaches the Jewish people that besides being careful about what comes out of our mouths, we need also be cautious about what goes into our mouths. For a first time reader of the many verses that instruct about visible signs that put various domesticated animals and fowl and fish into the kosher category, there is a question that begs itself: for what possible reason did God create a huge variety of food in the world, only to restrict the Jew to a sliver of it? And why are those the outward signs of a kosher species and not other signs?

We find ourselves at the very last verse of Shemini to get a sense of what God had in mind: *L'havdil bein ha-tamei u'vein ha-tahor* (to distinguish between the impure and the pure.) There is more to it (a LOT more to it!), but the core of *kashrut* (Jewish dietary laws) is to differentiate and to discern, to learn how to make spiritual and God-connected choices and to recognize differences.

There are gentiles who are careful to avoid pork and shellfish, eating what they call biblically clean, though not necessarily kosher. Discernment in food choices easily leads to having greater clarity in other life choices and is a beneficial proficiency to which to aspire.

TZEDAKAH (charity) and CHESED (deeds of loving kindness)

Many years ago, synagogues had an idea that revolutionized the Bar and Bat Mitzvah: the Mitzvah Project. It was felt that the event itself, the synagogue performance and the subsequent celebration, focuses so heavily on the child. What if we suggested that as part of their milestone event, a mitzvah project was done, to help each student climb out of themselves and see a bigger world and its many challenges and needs?

Many raised money or collected things or brought awareness of an urgent need to their guests. The idea was a huge success, and it continues to this day. Tzedakah/chesed is a major pillar of both Judaism and Islam, and for good reason. While the words tzedakah and chesed have a wide variety of applications, and the Torah has many examples of urging charitable and compassionate giving, at their core is the idea of repairing the world, sharing with others who have less, opening our eyes and hearts to need and challenge and shortage. Teaching the Nations the commandment as well as the privilege of tzedakah and chesed can affect a spiritual rehabilitation of our world.

TEN COMMANDMENTS

Jewish tradition is rich with rabbinic commentary about who was actually standing at Mount Sinai for the giving of the Ten Commandments. Some say it was all souls present, past and future. Others say it included the souls of all who would eventually convert to Judaism and the souls of those among the Nations who wished to be under God's command, even though their nation refused the Torah when it was offered.

You do not have to be Jewish to acknowledge that what happened on Mount Sinai was one of the most important moments in the history of civilization. God gave His commands, not in the Land of Israel, but in the desert, which is ownerless, and therefore belongs equally to everyone.

And His words weren't intended for just one people. They were meant for the whole world, because they represent the key to universal survival. Emblazoned on stone was the concept that some things are right and some are wrong, decided by Divine Will and not by a committee or society.

From the mountaintop of Sinai, God taught the world that there are absolutes and rules to abide by. He made us aware, through two tablets side-by-side, to be equally conscious of how we relate to Him as well as our fellow men and women. The entire world was challenged to channel our deeds, as well as our thoughts and intentions, heavenward. **And the Jewish nation was called upon to invest in teaching the Nations these basic tenets.**

PRAYER

In our *siddurim* (prayerbooks), there are many prayers for various reasons. Some are long prayers, such as the *Musaf* (additional service) Amida for Rosh Hashanah, and some are very short, such as *Moshe's* (Moses') prayer for healing for his sister Miriam: *El Na, Refa Na La* (please God, heal her!) There are many instances of prayer in the Torah, all efforts to reach and beseech God to consider our dire situation and respond with favor, or hearts pouring out in thankfulness for His grace and salvations.

The Torah teaches us that there are various ways to link heaven and earth, and one of the most primary is through prayer – the idea that what we say and do *here* is heard *there*. It's quite a distance to traverse.

A teaching from *Pirkei Avot* (Ethics of the Fathers) says that one miracle done repeatedly in the *Beit HaMikdash* (Holy Temple) was that the column of smoke that rose from sacrifices remained unaffected by winds. If sacrifice was prayer, one could vividly see and feel that connection, that channel. Lacking that vision today, we still have absolute confidence that our words can leap from our lips and find their place in the hearing of the Almighty. God and His Torah have given us, and from us to the Nations, a most powerful way to bathe our world in hope.

DERECH ERETZ

It has often been said that there should be a fifth section of the *Shulchan Aruch* (Code of Jewish Law) following the well-known four major sections, and it should be called *Derech Eretz* (acts of decency and courtesy). I would suggest it might even be better positioned as the first section, in honor of the teaching that *derech eretz kadma laTorah*, that being careful to be kind, sensitive, compassionate and refined has to be the foundation of a life of commitment to Torah and *mitzvot* (Divine commandments).

There is a teaching that for the three days prior to the receiving of the Torah, the Israelite nation was told to practice derech eretz with each other. Equally weighty is noting that Pirkei Avot is placed in the order of *Nezikin* (damages) in the *Mishna* (central part of the Oral Torah), in order to make the point that when we, as Jews, fail to keep the Torah with derech eretz, we can damage not only our individual reputation, but also that of the entire Jewish people, and even God Himself.

Rambam (important Torah scholar who lived 1138-1204 CE) teaches that when we do the right thing with the right attitude and kindness and sensitivity, it is a *kiddush Hashem* (sanctification of God's Name), making Him look very good in the world, and when we do the opposite, it is a *chillul Hashem* (desecration of God's Name), embarrassing and insulting to Hashem and His great Torah. **As Jewish people, our obligation to teach and model derech eretz is no less to the Nations, who see us as the preservers and the teachers of God's Holy Word.** Upgrading everyone's derech eretz is a magnet to bring Mashiach.

FAITH

We are the people who taught the world *Amein* (Amen), an acronym for the words *El Melech Ne'eman* (God is a faithful King). In saying Amein, we confirm our belief that whatever the blessing made entailed, we know it was God who made it happen, and will continue to make it happen again and again in the future.

We are a people of *emunah* (faith) and even more, *bitachon* (tested faith). Emunah is standing at the top of a staircase, waiting to jump into a parent's arms, believing that they will not let you down and will catch you. Bitachon is trusting them repeatedly because they have shown themselves to be trustworthy and consistently dependable.

Over and over, the Jewish people have put their collective trust in Hashem, Creator and Sustainer, knowing with surety that He loves us, cares for us, does only the best for us, and wishes to have the same relationship with all the Nations of the world. Faith is hardly sectarian; it is an equal opportunity lifter and supporter for all mankind. There is no better people to teach this faith to others than the People of the Book and the People of emunah and bitachon.

REWARD AND PUNISHMENT

In Rambam's 13 Principles of Faith, number 11 is summarized in a familiar passage as recorded in *Yigdal* (Jewish prayer based on the 13 Principles of Faith). "God repays the person of chesed for his deeds, while He punishes the evildoers in accord with their transgression."

At the very height of the Jewish experience at Mount Sinai prior to receiving the Torah, the Jewish nation asserted enthusiastically, *Naaseh Venishma* (We will do and then we will hear.)

If only that doing and following and observing would have been the hallmark of our nation. Alas, our history has been one of joyous following of the Torah, as well as joyous abandoning of the Torah. Not angels, we are human, susceptible to temptations and seductions of all kinds, drawing us from the service of God that we promised.

We therefore find statements in the Torah such as this one, the thrust of which is replicated many times in our Tanach: *"Behold it will be that when you listen to my commands...to love and to serve Hashem with all your heart and soul, that I will give rain in its season and plentiful crops and you shall eat and be satisfied. Be careful that your heart does not get tempted, causing you to worship other gods, and I will halt the rains and cancel your crops."* (Deuteronomy 11)

When we do good, it is acknowledged and rewarded in kind; when we do bad, that too is acknowledged and repaid in kind. While there are many in the Nations who feel that God's Grace, not our good deeds, bring the Kingdom of God to rest on earth, we teach and model the intrinsic value of doing good. Doing good helps us not only to avoid punishment, it also shapes and polishes our character and soul. Teaching this pillar of Judaism to the Nations helps polish the rough diamonds among us.

GRATITUDE

Our Jewish day begins with gratitude, when we arise and say *Modeh/Modah Ani* – "I thank you, Hashem, for compassionately restoring my soul to me, great is your faithfulness." This brief prayer inaugurates a day filled with blessing and praise, thanks and recognition for all that Hashem does for us, for others and for the world.

When we make a *bracha* (blessing), we call God the God of the entire world, *Melech ha'olam* (King of the world), understanding that, just as He created the world, he remains intimately involved with all its aspects and all its people.

Teaching and modeling gratitude to the Nations has a benefit beyond the spiritual; our health care professionals remind us of the importance of being thankful to each other and even to ourselves. In their estimation, being thankful and expressing it, is one of the most critical ingredients, perhaps even the main ingredient, to happiness and contentment. Our keen and detailed observations of God's goodness and kindness, even when we experience hardship and challenge, give us a helpful prism through which we can love God and our fellow men and women as well as ourselves. All Nations can benefit tremendously from the Jewish priority of gratitude.

MASHIACH/REDEMPTION

In the same way that a person starts dying from the moment he or she is born, the Jewish people have waited for the Mashiach and his redemption from the formation of Adam and Eve. From those first seconds of human life, we have anticipated the arrival of a worldwide Messiah, one who will bring us to a spiritually-drenched new epoch of existence, free of trial and pain and sickness and evil. Anxiously anticipating Mashiach has been a pursuit across the millennia, and it has helped the Jewish people cope with innumerable atrocities and challenges, personal and national, by knowing that Hashem's saving is coming, even though there might be a bleak outlook in the present.

It is a promise from God, veiled in the Five Books of Moses but clear in the rest of Tanach, that a Redeemer will come to Zion, and that Hashem will bring the Mashiach at the End of Days, to redeem and vindicate those who unstintingly awaited his arrival every day. Teaching the Nations about Mashiach and redemption is a priceless and indispensable gift to a fractured world that needs hope and optimism. *Od Lo Avda Tikvateinu* (Our hope is not yet lost). Who but a nation that, for 2,000 years, has not lost hope to return to our Homeland can so fervently spread this Messianic ideal to the Nations?

Rabbi Elan Adler was born in Israel to Hungarian Holocaust survivors. After receiving his rabbinic ordination from Yeshiva University, he served Orthodox congregations on the east coast of the US over a 25-year period. During that time, he was active in interfaith initiatives, and developed multi-faith relationships. In Israel since 2010, he teaches in a girls' high school and in several local programs of Jewish and biblical content and also does counseling for individuals and couples.

The Land of Israel Fellowship (A Case Study)

DR. RIVKAH LAMBERT ADLER

The Arugot Farm is located in the Biblical mountains of Zif which are mentioned in the Book of Joshua (15:55). This area is where King David served as a shepherd and where he escaped while being pursued by King Saul.

"The Arugot Farm is for people who want to touch the history of Israel and get a feeling for the destiny to come. We are literally building the vision of the prophets and turning the barren land into a garden of Eden-like oasis," shared Rabbi Jeremy Gimpel who lives on the farm with his wife and children.

At the heart of the Arugot Farm is a spiritual retreat center geared to spiritual tourism focused on prayer, music and Torah that are connected to the Land of Israel. "According to Jewish tradition, most of the Book of Psalms was written here in these very mountains by David before he became the king. Psalm 23 – *The Lord is my shepherd; I shall not fear*' was written right here when David was still a young man, tending to his flock.

"Creating a center based on prayer and music simply unveiled what this place was destined for long before we ever arrived here," Gimpel explained.

When COVID-19 froze tourism to Israel, the Arugot Farm went dark.

"When the coronavirus hit Israel and all international flights were banned, it felt like a death sentence for me, my family and my work. I don't remember being so confused, anxious and lost in a long time," Gimpel admitted.

The darkness eventually passed, and in its place came a dynamic inspiration. "If I can't bring people to Judea, I will bring Judea to them!" Gimpel declared. "It's where I felt I was being led. There are prophecies and guidance in Tanach that encouraged me on the way."

"For in those days it will happen that ten men from the Nations will grab hold of the corner of a Judean man saying 'Let us go with you for we have heard that God is with you.'" (Zechariah 8:23)

From this inspiration was born The Land of Israel Fellowship. With people around the world banned from, or nervous about attending, their local houses of worship because of the coronavirus, the Land of Israel Fellowship offered a virtual replacement.

Gimpel elaborated, "We are pioneering a new way in the world. The Land of Israel Fellowship is **a virtual house of prayer for all Nations**. People from all over the world, from different religious backgrounds, looking for something real and something different, have joined."

He and his partner, Rabbi Ari Abramowitz, who also lives on the farm with his wife and daughter, have been translating the universal wisdom of Torah for international audiences for many years. Now they are applying their experience and personal charisma into a soulful weekly virtual fellowship anyone with an internet connection can join. Already, hundreds of people representing 28 different countries have participated in the live Sunday broadcasts.

Fellowship member Levi Schwiethale, a young, Israel-loving Christian living in Colorado said, "We are purposely meeting every Sunday morning with a group of about 15 people to learn from Rabbis Jeremy and Ari. We call it our 'church' and we begin prior to the lesson by reading the Torah Portion for the new week. We feel like we are redeeming, in part, two millennia of Sunday church teachings against the Jewish people and the

Torah by centering our 'church' around lessons from Jewish rabbis and the Torah."

Gimpel explained that, "So far we have agnostic, atheist, Orthodox and even a Buddhist Jew, Christians from all backgrounds including a Catholic nun and a Muslim member. [The Fellowship] is forcing us, as representatives of the Jewish people, to create **a universal language that makes the Torah accessible and meaningful for all of humanity**.

"Our Fellowship is the virtual reality of our physical reality in Judea, and the members of the Fellowship are the agents who are facilitating the manifestation of this vision into the world.

"**It's not our vision, but the ultimate vision of the Bible**. We are witnessing and participating in the beginning stages of biblical prophecy being fulfilled in the Land of Israel. Without the values and spirit of the Bible, the world will perish. Look at America today, disconnected from God.

"**Our mandate is to be light unto the Nations. It is time for the Jewish people to take responsibility for the world and share the Torah from Zion and the word of God from Jerusalem,** as the prophet Isaiah says:

> And the many peoples shall go and say: "Come, Let us go up to the Mount of Hashem, To the House of the God of Yaakov; That He may instruct us in His ways, And that we may walk in His paths." For instruction shall come forth from Tzion, The word of Hashem from Yerushalayim. (Isaiah 3:2)

"As I see the vision of the prophets unfolding in Israel, the Jewish people and the righteous among the Nations who are participating in this experiment are the next step in the process of redemption," Gimpel articulated.

The Land of Israel Fellowship meets live every Sunday 18:00 Israel time and has hundreds of people tuning in live from dozens of locations worldwide, including Australia, New Zealand, Germany, Hawaii and Idaho.

"Seeing my new friends wake up at 3 AM to join us live from New Zealand and seeing all the faces from all over the world praying and learning at the same time is exhilarating. It feels like we are, in our very own way, fulfilling prophecy by covering the whole world with prayer and Torah," Gimpel enthused.

Since they have been welcoming Bible-loving non-Jews to Israel for many years, Gimpel and Abramowitz are very familiar with Christians who celebrate the Biblical feasts. "The Fellowship is opening its virtual gates to people from all backgrounds who want to prepare for the Biblical feasts alongside the Jewish people, while learning authentic Torah wisdom from the Land of Israel.

"The prophet Isaiah says the Nations will *stream* to Jerusalem. I never knew that prophecy meant live streaming on Zoom!" Gimpel joked.

On Gentiles Studying Kabbalah and Chassidut

RABBI AMICHAI COHEN

Live Kabbalah Was Reborn Through the Generosity of a Gentile

It was a regular wintery Tuesday morning in the mountainous region of Tzfat in northern Israel when I opened an unusual email. The email was from a non-Jewish businessman from Sweden. "Why is your site down?" he asked. "Your content is the best content out there on the Internet."

Upon moving to Israel from Florida, my students wanted to continue learning on Zoom. A friend thought it would be a great idea to start a website and stream these classes more globally. That's how LiveKabbalah.com was born.

After more than a year of teaching online, we had not yet devised a way to monetize our efforts, so we dropped LiveKabbalah.com. That decision left the Swedish businessman without access to our classes.

A week later, he was in Israel and insisted on meeting with us in Tzfat. He so believed in what we were doing that he personally invested in Live Kabbalah. His gift allowed us to purchase new computer and audio equipment. We now had the time and ability to produce professionally filmed classes, brand our website and focus on marketing.

We, as Jews, believe that everything is divinely ordained and that there are no coincidences. The fact that Live Kabbalah was reborn through the generosity of a gentile was, and still is, one of the most eye-opening and extraordinary events of my life.

Live Kabbalah's Next Stage

As Live Kabbalah grew, we met more gentiles interested in *Kabbalah* (the mystical tradition in Judaism) and *Chassidut* (the teachings of the Chasidic movement which focus on spiritual revival and the inner, mystical aspects of Judaism). The fact that we experienced such interest was surprising and intriguing.

For a long time I internally debated whether I could teach gentiles the more esoteric paths of the Torah. After all, Kabbalah is the most profound way certain souls need to be nourished.

Intuitively, I felt like I knew the answer from the beginning. It is often after much research and deliberation when we arrive back at the simple point of truth.

The Light of Torah

Our Sages tell us that this world was a garden of paradise and it is incumbent upon all of humanity to bring back the world to a state of paradise. The primordial sin represents the disconnection between the internally, God-centered reality versus the external, sensory association with the worldly pleasures.

Kabbalah teaches that the Torah is called The Tree of Life as it connects man to the internal purpose of creation, which is oneness with God. Kabbalah also teaches that there are two aspects of the Torah.

"It is told about King David," the rabbi said, "that when he wanted to bring people closer to an authentic Torah life, he would teach them the secrets of Torah.

> *"Just as there is a body and a soul, there is a body and soul of the Torah. Kabbalah is the soul of the Torah."*
> (Introduction to *Tikunei Zohar* – a main text of Kabbalah)

The bottom line is that all of us, Jews and gentiles, want to taste from the Tree of Life in the Garden of Eden. The world is beyond chaotic and without the guidance of the Torah, it is difficult, if not impossible, to make sense of what is transpiring in our world and where we are going.

The simple answer which I have found is that pure-hearted and well-meaning gentiles see the light which the Torah has given humanity.

I have come in contact with many Christians and Muslims who have been on challenging, and sometimes impossible, journeys to seek truth. Many have been through hell and back to find God and true happiness in their lives. It has evoked within me immense respect and admiration for their difficulties (including a lack of community) and courage. The gentile's pure fascination is something which has inspired me and caused me to reach deeper within my simple desire to connect to that root of life, the bedrock of existence.

The study of inner Torah, Kabbalah, gives one the inner answers to questions of why and how. Time and time again, I delight in seeing ideas register and associations made. The dots finally connect and inner healing and fixing is brought to tumultuous lives. This truth-seeking sincerity is the hallmark of the Jewish people, paved by Abraham, the first Jew, who left his familiar society to find God.

"Like cold water upon a thirsty soul," **the study of Kabbalah has the most universal, life-quenching solutions in the world.**

> *As cold water to a faint soul, so is good news from a distant country.* (Proverbs 25:25)

A Light Upon the Nations

The Jewish people have been entrusted to be a Light Upon the Nations. However, for many centuries, under the duress of anti-Semitism, pogroms, etc., we were unable to live as the shining examples of light to the world.

It is a fact that the Torah and Judaism, the oldest of the three monotheistic religions, changed the course of history and reshaped the trajectory of humankind. The wisdom of the Torah has served as a beacon of light for all of humanity.

Learn and observe [the Torah] for it is your wisdom and understanding in the eyes of the Nations, who will hear of all these laws and proclaim that this is truly a great, wise and understanding nation. (Deuteronomy 4:6)

In the famous Aleinu prayer, composed by Joshua, we reaffirm the goal of creation, that God's glory fills the entire earth - i.e., that ALL human beings recognize Him.

As we proclaim twice daily in the *Shema* (a central Jewish prayer), our perception of the Oneness of God will only be complete when God, Who is acknowledged now only by the Jewish people, will be the one God recognized by the entire world.

When God will be King over the whole world, on that day will He be One and His Name one. (Zechariah 14:9)

We, the Nation of Priests, are obligated to represent God to the world by our exemplary lifestyle, and imbue the world with knowledge of His existence.

I am the Lord; I called you with righteousness and I will strengthen your hand; and I formed you, and I made you for a people's covenant, for a light to Nations. (Isaiah 42:6)

During Temple times, the Jewish people brought 70 sacrifices on Sukkot for the benefit of the 70 Nations. The need for 70 distinct Nations is only a result of the Tower of Babel, when mankind united to deny God. As a consequence, God created divisions among them to thwart this attempt to countermand the purpose of man. The ideal, however, is that mankind should unite in the service of God, as the prophet Zephaniah proclaims.

Then will I return to the Nations a clear language so that they can all call on the Name of God and serve Him in unison. (Zephaniah 3:9).

As a Nation of Priests, the Jewish people have the obligation and privilege to share that light. *Rabbi Samson Refael Hirsch* (19th c. Talmudist and philosopher) expressed it like this:

"If, however, in the midst of a world which worships wealth and lust, Israel were to live a tranquil life of righteousness and love; if, while everywhere else the generation of man is sinking into the depth of sensuality and immorality, Israel's sons and daughters should bloom forth in the splendour of youth, purity and innocence, ah, what a powerful instrument for good Israel could be! **If...every Jew would be a mutely eloquent example and teacher of universal righteousness and universal love; if thus the dispersed of Israel were to show themselves everywhere on earth as the glorious priests of God and pure humanity; if only we were, or would become that which we should be, if only our lives were a perfect reflection of our Law - what a mighty force we would constitute for steering mankind to the final goal of all human education!** This would affect mankind more quietly, but much more forcefully and profoundly than ever our tragic record of suffering." (*The Nineteen Letters*, p. 65).

The Seven Laws of Noah

Yad Hachazaka, the encyclopedic work of the 12th century scholar Rambam, covers all of the laws incumbent by a Jew in the time of exile as well as when there is a Temple. The Rambam left no room for question, detailing every aspect of Jewish law.

In the very last laws of his work called "Kings and Wars" (*Melachim uMilchamot* chapters 11-12), the Rambam speaks about the identity of Moshiach as well as what will happen in the world at that time. In chapters 8-11, he speaks about the obligation of the Noahide in the world, **including the Jewish people's responsibility for ensuring that their non-Jewish brothers and sisters are committed to their Godly obligations.**

The Rambam wrote: "Moses was commanded by the Almighty to compel all the inhabitants of the world to accept the commandments given to Noah's descendants. Anyone who accepts upon himself the fulfillment of these seven mitzvot and is precise in their observance is considered one of 'the pious among the gentiles' and will merit a share in the world to come.

"This applies only when he accepts them and fulfills them because the Holy One, blessed be He, commanded them in the Torah and informed us through Moses, our teacher, that Noah's descendants had been commanded to fulfill them previously. However, if he fulfills them out of intellectual conviction, he is not a resident alien, nor of 'the pious among the gentiles,' nor of their wise men."

The Lubavitcher Rebbe, Rabbi Menachem Mendel Schneerson (20ᵗʰ c. leader of the Chabad-Lubavitch Chassidic movement) profusely quoted the Rambam's view on the Jewish obligation to help spread the Noahide laws to every human, thereby helping usher in the time of redemption. The Rebbe wrote, "**An integral component of the Jew's task is to see to it that all peoples, not just Jews, acknowledge God as creator and ruler of the world.**"

The Rebbe saw the shift in Jewish prominence and influence in the world as an omen of positive tidings for all of humanity. The Jewish people can finally rise up to their role as a Nation of Priests. "In previous generations, any attempt to influence the Nations of the world in matters of faith entailed danger to one's life, and therefore it was not possible to fulfill this command. In our generation, however, not only is there no danger involved, on the contrary, this increases the honor of the Jewish people in the eyes of all the Nations when they see that the Jewish people care not only about themselves but also about the civilization of the entire world by people behaving according to righteous and just ways," he wrote.

As proof, the Lubavitcher Rebbe referred to the enthusiastic endorsement of the then-President of the United States, Ronald Reagan, to announce to all citizens of the U.S. to unite around the fulfillment of the Seven Noahide Laws, as well as the declaration of both the Congress and the Senate that the Seven Laws should be upheld. From this, the Rebbe concluded, "The very fact that the President publicly announced the fulfillment of the Sheva Mitzvah B'nai Noach ought to greatly increase the efforts of Jews in this regard on all people of the world."

The Ba'al Shem Tov

It is well known that the *Ba'al Shem Tov* (18th c. mystic and the founder of Chassidic Judaism) had the wondrous abilities to catapult his soul to various heavenly realms. On Rosh Hashana in the year 1734, the Ba'al Shem Tov's soul entered the academy of Moshiach. Speaking to the soul of Moshiach, the Ba'al Shem Tov asked, "When will master arrive?" The soul of Moshiach responded, "When your teachings will spread outwards."

There is a direct correlation between the spreading of the esoteric teachings of the Torah, namely Kabbalah and Chassidut, and the arrival of Moshiach and the redemption of mankind.

The schools of Chabad and *Breslov Chassidut* (a branch of Chassidut founded in 18th c. by Rebbe Nachman of Breslov) in particular took the words of the Ba'al Shem Tov and Moshiach literally. Chabad is known to set up Chabad Houses all over the world, all with the aim of bringing unaffiliated Jews back to Judaism by spreading the teachings of Chabad Chassidut, which is an in-depth Kabbalistic understanding.

In the midst of serving Jews, the Chabad emissaries come in contact with and directly influence many non-Jews in keeping the seven Noahide laws, deepening their spiritual connection.

Rabbi Shmuel Eliyahu and Rav Yehuda Leib Ashlag

During an interview with a popular media resource, Rabbi Shmuel Eliyahu, the chief Rabbi of Tzfat said, **"I believe that the study of the Zohar by gentiles, as in the common phenomenon**

we see today with non-Jewish musicians and entertainers studying Kabbala, is a positive phenomenon - as long as it is done in the right way." He explained that it should not just be a matter of curiosity, but of a genuine search for the "Torah of life".

Rabbi Eliyahu addressed the matter in light of the jump in sales of books of Kabbalah. According to Meir Bar-El, Deputy Director of the Manufacturers Association of Israel, exports of such books have tripled in recent years due to the world-wide awakening to the study of Kabbalah. He reported that US$35 million worth of Kabbalah texts were exported around the world from Israel in 2005, and that total exports of Jewish holy books in 2005 grew by 119% over the year before and totaled 70% of all book exports from Israel. He even said that there are not enough professional printers now in Israel to meet the continuing demand for holy books from Israel and that more training courses are needed.

"This is exactly what Elijah the Prophet told *Rabbi Shimon Bar Yochai* (2nd c. sage and author of the Zohar, Kabbalah's foundational text) and his group when they began writing the Zohar," Rabbi Eliyahu said, "that in the course of time, people will begin making a living from this work. Of course, Elijah was referring to the fact that it would have a spiritual effect on those who study it, but it can be understood this way as well."

Early 20th c. Kabbalist Rav Yehuda Leib Ashlag was a strong proponent of learning Kabbalah. His disciple was Rabbi Yehuda Brandwein who taught Philip Berg who started the Kabbalah Centre.

There is no doubt that the Kabbalah Centre[23] had a worldwide effect of spreading Kabbalah out to the world. Whatever one's opinion is about "The Centre", we can say that they were directly involved with the worldwide fascination with Kabbalah. From

---

[23] The Kabbalah Centre is a cultural phenomenon. It is not a reputable source of authentic kabbalistic teaching.

celebrities to high profile business executives, people were drawn to Kabbalah en masse.

Rav Ashlag, who wore a *spodik* (a tall, black fur hat worn by some Chassidic men) and lived a *Charedi* (subset of Orthodox Jews characterized by their cloistered lifestyle) lifestyle, was far more conservative than Berg was in spreading his message. Nevertheless, his teachings are revolutionary and very universal. In the teaching of Rabbi Ashlag, both secular Jews and gentiles can find the applicability of these deep concepts within their lives.

Regardless of whether or not they were halachically observant (a point which many of the detractors of Rav Ashlag used as a way to condemn his approach) everyone was invited inwards to do the "inner work". In his opinion, only when we can shift our inner conscious can the outer conscious of the world follow suit. The work must be done and **all must take part, including the non-Jewish world.**

Here is a quote from *Matan Torah*, Rav Ashlag's treatise on learning Kabbalah:

"Now you must know that everything has an inner aspect and an outer aspect. In the world as a whole, Israel, the seed of Abraham, Isaac and Jacob, is considered to be the innermost aspect. The seventy Nations are considered to be the outer aspect of the world. Within Israel itself, there is an inner aspect which consists of those people who are seriously committed to their spiritual work of serving G-d, and there is an outer aspect consisting of those who are not involved in spirituality. Likewise, amongst the Nations of the world, there is an inner aspect which consists of the saints of the world and an outer aspect which consists of those who are destructive and coarse.

"Do not be surprised by the fact that an individual person, through his or her deeds, can cause an elevation or degradation of the whole world. There is an unalterable law that the macrocosm [the totality] and the microcosm [the individual] are as like to each other as two drops of water. The same procedures that occur with respect to the macrocosm occur with regard to the individual and vice versa. Furthermore, it is the individual components themselves which make up the macrocosm and thus the macrocosm is only revealed through the manifestation of its individual components according to their measure and their quality. So certainly, the act of a single person, according to his or her capacity, may lower or elevate humanity as a whole.

"This is how we can understand what is stated in the *Zohar*, that through the study of the *Zohar* and the practice of the true wisdom, we can bring about an end to our state of exile and a complete redemption."

The Fourth Revolution

Rav Yitzchak Ginsburgh, one of the foremost thinkers and Kabbalists of our generation, has spoken extensively about the need to spread Kabbalah and Chassidut to the Nations. In an in-depth talk, Rabbi Ginsburgh spoke about the revolutions which occurred within Torah. The first revolution was orchestrated by Rabbi Judah the Prince, who permitted the Oral Torah to be written. The second was for women to learn Torah. The third was the spreading of the mystical teachings as spoken by the soul of the Moshiach to the Ba'al Shem Tov. The fourth revolution is that the Kabbalistic teachings are now meant to permeate all of existence and spread to all of mankind.[24]

Whatever one's approach is to this phenomenon, at the end of the day, we understand that we don't understand.

In the words of the *Rashab* (Rabbi Shalom Dov Bear, the fifth Rebbe of Lubavitch - 20th c.), "[A]t the end of days, none of us know the extent of things." We do not understand why we meet certain souls and what is the greater cosmic purpose. Just as

---

[24] See the chapter "The Fourth Revolution in Torah Learning" for Rabbi Ginsburgh's explanation

Abraham called out the name of God to all wayfarers, so too he taught his offspring to exemplify the loving kindness of their Creator and become the beacon of light for all of humanity.

My mentor, Rabbi Schneur Zalman Gafne, heard from a close disciple of the Rashab that before the coming of Moshiach, things will be as inexplicable and unexplainable to us as "a goat staring at the moon."

It is with great humility and honor that I find myself a facilitator of spiritual growth for all those, Jew and gentile, whom Hashem has placed before me.

Rabbi Amichai Cohen is the Founder and Director of Live Kabbalah Online School (livekabbalah.com), internationally acclaimed speaker and lecturer, scholar, spiritual teacher and sought-after mentor based in Tzfat, Israel.

China Discovers Talmud and Kabbalah (A Case Study)

RABBI DR. YAKOV NAGEN

China Discovers Talmud and Kabbalah

Several years ago, Amit Elazar, an Israeli living in Beijing, founded *Shofar from Zion*, an organization dedicated to spreading Jewish culture and wisdom in China. A group of Chinese volunteers has translated hundreds of articles and books about Judaism into Chinese, including my book on Jewish spirituality titled *Be, Become, Bless - Jewish Spirituality between East and West*.

In the wake of the translation, I was invited to China to deliver a series of lectures. During my trip, I was astonished to discover the depth of interest and knowledge about Judaism of many of those who I was privileged to meet.

One of my translators gave me, as a gift, a coin of emperor Song Huizong (1082-1135), the last emperor of the Northern Song Dynasty. "I love Rashi!" he told me. "This coin was minted at the same time that Rashi lived. You are a Jew, so I want this coin to be yours."

Another young woman told me that her study group had just completed studying the commentary of the *Ain Yakov* on the exegetical texts of the Talmudic tractate Brachot. I also met, for the first time after years of correspondence, Yong Zhao, author of *Midrash Sinim, Hasidic Legend and Commentary on the Torah*.

The Waiter as Individual

One of the lectures I delivered was devoted to individualism in light of *Rabbi Kook's* (first Ashkenazi Chief Rabbi of pre-state

Israel and one of the early religious Zionists) conception that the image of God in each of us is expressed by our ability to choose. The next day, one of the participants, Paul, told me that after the lecture he went to a restaurant where a waiter dozing off in a corner caught his attention. "In what way is the image of God manifested in this waiter who seems so ordinary and anonymous?" thought the student to himself. Suddenly the waiter noticed that he was being looked at, and the waiter responded by breaking out in a broad smile.

Paul, now filled with excitement continued: "By smiling, the waiter made a conscious choice of how to respond. He could have ignored me or become angry at me. It is in his making of a choice, this is what expresses his individuality, the image of God inside him!"

Two Jews, Three Opinions, One Heart

Another lecture was devoted to the Jewish discourse of debate, disputes and multiple truths. I shared with them the teaching of the Zohar, that the Hebrew word for peace, *shalom* is connected to the Hebrew word *shalem*, which means whole. The word *shalom* begins with the letter *shin*, which in Hebrew represents fire, and ends with the letter *mem* which represents water. *Shalom* is the linkage and harmony between opposites: fire and water, female and male, left and right.

The Chinese were quite surprised when I told them that, in Jewish mysticism, women are fire and men are water. A member of the audience remarked, "For Chinese, men are fire and women water. It is therefore dangerous for a Chinese man to marry a Jewish woman. Too much fire!"

We then clapped our hands to create a meeting between the left hand and right hand which as Rabbi Menachem Froman (21st c. leader in Arab-Israeli reconciliation) has taught, symbolizes the meeting between opposing sides and thereby creates Shalom. I concluded by quoting Rabbi Dov Singer's proverb, "Two Jews, three opinions, one heart".

A young Chinese woman then stood up and taught me: "I would like to explain why in the proverb it is three opinions and not two opinions. At first, two people have two opinions. However, if they meet with one heart, truly listening to each other, a new opinion will emerge; this is the third opinion." This is what happens when we clap our hands. At the beginning, we have two hands, left and right, but when they meet, something new is created - the sound emitted by clapping.

China and Israel: A Brotherhood of Fire and Water

At the conclusion of the lecture series, my hosts gave me a gift – two artistically designed teacups, one red, the color of China's flag, the other blue, the color of Israel's flag; they named the creation *Shevet Achim* (Brothers Together), to express the friendship between China and Israel. Red and blue are also the colors of fire and water which, by forging together, create *Shalom*. Fire can symbolize *doing* and water *being*.

Israelis are often proud of our progress in technology, a reflection of *doing*, but in our encounter with China, what we most have to offer them is the spiritual, the *being*.

In China, the economy is surging ahead and the trains rush forward at 350 kilometers an hour, but while the body races ahead, it is important not to leave the soul behind.

Tents of Abraham

Our patriarchs, Abraham, Isaac and Jacob were each told that through them, blessing would come to the Nations of the world.

> *And I will multiply your seed like the stars of the heavens, and I will give your seed all these lands, and all the Nations of the earth will bless themselves by your seed,* (Bereshit - Genesis 26:4)

> *And your seed shall be as the dust of the earth, and you shall gain strength westward and eastward and northward and southward; and through you shall be blessed all the*

families of the earth and through your seed. (Bereshit 28:14)

After the giving of the Torah at Sinai, the Jewish people are called upon to be a nation of priests, which many commentaries understand as a call to service the spiritual needs of humanity. **We are privileged to live in a time of the realization of the biblical prophecies of the redemption. Part of this vision of the future is for Torah from Zion to reach the corners of the world.**

> *And many peoples shall go, and they shall say, "Come, let us go up to the Lord's mount, to the house of the God of Jacob, and let Him teach us of His ways, and we will go in His paths," for out of Zion shall the Torah come forth, and the word of the Lord from Jerusalem.* (Isaiah 2:3)

The founding fathers of Israel chose the menorah as the nation's symbol to represent this role of the Jewish people to be light unto to the Nations

> *And He said, "It is too light for you to be My servant, to establish the tribes of Jacob and to bring back the besieged of Israel, but I will make you a light of Nations, so that My salvation shall be until the end of the earth."* (Isaiah 49:6)

The time has come to fulfill our destiny.

Throughout the world there are thousands of *Chabad* (large Chasidic group known for outreach to unaffiliated Jews) houses tending to the needs of each and every Jew. My vision is that there will one day be additional places that are open to all people to spread light and blessings. This would be a return to Abraham's tent, which was a center where all were welcome. The Tent of Abraham provided for the material and spiritual needs of all. Even before realizing this vision, there is so much we can each do towards this vision. In 2019, Israel welcomed a record 4.55 million tourists. Most of them are not Jewish and many have come because they are striving for a connection to the Holy Land.

Let us, like the Chinese waiter in the story, choose to greet them with a smile.

It will do good for them. It will do good for us.

Rabbi Dr. Yakov Meir Nagen is an Israeli rabbi and author. Nagen teaches at Yeshivat Otniel and has written extensively about Jewish philosophy and Talmud. He is a leader in interfaith peace initiatives between Judaism and Islam and in encounters between Judaism and Eastern religions. Nagen is also the Director of the Blickle Institute for Interfaith Dialogue and the Beit Midrash for Judaism and Humanity. In 2016 Nagen was profiled in Tablet Magazine as one of the 10 "Israeli Rabbis You Should Know".

Nagen is active in spreading Judaism in China and many of his writings have been translated into Chinese. In 2017, he gave lectures in Beijing and Shanghai. He also taught Torah to a group of Christian pastors from Taiwan who came to Yeshivat Otniel to study. Nagen is a member of the Tzohar and Beit Hillel rabbinical organizations that focus on the relations between the religious and secular communities in Israel.

Sheva Mitzvot Bnei Noach and The Jews

RABBI YITZCHAK MICHAELSON

I can still remember a conversation I had with several colleagues when I was on staff with Jews for Judaism, the leading counter-missionary organization, about eight years ago. We were discussing how in the world rabbis dedicated to protecting Jews from the missionary threat were suddenly inundated with calls, emails and text messages on social media from non-Jews. Not only non-Jews, but those who were or had been practicing Christians.

What we soon learned is that a shift was taking place. It was as if the words of *Rambam* (Rabbi Moshe Ben Maimon) written in the *Mishne Torah* (Code of Jewish Law) so long ago were suddenly coming true. Christians were waking up to the fact that the Torah was true, and that Jews and Judaism had the answers they were seeking. This is when that shift turned into a paradigm shift, one that has produced a wave that could potentially cause a spiritual tsunami if we are not paying attention. With that in mind, I would like to share a *mashal* (short parable with a moral lesson) with you.

Summers in the housing projects of Brooklyn, New York where I grew up could be brutal. The only respite we had were days when Mom and Dad would pack up the cooler with some sandwiches and snacks, load me and my sister into the car and off we went to Rockaway Beach. If I close my eyes, I can still smell the salt air and feel the coolness of the Atlantic Ocean against my skin.

There I am, in the water up to my waist, when suddenly Mom calls from the edge of the water to tell me to come out and have something to eat. I yell back, "Just a little longer." Just as I turn back to the ocean, I am suddenly bowled over by a wave that I never saw coming. **I tell you this little short parable or moral lesson to emphasize how important the role of the Jewish people is in not turning our backs on the current wave that will surely bowl us over if we ignore it.**

The Torah is very clear about our marching orders. The prophet Isaiah, speaking during the years when the Assyrians sought to subdue Israel, said the following:

> For He has said: "It is too little that you should be My servant In that I raise up the tribes of Jacob And restore the survivors of Israel: I will also make you a light of Nations, That My salvation may reach the ends of the earth." (Isaiah 49:6)

All too often I have heard this verse mistranslated or misinterpreted as speaking only about the Jewish nation. One could make that argument only if they choose to merely read the first part of Isaiah 49:6. However, a very simple reading of the entire text makes it clear that the will of the Creator is for His salvation to reach to the ends of the earth.

As a matter of fact, if one were to compare this to some other very important prophecies of Isaiah, one could translate that word "light" in the context of our mission as the Jewish people as "agents of good fortune" to the rest of the world.

Judaism is not now, nor ever has been, unconcerned with non-Jews. While it is clear that we the Jewish people have a special covenant with Hashem through the giving of the Torah at Sinai, this was not the first or only covenant established by the Creator.

Prior to the revelation at Sinai, God initiated and established covenants with both Adam and Noah. In essence, the Torah enables both the Jew and the non-Jew to enter into covenant with God. Judaism and Torah is the path by which a Jew is in relationship with God, while the covenants with Adam and Noah, or what has become known as the Noahide Laws, allows the non-Jew to also be in relationship with the God of Abraham, Isaac and Jacob.

What separates Judaism from other religions like Christianity is action. Christianity has often chosen to set itself apart as the religion of love while relegating Judaism to the religion of law. However, within Judaism love and law are not mutually exclusive. One could go so far as to say the very reason we keep the law is out of love. Unlike Christianity, Judaism is not solely based on *emunah* (faith) but there is the added concept of *bitachon* (trust). I heard an amazing story that I would like to share that illustrates the connection and distinction between faith and trust which sets Judaism apart from other religions.

Every year, a rabbi would take his students to the botanical gardens on Rosh Hashanah for *tashlich* (a Jewish atonement ritual performed near water) as there was a lake there. Every year, the caretaker of the gardens would leave the gate open, knowing the rabbi would come. However, one year, the rabbi and his students came to the gate of the botanical gardens on Rosh Hashanah afternoon to find the gate chained and locked.

As the students were discussing their dilemma, nobody noticed the elderly rabbi had already somehow climbed the gate and was walking toward the lake. One by one the students jumped over the gate and ran to catch up with the rabbi.

When they all had caught up, they gathered around the rabbi and he related the following to them, "Emunah is making your way to the locked gate, but bitachon is how you react when you're confronted with a chained and locked gate. Will you just stand there and be defeated, or will you overcome the challenge? Climbing over the gate to the other side shows that you also have bitachon."

This story illustrates the plight of those non-Jews who have chosen the path of the Noahide. By committing, at a minimum, to keeping the seven Noahide laws, they have confronted the gate of faith and they have overcome the challenge presented by climbing over to the other side. I say minimum because there are distinctions even in our own rabbinic sources regarding references to a Noahide, a complete Noahide, and one who is described as *Chasidei Umot HaOlam* (the pious of the Nations). For instance, a simple Noahide might be someone who has chosen the path of the seven laws but has not given up the concept of *shituf* (the worship of God in a manner which Judaism does not deem to be purely monotheistic.)

This concept of shituf or partnership is something that is permissible for a non-Jew but forbidden to the Jew. A complete Noahide or one who carries the designation of Chasidei Umot HaOlam would be one who has not only committed to the seven laws and its categories, but has committed to keep them carefully while totally rejecting shituf.

As expressed earlier, the Jewish people have a covenant with God through the giving of the Torah which obligated us to keep the 613 *mitzvot* (commandments/laws). Through the observance of these commandments, we express the will of Hashem. Based on this, we would have to agree that the covenants made with Adam and Noah which produced what we now know to be the Sheva Mitzvot Bnei Noach, or Seven Noahide laws, affords the non-Jews a similar opportunity to express the will of Hashem in this world.

I am reminded as I write these words that thirty-seven years ago, on the 19th of Kislev, (December 25, 1983) one of the most respected Jewish leaders of the modern time, Rabbi Menachem Mendel Schneerson z"l shared in a message what would become a major campaign of the Chabad Lubavitch movement to bring awareness and observance of the Seven Noahide Laws to the whole world.

In his message to a packed crowd at 770 Eastern Parkway, the Chabad Headquarters in New York, he started off by stating that **it was our obligation according to the *psak din* (ruling in Jewish law) given to us by Rambam in Mishne Torah to teach the world about, and to make the world more civilized,**

by introducing these laws and encouraging non-Jews to live by them. He went on to state that we are only exempted as Jews from our obligation to Torah when things are beyond our control. However, we are no longer in ghettos or suffering the type of persecution that requires our silence.

He even chided Jewish leaders who opposed such outreach by reminding them that, in the same way that the 613 laws of Torah can never be annulled, it was equally impossible for the Seven Noahide Laws to be annulled, as they were reiterated and solidified when the Torah was given at Mt. Sinai.

We as Jews no longer have the luxury of dwelling on the past when we suffered the sort of persecutions or were silenced in a way that exempted us from this obligation. There is far too much at stake, considering all the world is suffering right now. These words of the Rebbe are as fresh today as they were on that fateful day in 1983:

"As Gd's 'light unto the Nations,' it had always been the Jew's mission to bring all peoples of the world to a belief in Gd. For many centuries, however, the circumstances of our exile did not allow this to be done. Now, is the time to revitalize this long-dormant aspect of our role as a people."

Of course, the Lubavitcher Rebbe shared the obvious distinction between the 613 mitzvot of the Jew and the Seven Noahide laws of the non-Jew. However, he was clear in his message that those seven laws were not static. He told his followers that we must teach the world these seven laws, and I quote, "their derivative laws."

What the Rebbe knew, as do all those who seriously look at our Jewish sources, is the very simple fact that the Sheva Mitzvot Bnei Noach are actually categories. In fact, while there are differing opinions within *Chazal* (Jewish sages) as to the exact number, most would agree that these categories can be expanded out to about 60 to 70 mitzvot in total. Considering that we as Jews no longer have a Temple, we also are limited in the mitzvot we are able to fulfill. While we certainly differ in our obligations and responsibilities as Jews and non-Jews from a numbers standpoint alone, there may not be as great a divide between the number of mitzvot each of us are able to accomplish within our relative context.

Now more than ever we must heed the words of Hashem as spoken through His prophet Isaiah:

> For He has said: "It is too little that you should be My servant In that I raise up the tribes of Jacob And restore the survivors of Israel: I will also make you a light of Nations, That My salvation may reach the ends of the earth." (Isaiah 49:6)

This mission was understood by Rambam, the Lubavitcher Rebbe and so many others.

The mission now falls to us. There are many of us who have had no choice but to confront this wave. It is a wave that will not and cannot be stopped or ignored. It is moving across this planet growing taller and wider each day. We can either see it as destructive or recognize that this wave in fact has its own mission. It is a wave of the wisdom of the Torah that is sweeping across the world and must fulfill the words also given to us through the prophet Isaiah, words that are part of our daily prayer services at the end of what is known as the Aleinu prayer.

> They shall not hurt or destroy in all my holy mountain; for the earth shall be full of the knowledge of the LORD as the waters cover the sea. (Isaiah 11:9)

> And the LORD shall be king over all the earth; in that day there shall be one LORD with one name. (Zechariah 14:9)

The dissemination of Torah to the Nations and our mission to encourage them to follow these ethical laws is, at a minimum, an imperative. There is no longer room for an "us and them" mentality. **If geula is to come, bringing our long awaited and promised Moshiach, our responsibility is to see that the**

knowledge of Hashem sweeps across this world. This can only be accomplished if we choose to allow it, rather than trying to block it. May we all come together for this purpose and merit to see this come to pass soon, speedily, and in our days. Amein!

Rav Yitzchak (Ira) Michaelson has been a student of Kabbalah, Chassidut and other religious topics for over 40 years. Rav Yitzchak previously worked with Jews for Judaism as the East Coast Outreach Coordinator and most recently with Rav Dror Moshe Cassouto founder of Emunah Project as Executive Director. Now he has launched the Kabbalah Project. He currently lives in Tzfat, Israel with his wife where they work together on behalf of the Jewish people as well as people from all nations, helping them to draw closer to the Creator.

My Lesson in Unconditional Love (A Case Study)

BY DR. JAIR JEHUDA

Introduction

During Hanukkah 5781 (December 2020), a popular song in public candle lightings was *Or Ha-Ner* (light of the candle). The words were written by Rabbi Avraham Yitzchak HaCohen Kook about becoming a light unto Nations.

> *Every person should know and understand that deep inside burns a candle,*
> *a unique candle unlike any other.*
> *Every human being has such a candle, and each must toil to reveal their light, so that these candles together can illuminate the entire world.*

A chance encounter with a gentile in 2010 sparked in me a love of Torah and humanity coupled with a sense of purpose that many years in *yeshiva* (school for advanced Torah study) failed to instill. Hashem's words before the giving of the Torah suddenly resonated with new relevance and meaning.

> *"'Now then, if you will obey Me faithfully and keep My covenant, you shall become My treasured possession among all the peoples. Indeed, all the earth is Mine, so you shall be to Me a kingdom of Kohanim (priests) and a holy nation.' These are the words that you shall speak to the children of Israel."* (Exodus 19:5-6),

As in Psalms 126 that we sing before reciting *Birkat Hamazon* (grace after meals), an awakened gentile provoked me into a new consciousness.

Then our mouths will be filled with laughter and our tongues with songs of praise; **then they will say among the Nations,** *"The Lord has done great things with these."*

"The Lord has done great things with us; we were happy." (Psalms 126:2-3)

We studied Torah together via the internet on a weekly basis and others joined us. We sought guidance together with rabbis and developed a joint program called e-Noam, in the hope that we would find that *"the ways of the Torah are pleasant, and all of its paths are peace."* (Proverbs 3:17)

What follows is our case study, including what we learned from it, the existential questions that it raised and potential answers. The song "Or Ha-Ner" implies that becoming a light unto Nations is an organic, grass-roots process that wells from deep within us. It tells us that **all people have a unique light to contribute.** Discovering and revealing that light is challenging and entails a joint effort.

The *Kohen Gadol* (high priest) is tasked with improving the candles so that the light emanating from the Temple is pure and enduring. We, as a kingdom of *Kohanim* (priests), appear to be similarly tasked with the candles of all humanity.

How do these beautiful analogies translate into concrete terms? How can we possibly fulfill such a role? Our case study endeavors to offer possible answers.

Case Study

Our story begins with a Christian tour of Israel. I live in Mitzpe Netofa in northern Israel, where a Christian tour group came to visit friends who, with their assistance, had made *aliyah* (immigrated to Israel) to our community. The tour group sought to vicariously experience aliyah through them.

They also asked to meet with additional residents, whereupon I was called upon as a veteran *oleh* (immigrant to Israel). They believed that meeting Israelis engaged in the fulfillment of biblical prophecies would help them learn how to join, as prophesied by Zechariah.

> *"And many Nations shall join themselves to the LORD in that day and shall be My people."* (Zechariah 2:15)

I was told that they need our assistance to better understand the biblical texts, their roles and how they can fulfill them. In the spirit of Isaiah, they want to carry us on their shoulders so that they too might join us.

> *And they shall bring all your brethren from all the Nations as a tribute to the Lord, with horses and with chariots, and with covered wagons and with mules and with joyous songs upon My holy mount, Jerusalem," says the Lord, "as the children of Israel bring the offering in a pure vessel to the house of the Lord.* (Isaiah 66:20)

Even as Christians, they understand that the replacement theology taught by their church has been proven wrong by the return of the Jewish people to the Land of Israel. In the words of Jeremiah:

> *O Lord, Who are my power and my strength and my refuge in the day of trouble, to You Nations will come from the ends of the earth and say, "**Only lies have our fathers handed down to us**, emptiness in which there is nothing of any avail!* (Jeremiah 16:19)

Having lost their way, they must now reconnect with their authentic Hebrew roots. To this end, they hope to awaken us to *our* destiny as teachers of Torah so that we can help them learn to walk in His ways as independent Nations within Avraham's family of Nations.

When I was first asked to study Torah together with a Christian on a regular basis, I was taken aback and skeptical - but I could not refuse. This was the first time I heard a gentile speak of us as a kingdom of priests, with a calling towards all mankind.

Was he perhaps a sophisticated missionary? Is Torah study with gentiles even permissible? How long can we ignore the elephants in the room, like their faith in Jesus as the only son of God? Was this kind of Christian an anomaly or, perhaps, a growing trend? And how can we help them if we do not understand our own role as a kingdom of priests? How can we help others to hear the word of God, when we ourselves do not hear His voice, understand our calling?

I was cautious and kept my guard up.

At one point, I spent Shabbat with 40 Christians connected to the original group I met in Mitzpe Netofa. It was the Shabbat of *Parshat Balak* (Numbers 22:2-25:9) and we studied the Torah together for about 15 hours. For the first time, **I was inspired and stirred by a sense of calling to these people.** I could not ignore it.

Together we studied controversial Talmudic sources regarding the gentile who studies Torah, whether he must die or whether he is considered a High Priest. We delved into sayings like, "It is the natural law (*halacha*) in the universe that Esau hates Jacob."

We sat in on conversations between Judah the Prince and Antonius the Roman leader that occurred 2,000 years ago but still feel fresh and relevant today. We focused on biblical figures who are not the sons of Abraham, Isaac and Jacob. Though we talked about the elephants in the room, and indeed perhaps *because* we faced those elephants, the bond between us only grew stronger.

After studying together for several months, we felt the need to venture out and share what we had learned with others. We gave a series of lessons together at the Limmud Conference in England. At the same time, we discovered that we are not alone.

I initiated a meeting in Jerusalem, attended by a representative of the Bnei Noach tribunal of Rabbi Steinsaltz, a secular professor who was a chief scientist at the UN, an ultra-Orthodox rabbi who cultivates dialogue with Islam, a large group of ministers and a Muslim Imam from Germany. At this meeting, each participant presented a summary of their doctrine of Abrahamic blessing in peace. The meeting moved everyone to tears.

We decided to set up a virtual framework and format that would allow this type of study to continue on a regular basis. Thus, e-Noam was born: a small group of Jews and Christians from Canada, Israel and Africa who meet every Sunday to study the week's Torah portion. We have been meeting for the past ten years.

Ours is not a one-way attempt to influence the other. Both sides in this ongoing dialogue are sincerely trying to understand our unique paths, to see the light of the other, to discover what God wants us to do in this world which He created, a world made up of different faiths and all kinds of people.

On *Shavuot* (holiday marking the giving of the Torah on Mt. Sinai) 5779 (2009), my wife and I invited 17 Christians from four continents to our home. For most of them, it was their first experience with observant Jews. At the beginning of the gathering, they were embarrassed, mixed with fear and generosity. By the end of Shabbat, everyone testified that the meeting fundamentally changed their attitude toward the Jews, the Covenant of Israel and our Torah.

As a result of the gathering, they came to the conclusion that it is not enough to support Israel in order for them to be blessed or to gain inspiration from Israel's status as a Start-up Nation. Now they sought to learn Torah from Jews on a regular basis and to receive from this Torah everything that was relevant to them.

The Shavuot gathering demonstrated to me how the Torah of Israel can become an engine of blessing and peace in the world, in ways I could not imagine. I saw how much we must study and teach Torah in a way that is relevant to the Nations and to ourselves.

The Serpent's Poison and the Zero-Sum Game

Baseless hatred, like a virus, endangers the whole world because it is contagious. The contagion of hatred is exponential. In the story of Kamsa and Bar Kamsa[25], the Talmud (Gitten 55b) relates how a chain of baseless hatred destroyed the Second Temple. Hence, the upcoming Third Temple can only be built from unconditional love.

The main barrier to unconditional love is a zero-sum game consciousness, the belief that what another receives is at our expense. In rabbinic language, the main barrier to world peace since the expulsion from Eden is the filth of the serpent, which gives rise to this mode of thinking.

Indeed, man was created in a reality of abundance and intimacy - God walks within the garden, and man is naked, his light visible to all, without shame. It is the serpent within us that brings enmity and competition into the world, making us feel threatened by others. It's not surprising that the brain stem, which protects us with involuntary reactions such as fight or flight, is called the reptilian brain.

This part of the brain protects us as part of the survival developmental process and therefore is an important part of nature. But if one stays at that stage, development is delayed.

If only we listened to the voice of God instead of to the serpent, what a world that would be! The only way to do this is unconditional love, which encourages partnership instead of competition, mutual family responsibility instead of rivalry. For cooperation and unity, the Torah promises abundance, freedom, and endless peace, instead of the curses meted out to Adam and *Chava* (Eve).

Encounters with non-Jews have proven to me how a change of consciousness can break the chains of baseless hatred that drag us into exile, war, famine and plague. These encounters give our existence the purpose and meaning we all long for. Because the capacity for unconditional love is inherent within us, change

---

[25] See https://www.chabad.org/library/article_cdo/aid/404863/ jewish/Kamtza-and-Bar-Kamtza.htm for a version of the story

in our mode of thinking is not only possible, but can happen relatively quickly and easily.

Beyond serving as a vehicle for learning our role as a priestly kingdom and holy nation, e-Noam can also be a model for a different, better relationship between Jews and Christians. **The Christians that we study with, for example, see us as their older brother – a source of ancient wisdom that they must tap rather than proselytize.** I could not even imagine such conclusions before I experienced it myself. Since meaningful relationships and a sense of purpose and meaning is so necessary for all of us, even in a self-focused generation, unconditional love for the other is possible.

Torah of the Land of Israel and Torah Abroad

The nature of the Torah of the Land of Israel can be learned from the teachings of Rabbi Yehuda Ashlag and Rabbi Avraham Yitzchak HaCohen Kook. According to Rabbi Ashlag, the name Israel means "that he has a direct will to God, meaning, that he has no desires of self-love, but of the love of others." The purpose of the people of Israel is to instill this consciousness in the whole world.

The Nation of Israel was established as a kind of transition, through which the sparks of purification pass to all of mankind, until the rest of humanity develops to the point where they can understand the peace and serenity of others.

Rabbi Kook wrote similar things. "The last purpose is not a definition of national unity alone but is the ambition to unite all those in the world into one family... Out of these things we see that God has made us a heart to the world in which people give up self-love and choose, out of their own free will, to love others.

"We must be aware that there are shortcomings in the balance of private love in 'limited nationality,' as it reflects the poison of the snake from which we must abstain. To fulfill our destiny as a kingdom of priests, we are required to elevate the limited nationalism to a place where there is unconditional love for all mankind."

The Torah of the Land of Israel cannot exist in kingdoms ruled by the poison of the serpent. Therefore, when Israel is in exile, we build protective shells (*klipot*) that help us survive - but at the cost of division, which we often experience today. As we return to Israel, we cannot let the Torah of the exile and its mentality perpetuate the zero-sum game mindset even in the land of Israel. This consciousness is not suitable for Zion and the Temple, whose purpose is to reconcile and unite.

A profound change of consciousness is needed to move from an exile mentality to the Torah of *Eretz Yisrael* (Land of Israel). The Talmud tells of rabbis in the Diaspora who fasted for many days before immigrating to Eretz Yisrael. They needed to unlearn their exile consciousness in order to cultivate the unconditional love needed to fulfill their destiny.

The Torah of the Land of Israel today requires an abundance (*shefa*) mentality, one that is a blessing for the whole world. This requires strong hearts. The doctrine of the Land of Israel cannot exist and develop without unconditional love for the whole world.

Redemption And Change of Consciousness

It follows that the key to redemption is a change of consciousness. We must believe, take in and demonstrate that a significant core of loving others is more helpful, blessed and powerful than self-love.

There is now a broad consensus on the need for a consciousness change. At a recent meeting attended by a highly respected representative of rabbis, it was agreed that Israel must free itself from the survival mentality and begin to think of our purpose in the world as a light to the Nations. The current generation is not content with a narrow national identity; it seeks an identity that will enable connection to the whole world. Survival consciousness cannot supply this.

Such a change of consciousness is extremely challenging. Personally, it took me and my friends years to internalize this worldview and to be a conduit of influence to all our circles, from the most intimate spheres of relationships and family, to a much larger community. **It was through relationships with non-Jews that my eyes were opened to the reality that we, as Jews, have responsibilities way beyond what I had previously believed.**

Over the past decade of study with Jews and Christians, many mitzvot took on additional dimensions connected to free will and choice. The Torah commandments became a blueprint for the fulfillment of our destiny as a kingdom of spiritual guides for the whole world.

According to Rabbi Kook, as stated, the trend of Israel and the Temple is "to unite everyone in the world into one family." Our experience showed us how much the destiny of being a kingdom of Kohanim and Holy Nation is relevant and possible. When the Nations of the world are interested in the commandments we are following, deeds that we are used to suddenly acquire deeper significance and holiness.

A Kingdom of Priests?

A decade of joint Bible study taught me that it isn't our diverse heritages that divide us - it is the superficial and narrow interpretations of our heritages that divide us. A more profound understanding of our heritages reveal that all major faiths draw from the same wells dug by our joint forefathers. Joint Bible study enables us to demonstrate by example how we deepen and expand our understanding of Torah.

The roadmap to achieving redemption for all mankind is an ancient one, foretold in the Bible. All the necessary tools are now available and the growing thirst for Torah is evident. We now know that joint Bible study with people from different backgrounds can be transforming, purifying and unifying for all participants.

Like *Moshe Rabeinu* (Moses our teacher), we have to aspire to utmost humility. Our Torah must be just, with an unconditional love that characterizes the Torah of Eretz Yisrael. Moshe makes himself accessible to everyone by pitching his tent outside – anyone seeking the word of Hashem must have a tent to go to.

As the mounting multitudes of gentiles come to Israel, more and more will seek out Torah observant Jews and a minyan of gentiles will be hosted by every Jew, as Zechariah predicted:

> *So said the Lord of Hosts: In those days, when ten men of all the languages of the Nations shall take hold of the skirt of a Jewish man, saying, "Let us go with you, for we have heard that God is with you."* (Zechariah 8:23)

To prepare for this role, each of us must discover and expose an inner light capable of sparking others to seek their own internal light, rather than impose our light on others. Hence our light must be pure – never triumphant or condescending. When we speak of seventy faces to the Torah, we must acknowledge that each of the seventy Nations has their own unique face of Hashem and that every human being has a unique light that isn't necessarily Jewish.

When we teach others, it has to be an act of selfless love – never for personal gain. Our role is to facilitate by example and to make the Torah accessible to them so they can discover their unique inner light through their own effort. When we meet at the Temple, our inner lights will be visible to all others and through this Hashem's visible multi-spectral light will intensify and be celebrated. This is an antithesis of an authoritarian priesthood that tells others what to do.

Like the Kohen Gadol, we must become super facilitators, helping each candle better align to highlight facets of Hashem's Face. Only then can we honestly pray: *"We have blessed our Father all with one another in the light of Your face. For in the light of Your face You have given us the doctrine of life and the love of grace and charity and blessing and mercy and life and peace."*

Prior to giving us His Torah, Hashem specified a clear goal in Exodus 19:6: *"And you shall be to Me a kingdom of priests and a holy nation."* Our circles of unconditional love must expand to include the whole world.

Dr. Jair Jehuda was born on Israel Independence Day 1954 in San Antonio, Texas. His family immigrated to Israel when he was 15. In 1972, he joined the IDF Hesder Yeshiva Program in Alon Shvut, serving as a tank commander and later as a naval reserve officer. Technion degrees in Electrical Engineering and Computer Science paved the way to 17 years of defense work in Rafael, ultimately serving as Chief Software Engineer.

He and his wife Dina co-founded the Mitzpe Netofa community, an innovative, cross-cultural community in the Lower Galilee, in 1985. This is where they brought up seven sons and one daughter. Several of their married children and grandchildren remain in Netofa today.

With entrepreneurial hi-tech aspirations, Jair founded Kinor Technologies ("Live Meaningful Data") in 2002 and e-Noam ("Meaningful Experiences Together") in 2010. The technological and social platforms being developed by these start-ups are now setting the stage for educational programs designed to cultivate a cross-cultural family spirit between Israel and the Nations as well.

IN THE MESSIANIC ERA

Universal Recognition of the God of Israel in the Messianic Era

DR. RIVKAH LAMBERT ADLER

Once our understanding of the Jewish responsibility to the Nations begins to shift, we begin to notice something we've never noticed before. **The theme of the eventual, universal recognition of the One True God of Israel appears over and over again in Hebrew scriptures and in Jewish prayer.**

In this chapter, we will look at some sources that amplify this. In my experience, *Sefer Tehillim* (Book of Psalms) is the richest repository of verses on this theme. The sources presented here are not intended to be comprehensive, but rather, my aim is to make the case that **the universal worship of the One God, the God of Israel is, and always has been, a Torah intention.**

Taken together, my contention is that these sources demonstrate an unmistakable theme in *Tanach* (complete Hebrew Bible) and in our prayers, that, **at the End of Days, the entire world will recognize, worship and obey the One True God of Israel.**

NOTE: In Hebrew, different terms are used to refer to Nations or peoples. Since the sources are being presented in English translation, where appropriate, I've included a transliteration of the specific Hebrew word used to refer to people who are not from the Nation of Israel.

TANACH
Melachim Alef (1 Kings) 8:41-43

*As for the foreigner (**hanachri**) who does not belong to your people Israel but has come from a distant land because of your name—*

for they will hear of your great name and your mighty hand and your outstretched arm--when they come and pray toward this temple,

*then hear from heaven, your dwelling place. Do whatever the foreigner (**hanachri**) asks of you, so that all the peoples of the earth (**amei haaretz**) may know your name and fear you, as do your own people Israel, and may know that this house I have built bears your Name.*

When *Shlomo HaMelech* (King Solomon) dedicated the first *Beit Hamikdash* (Holy Temple) on *Sukkot* (Feast of Tabernacles), he specifically asked Hashem to answer the prayers of the foreigners who came there to pray.

Both Temples were built with non-Jewish assistance. In the case of the First Temple, Hiram of Tyre offered Shlomo HaMelech material assistance. The Second Temple was built with the help of *Koresh* (Cyrus), the ruler of Persia. Thus, it should not come as a surprise that righteous non-Jews will also be part of the construction of the Third Temple.

The involvement of non-Jews emphasizes that the Holy Temples in Jerusalem were never intended for the exclusive use of the Jews. *Yeshayahu* (Isaiah) himself reminds us that the Beit Hamikdash was always intended to be "a house of prayer for all Nations." (Yeshayahu 56:7)

Yeshayahu (Isaiah) 2:2-3

*And it shall be at the end of the days, that the mountain of the Lord's house shall be firmly established at the top of the mountains, and it shall be raised above the hills, and all the Nations (**goyim**) shall stream to it.*

*And many peoples (**amim**) shall go, and they shall say, "Come, let us go up to the Lord's mount, to the house of the God of Jacob, and let Him teach us of His ways, and we will go in His paths," for out of Zion shall the Torah come forth, and the word of the Lord from Jerusalem.*

The words "at the end of the days" is a reference to a time when evil will cease to exist. The Vilna Gaon suggests that the streaming will be literal. That is, people who live outside of Israel will stream to the Temple across waterways by boat. Alternately, the stream will be a beacon of light that will emerge from the Third Temple and will attract the attention of the Nations.

The teacher of the Nations is either a reference to Hashem or to *Moshiach* (the messianic redeemer) who will teach God's ways to people from the Nations. The Nations will desire to visit the Temple because they will understand that it will be the source of Torah law and moral instruction.

Yeshayahu (Isaiah) 11:9

For the Earth shall be filled of knowledge of the Lord, as the waters cover the sea.

In the Messianic period, hatred, fighting, jealousy, competition and false beliefs will no longer exist. Everyone will know God and will spend their time studying the Torah of Moshiach and being connected to Hashem.

Yeshayahu (Isaiah) 49:6

And He said, "It is too light for you to be My servant, to establish the tribes of Jacob and to bring back the besieged of Israel, but I will make you a light of Nations, so that My salvation shall be until the end of the earth."

In this verse, God is speaking to Yeshayahu, reminding him that his mission includes sharing his prophetic messages with both the Jewish people and the Nations. Additionally, **it is the job of the Nation of Israel to show the rest of the world that Hashem is the Only God and that His laws apply to all of humanity.**

Yeshayahu (Isaiah) 56:6-7

*And the foreigners (**hanechar**) who join with the Lord to serve Him and to love the name of the Lord, to be His servants, everyone who observes the Sabbath from profaning it and who holds fast to My covenant.*

*I will bring them to My holy mount, and I will cause them to rejoice in My house of prayer, their burnt offerings and their sacrifices shall be acceptable upon My altar, for My house shall be called a house of prayer for all peoples (**ha'amim**).*

After the coming of Moshiach, Jews and gentiles will come to Jerusalem to pray at the Third Temple. These words are part of the *Yom Kippur* (Day of Atonement) liturgy, when we pray for this to actually occur.

Yeshayahu (Isaiah) 60:3

*And Nations (**goyim**) shall go by your light and kings by the brilliance of your shine.*

The Nations will eventually be drawn to the spiritual light that shines from the Torah.

Yermiyahu (Jeremiah) 23:7-8

Therefore, behold days are coming, says the Lord, when they shall no longer say, "As the Lord lives, Who brought up the children of Israel from the land of Egypt," But, "As the Lord lives, Who brought up and Who brought the seed of the house of Israel from the northland and from all the lands where I have driven them, and they shall dwell on their land."

These verses refer to the ultimate reunification of the Twelve Tribes. Here, "the house of Israel from the northland" is a reference to the Lost Tribes of the Northern Kingdom. It's important for the Jewish people to be aware that, even if we don't know exactly how it will play out, this reunification is considered part of the process of geula.

Although it's not a universally accepted understanding, there are those who believe that many of the non-Jews who feel drawn to Torah in our day may be spiritual, if not also physical, descendants of members of the Ten Tribes. See the chapter "Rachel Weeps for Her Children: The Return of the Ten Tribes" by AnaRina Bat Tzion Kreisman for more on this theme.

Yermiyahu (Jeremiah) 31:9-11

*Hear the word of the Lord, O Nations (**goyim**), and declare it on the islands from afar, and say, "He Who scattered Israel will gather them together and watch them as a shepherd his flock.*

For the Lord has redeemed Jacob and has saved him out of the hand of him who is stronger than he.

And they shall come and jubilate on the height of Zion, and they will stream to the goodness of the Lord, over corn, wine, and oil, and over sheep and cattle, and their soul shall be like a well-watered garden, and they shall have no further worry at all.

The Nations will recognize God's Hand in redeeming the Jewish people and they will come and celebrate with us.

Yermiyahu (Jeremiah) 31:33

And no longer shall one teach his neighbor or [shall] one [teach] his brother, saying, "Know the Lord," for they shall all know Me from their smallest to their greatest, says the Lord, for I will forgive their iniquity and their sin I will no longer remember.

When Moshiach ben David comes into the world, he will teach the *pinimius* (the hidden, inner dimension) of Torah. Everyone, Jew and gentile, will be able to connect to God directly through these teachings.

Tzefaniah (Zephaniah) 3:9

*For then I will convert the peoples (**amim**) to a pure language that all of them call in the name of the Lord, to worship Him of one accord.*

One way of understanding this verse is that, in order to be able to express spiritual reality, all people will speak Hebrew in the Messianic age so that they can call out to God in the most proper and accurate manner.

Zechariah 8:23

So said the Lord of Hosts: In those days, when ten men of all the languages of the Nations shall take hold of the skirt of a Jewish man, saying, "Let us go with you, for we have heard that God is with you."

According to *Rashi* (preeminent commentator on the Torah and Talmud who lived 1040-1105 CE), there will be ten men from each of the seventy Nations (700 people) clinging to each corner of a Jewish *tallit* (prayer shawl). Since a tallit has four corners, each Jew will attract the attention of 2,800 (700x4) God-fearing non-Jews. **This verse gives us a sense of the awesome responsibility we have to guide them toward an understanding of Who God truly is and what He wants from them.**

Zechariah 9:10

*...And he shall speak peace to the Nations (**goyim**), and his rule shall be from the sea to the west and from the river to the ends of the earth.*

Moshiach will communicate with the Nations and his rule will be over the entire world.

Zechariah 14:9

And the Lord shall become King over all the earth; on that day shall the Lord be one, and His name one.

Eventually, God's Kingship will be universally recognized by whoever survives until the End of Days.

According to Rabbi Pinchas Winston, "The goal of history, according to this verse, is the universal recognition of God as King over EVERYTHING. This means what it sounds like: no more atheism, no more agnosticism, and ALL OF MANKIND worshiping one God, the God of the Torah."

Tehillim (Psalms) 9:12

*Sing praises to the Lord, Who dwells in Zion; relate His deeds among the peoples [**amim**].*

David Hamelech (King David), and by extension, the rest of the Jewish nation, are urged to speak about the wonders that God has done for them whenever they interact with people from the Nations.

Tehillim (Psalms) 22:28-29

*All the ends of the earth shall remember and return to the Lord, and all the families of the Nations (**mishpachot goyim**) shall prostrate themselves before You.*

The Nations will eventually realize that, despite our history of degradation, Hashem will ultimately reward the Jewish people. When they see this, it will inspire them to turn to God.

For the kingship is the Lord's, and He rules over the Nations (**goyim**).

When the Nations come to see clearly that God is the King, it will inspire them to want to serve Him.

Tehillim (Psalms) 33:8

Let all the earth fear the Lord; let all the inhabitants of the world stand in awe of Him.

God created the world in such a way that there are aspects of nature that a person understands they simply cannot control. In this way, nature serves as a vehicle for all people to fear and respect God.

Tehillim (Psalms) 33:14

From His dwelling place He oversees all the inhabitants of the earth.

Every individual on earth is looked after by God Himself.

Tehillim (Psalms) 46:11

This whole chapter is about the Messianic era. The Messianic era is a turbulent time, but one way to survive is to turn to God.

Desist, and know that I am God; I will be exalted among the Nations, I will be exalted upon the earth.

God is addressing the Nations, telling them to stop fighting against Jerusalem. He is both warning them and also urging them to recognize His Omnipotence.

Tehillim (Psalms) 47

This chapter of Tehillim is recited before *shofar* (ram's horn) blowing on Rosh Hashana. It is set in the future Messianic era when the Jewish people are no longer in exile, being persecuted by the Nations. Instead, all Nations will celebrate along with the Jewish people.

47:2 All peoples (amim), clap hands; shout to God with a voice of praise.

The Jewish people will blow shofar for Moshiach and the Nations will clap their hands, acknowledging that their Divine judgment at the End of Days has been fair.

47:3 For the Lord is Most High; yea, feared; a great King over all the earth.

At this stage, the Nations will unite with the Jewish people to serve God and recognize His dominion over the entire earth.

47:4 He shall plague peoples (amim) in our stead and kingdoms under our feet.

In the days of Moshiach, the Nations will acknowledge that the Jewish people have eternal worth and they will turn to us to teach them about God. At the same time, those Nations that were our enemies will suffer God's Wrath.

47:8 For God is the King of all the earth; sing a song composed with wisdom.

The future song will help the entire world see and believe in the Kingdom of God.

47:9 God reigns over peoples (goyim); God sits upon His holy throne.

Again, a reference to the Messianic future, when God will be universally recognized.

Tehillim (Psalms) 67:3-6

This chapter is a prayer for the Messianic era when all Nations will worship God.

67:3 That Your way should be known on earth, Your salvation among all Nations (goyim).

We are asking God to give us the tools we need to teach His Torah to the Nations because we want the entire world to recognize God's Ways.

67:4 Peoples (amim) will thank You, O God; peoples (amim) will thank You - all of them.

67:5 Nations (leumim) will rejoice and sing praises, for You will judge peoples (amim) fairly, and the Nations (leumim) on earth You will guide, Selah.

67:6 The Nations (amim) will acknowledge You, O God; peoples will thank You, yea, all of them.

First, only the Jewish people will recognize God. Then the leaders of the Nations will defer to Him. Eventually, His Word will spread throughout the world and all people will have a direct relationship with the Master of the Universe.

Tehillim (Psalms) 86:9

All Nations (goyim) that You made will come and prostrate themselves before You, O Lord, and glorify Your name.

Where will this happen? In the Temple in Jerusalem. All the Nations of the world will come to Jerusalem to experience the Divine light that will emanate from the Temple.

Tehillim (Psalms) 96:3

*Tell of His glory among the Nations (**goyim**), among all peoples (**amim**) His wonders.*

Whereas throughout history, the Jewish people have suffered at the hands of others, when God glorifies us in the Messianic era, the Nations will see it for themselves.

This verse also speaks plainly of our obligation to share God's glory and wonders with the rest of the world.

Tehillim (Psalms) 96:10

*Say among the Nations (**goyim**), "The Lord has reigned." Also the inhabited world will be established so that it will not falter; He will judge peoples (**amim**) with equity.*

Those from the Nations who come to offer a sacrifice at the Holy Temple in Jerusalem will be impressed by what they see and will return to their home country to report that God truly reigns in Jerusalem.

Each country will be judged by the God of Israel at the End of Days. Those who deserve reward will receive it and those who deserve punishment will receive what they deserve.

Tehillim (Psalms) 100:1

A song for a thanksgiving offering. Shout to the Lord, all the earth.

All people are commanded to pray to and bless the Master of the Universe.

Tehillim (Psalms) 102:16

*And the Nations (**goyim**) will fear the name of the Lord, and all the kings of the earth Your glory.*

When they see the miracles that God will bring when He redeems the world, even earthly kings will be in awe of Him.

Tehillim (Psalms) 105:1

*Give thanks to the Lord, call out in His name; make His deeds known among the peoples (**amim**).*

Those who know God are obligated to speak of His greatness to everyone.

Tehillim (Psalms) 117:1

*Praise Hashem, all Nations (**goyim**), laud Him, all the states (**haumim**).*

With just two verses, this is the shortest chapter in the Book of Tehillim. Its simplicity echoes the nature of the world after Moshiach comes. This first verse addresses different kinds of Nations, from primitive ones to important ones, and invites them all to praise God equally.

Tehillim (Psalms) 145:18

The Lord is near to all who call Him, to all who call Him with sincerity.

The greatness of Hashem is that He can respond to anyone, anywhere, if only they turn to Him. This applies equally to Jews and to the Nations.

Tehillim (Psalms) 150:6

Let every soul praise God. Hallelujah!

In this final chapter of Tehillim, the human soul is called on to praise God 13 times. There is no praise greater than a human being who applies all their strength and gifts to the service of the Divine. This is a universal goal of every person, regardless of their nationhood.

Divrei Hayamim Alef (I Chronicles) 16:8

Give thanks to the Lord, call out in His Name; make His exploits known among the peoples (amim).

Divrei Hayamim Alef (I Chronicles) 16:23-24

Sing to the Lord, all the earth; announce His salvation from day to day.

Tell of His glory among the Nations, among all peoples (amim) His wonders.

Divrei Hayamim Alef (I Chronicles) 16:31

The heavens will rejoice and the earth will exult, and they will say among the Nations (goyim), "The Lord has reigned."

On one level, these verses from chapter 16 all refer to the time of David Hamelech. But it is not hard to extrapolate that these goals will also be relevant in the time of Moshiach ben David.

TEFILLAH (Prayer)
Nishmat Kol Chai

For every mouth will offer thanks to You and every tongue will swear allegiance to You and every knee will bend to You and every upright spine will prostrate itself before You.

Nishmat Kol Chai (literally the soul of all living beings) is part of *Pesukei d'Zimra* (verses of praise) on *Shabbat* (Sabbath) and *Yom Tov* (holiday) morning. This verse speaks about the universal recognition of the uniqueness of God.

Second paragraph of Aleinu

Therefore, we put our hope in You, Hashem our God, that we may soon see Your mighty splendor, to remove detestable idolatry from the earth, and false gods will be utterly cut off, to perfect the universe through the Almighty's sovereignty. Then all humanity will call upon Your Name, to turn all the earth's wicked toward You. All

the world's inhabitants will recognize and know that to You every knee should bend, every tongue should swear.
(Isaiah 45:23)

Before You, Hashem, our God, they will bend every knee and cast themselves down and to the glory of Your Name they will render homage, and they will all accept upon themselves the yoke of Your kingship that You may reign over them soon and eternally. For the kingdom is Yours and You will reign for all eternity in glory as it is written in Your Torah: Hashem shall reign for all eternity.
(Exodus 15:18)

And it is said: Hashem will be King over all the world – on that day Hashem will be One and His Name will be One.
(Zechariah 14:9)

Aleinu ("It is upon us") closes every communal prayer service and is one of the most frequently recited prayers in our liturgy. This text is from the second paragraph in which we pray for the universal recognition of God ("and all humanity will call upon your name").

Rosh Hashana and Yom Kippur Evening Service

Our God and God of our ancestors, reign over the entire universe, all of it. Be upraised in Your glory over the entire world. Reveal yourself in the majestic grandeur of your strength over all the dwellers of the inhabited world, Your earth. Let everything that has been made know that You are its Maker. Let everything that has been molded understand that You are its molder. And let everything that has life's breath in its nostrils proclaim, "The God of Israel is King and His Kingship rules over everything."

On the holiest days of the year, we acknowledge the goal of the universal recognition of Hashem.

Editor's Caution to Christian Readers: I am aware that, more than any other part of this book, this chapter, which presents a Jewish understanding of the eventual relationship between Jews and the Nations in the Messianic era, has the potential to offend Christians with its understanding of Isaiah 49:23.

I discussed the pros and cons of including this chapter with a number of Jewish and non-Jewish beta readers before deciding whether or not to include it. In the end, my desire to represent authentic Torah truth in my work as a bridge between faith traditions, no matter how awkward or uncomfortable, prevailed.

Christian readers might prefer to skip this chapter entirely.

Redemptive Servitude: A Commentary on Isaiah 49:23

FRAIDIE LEVINE

And kings shall be your nursing fathers and their princesses your wet nurses; they shall prostrate themselves to you with their face on the ground, and they shall lick the dust of your feet, and you shall know that I am the Lord, for those who wait for Me shall not be ashamed. (Isaiah 49:23)

We are told that, at the end of days, the gentiles will be our slaves, as the *gemara* (Talmud) in Tractate Shabbos (32:2) states, *"Each Jew will have 2,800 slaves"* and Isaiah prophesied *"Kings [of the Nations] will raise your children and their princesses will be your wet nurses."* (Isaiah 49:23).

When Jews were extremely oppressed and degraded by the gentiles amongst whom they lived, prophecies foretelling how those gentiles would come bowing and groveling before them must have been music to their ears. This would be such perfect justice! Instead of Jews being subject to them, they would be subject to the Jews. But in our society where discriminatory laws against Jews have been banned, and Jews have reached very respected governmental and social positions, turning the gentiles into our servants no longer resonates. Why would we want to do such a thing?

Furthermore, on Pesach 5646 (1886) the *Sfas Emes* (important Chassidic rabbi in 19th c. Poland) writes that the redemption of Pesach was mainly to bring redemption to the entire world. Since the redemption from Egypt foreshadows the future redemption, which will also be for the entire world, and since the exodus certainly involved freedom from subjugation and enslavement, how can the redemption possibly bring about a situation where others will be turned into our slaves?

And while on the subject of servitude, one may ask, how did the Torah, whose very basis is, *"What is hateful to you do not do to your friend,"* (Shabbat 31a) ever allow such a thing as slavery?

The truth is that most slavery that existed in the world is not condoned by the Torah; just the opposite. On Passover we celebrate how Hashem took the Israelites out of slavery and punished the cruel Egyptians. It was a case of the strong oppressing the weak, and it was very evil. Most of the world's slavery was of that type.

However, there is a type of slavery which is actually beneficial, as we find in *Noach's* (Noah's) statement, *"Cursed is Canaan, slave of slaves he will be to his brothers."* (Breishis/Genesis 9:25). What is the meaning behind this?

The Torah says that Cham, the father of Canaan, had seen his own father Noach become uncovered in the tent and he told this to his brothers, Shem and Yefet, who then went and covered their father, walking backwards so as to not see this. Chazal explain the incident further. Canaan, the son of Cham, had caused his father to have a homosexual relationship with his grandfather, Noach, while Noach was in a drunken sleep. Some say that he castrated Noach. The commentary *Da'as Zkeinim MiBa'alei Tosafos* (12th and 13th c, Torah commentary), brings in the name of a Rabbi Aharon, that a *midrash* (biblical exegesis) says that it was actually Canaan himself who had the homosexual relationship with Noach. So what does this have to do with slavery?

Rabbi Shimshon Rafael Hirsh explains that Noach was not actually cursing Canaan, but rather stating a fact; Canaan, through his terrible deed, had caused himself to be cursed. The only way for him to rectify this situation would be to become a slave to his brothers.

In 5649 (1889) the Sfas Emes on *Chayei Sarah* (Genesis 23:1–25:18) also teaches this. The Sfas Emes writes: "...Avraham was his [Eliezer's] means of serving God...he found sense and wisdom in his slavery [seeing that this connected him to God and using it to advance his spiritual status]...Eliezer was Canaan and it is written, "Cursed is Canaan, a slave of slaves shall he be."

Noach gave him advice how to get out of being cursed; to be a slave, because he [Noach] saw and understood that it's impossible for him [Canaan] to be on his own, because he's stuck in the curse [that he brought upon himself with his evil deed] and he advised to become a slave, so that through being a slave to someone who is blessed he can rectify his soul, and Eliezer understood this....for if Canaan were free he would destroy the world because the curse sticks to him... [Afterwards] he was freed (by Avraham) because he served him faithfully and was no longer in the category of being cursed, so certainly he [Avraham] was required to set him free..."

So we see that the institution of slavery in Judaism was primarily for the sake of the slave, to help them rise to a higher level.

But what does this have to do with the gentiles serving us at the time of the redemption?

As we said, the redemption is for the entire world, so why do they need to serve us?

The answer is that this will not be the type of slavery that existed in the past. The evildoers among the *goyim* (Nations) will not be around anymore. The Torah and the prophets say specifically that the evildoers will be wiped out. This servitude will be born of the desire to come closer to Hashem, to receive *Ruach HaKodesh* (a lower form of prophecy), and to merit *Olam Haba* (the world to come), in the merit of their service. Let's speak about this some more.

Hashem created this world so that people would be able to earn their reward in the next world. We are not referring here to *Gan Eden* (Garden of Eden) and *Gehinom* (spiritual realm where the souls of sinners are cleansed after death), although that is also true, but rather to the future world that will exist after the revival of the dead. Chazal said, "Today is to do them and tomorrow is to receive their reward." and "He who toils on Sabbath eve will eat on the Sabbath, but he who does not toil on Sabbath eve, what will he eat on the Sabbath?"

This means that one must toil in this world, which is compared to Sabbath eve, in order to eat the fruit of one's labors in the next world which is called Shabbat. In other words, you must have the merit of serving Hashem in this world in order to merit the next world.

This is the meaning of Chazal's words that Hashem wanted to create the world with *Midas HaDin*, the attribute of justice. In actuality Hashem partnered justice with the attribute of mercy, but He did not do away with justice as the Torah says, *"For all His ways are just."* (Deuteronomy 32:4) A person must earn their way to the next world.

Hashem is not discriminatory. Chazal said, "I bring heaven and earth to testify for me, whether a gentile or an Israelite, whether a man or a woman, whether a manservant or a maidservant, all according to the deed of the person Ruach HaKodesh rests upon him." (Brought in *Yalkut Shimoni* 4:4, from *Medrash Tanchuma* – rabbinic commentaries on the Torah from 9th -14th c.).

Ruach HaKodesh is a real relationship with Hashem, something akin to prophecy. It is one of the most pleasurable experiences a human being can have. But it must be earned, as it says "all according to the deed, does the Holy Spirit rest on him."

Chazal also said, "Hashem says, I love those who love Me... "Why does The Holy One Blessed is He love *tzadikim* (righteous people)? For they are not an inheritance, and they are not a family. You find that the Kohanim are a patriarchal house, the Levites are a patriarchal house...if a person wants to be a Kohen he cannot, to be a Levi, he cannot. Why? Because his father was not a Kohen and not a Levi. But if a person wants to be a tzaddik, even a non-Jew can..." (*Bamidbar Rabba*, Naso, parsha 8 – ancient rabbinic commentary on the Book of Numbers)

But again, to be beloved by Hashem you have to love Him, which means being willing to go all out for Him. Again, you have to do something to earn it. You don't get something for nothing.

So what will happen if Moshiach comes and most of the world didn't do something to earn Godliness? What will happen to all those people who, although not awfully evil, also did not serve Hashem? How will they get Ruach HaKodesh, how will they get into Olam Haba?

Olam Haba is formed by our keeping the Sabbath, which is called *me'ein Olam Haba* (Shabbat is compared to the World to Come). This doesn't only mean that the Sabbath resembles Olam Haba; it means that keeping the Sabbath actually creates our Olam Haba, according to the *Tiferes Shlomo* (Rabbi Shlomo Hakohen Rabinowicz – 19th c. Poland).

Yet a gentile is not allowed to fully keep Shabbat, because it is "a sign between Me and You" i.e. between God and the Jewish People (Exodus 31:13). Similarly, a gentile cannot eat of the

Korban Pesach (Passover sacrifice) which represents, among other things, being Hashem's people and having a very special relationship with Him.

So what will happen to all of these people who aren't Jewish? After the evil inclination is removed and the greatness of the Jewish People is revealed, everyone will want to become Jewish, only it won't be possible anymore. Conversion only means something when it involves a measure of sacrifice, just like the Jewish People had to sacrifice their desires, their livelihoods and often their lives for their Jewishness. After the Jews are so greatly respected, converts will no longer be accepted. So again, how will all those who didn't act in time, make it? If, as Chazal put it, they didn't toil on Erev Shabbat, what will they eat on Shabbat?

The answer is that Hashem left them another option. One cannot convert to Judaism when such conversion is so glittering and easy, but one can become an *eved Caanani*, a slave to a Jew, which is also a form of conversion. Such a slave must dip in a *mikvah* (a bath used for ritual immersion) in order to receive their position, a position which is spiritually much higher than that of a gentile. The Canaanite slave keeps Shabbat. He has a *brit milah* (ritual circumcision). A Caananite slave eats of the Pesach sacrifice. In fact a Canaanite slave keeps most of the mitzvot. True, they didn't choose to be a subject of God in time, but they can still make it to Olam Haba by voluntarily subduing themselves this way. They accrue merit and can get in on a Jew's ticket, so to speak.

To explain this idea with an allegory, let's take the case of a teenage girl who is consumed by the desire to travel to foreign countries and see the world. The problem is that she has no money for it. One day she sees an advertisement for a babysitter from a couple who is traveling around the world and looking for someone to watch their five-year-old. The girl runs to answer the ad and is accepted. She gets to stay in the best hotels, she flies and rides first class, and most of all, she gets to see the foreign countries. Her dream comes true. Yes, she does have to do something for it, she takes care of the child, but she's absolutely delighted with the job.

And so we see that the servitude at the time of the geula is not at all like the evil slavery that existed throughout most of world history. Good riddance to that evil institution! In our technologically-advanced world, there will probably be very little actual work to do, and there will be so many candidates for the position, they will probably be longingly waiting for their chance to actually do a little something for a Jew! In fact, the verse that Chazal say alludes to the fact that every Jew will have 2,800 slaves is the verse in Zechariah 8:23 which says that people of all the Nations will hold onto the corner (tzitzit) of every Jewish man saying *"Let us go with you, for we have heard that God is with you."* (Zechariah 8:23) So we see that they will be begging us for the job, for the opportunity to come along with us.

And of course, the Jews will treat them with respect and consideration, since this is how all people should be treated. After the evil inclination no longer exists, no one will oppress anyone. And perhaps, as was with Avraham and Eliezer, when the Jew will see that his eved Caanani has reached rectification, he will free him, as Avraham freed Eliezer, and then he will become a full Jew, for a freed eved Caanani automatically becomes a full Jew.

And then we can all go together to Olam Haba.

Fraidie Levine lives in Beitar Illit, Israel. She is the author of a book on equality and feminine redemption, and a booklet called Whatever Happened to the Atachalta DeGeula. *She is a lecturer and writer on various Torah topics and can be contacted at devorahfraida@gmail.com.*

Rachel Weeps for Her Children: The Return of the Ten Tribes

ANARINA BAT TZION KREISMAN

A Brief History Lesson

I always stand amazed at how little we know about our own history. When I made aliyah in 2012, the absorption center invested a lot of time in getting the new immigrants on par with modern-day Israel history. Apparently, there is a huge need for it. We came from all over the world, very much marinated in the history of the countries we lived in; for what it's worth – they were our homes.

Now we came Home and most of us only knew the broad strokes (expulsions, Holocaust, War of Independence, Six Day War, a few prime ministers that stood out above the rest) – those historical points in history that no Jewish consciousness can be ignorant of or deny, but then again - not even that is a given these days.

If that is how it goes with modern day history, then there is almost no hope for the older chapters of Jewish history. So much so that **we forgot that more than half of the family got lost a long time ago** and we don't even remember them, never mind miss them.

The situation gets even more dire when recognizing and unifying with them is a prerequisite for the *geula shlema* (full redemption). We somehow developed divine amnesia, caused and justified by a relentless *galut* (exile), where we were merely trying to keep our heads above water. Chazal tell us that we even miscalculated dates surrounding the Temples' destruction due to severe PTSD.

Still, we are commanded to remember, and that's why things got written down. And yet most Jews, even Orthodox Jews, have never sat down and read the full Tanach. We somehow get stuck in *Parshat haShavua* (weekly Torah portion) and its plethora of *perushim* (commentaries) and the Haftarah that we usually yawn through before Mussaf.

And this is where the gap in the geula process lies, a gap that, when properly studied, can bring much more insight and tolerance on an inevitable but divine process.

The gap goes something like this:

Just after the death of Shlomo HaMelech, the Kingdom split into two, the Southern Kingdom, also known as the House of Yehuda (Judah and Benjamin) or better known today as the Jews, and the Northern Kingdom or the House of Israel, sometimes also referred to as *Yosef* (Joseph) or Ephraim. Due to the youthful arrogance of David HaMelech's grandson, the young *Rehavam (Rehoboam)*, an insulted and equally hard-headed *Yerovam* (Jeroboam) decided to break away from Yehuda's authority and dragged ten tribes with him.

Yerovam faced some challenges as Jerusalem, the focal point of connection, stood center in the heart of Israel. So, he started a replacement campaign. He replaced Jerusalem with worship centers in Bethel and Dan, basically telling the Northern tribes that this is their "new Jerusalem".

He replaced Sukkot with an imitation of some sort, shifting it one month later and he appointed priests not ranking from Levite descent. As his flagship move, he exploited and enforced an already existing weakness in the House of Israel – deviant worship - by replacing God with two golden calves, leading the House of Israel down a steady slope to full-on idolatry. Any of this sound familiar?

Rehavam wanted to take action, but God warned him not to, *"for this thing has been brought about by Me."* (1 Kings 12:24), a sentiment and offset of a pattern to be painfully repeated a few centuries later when even the great Rabbi Gamliel told his followers to be hands-off when reports of a new religion reared its head. Happenstance?

No. A deeply embedded correlation.

As idolatry took its toll, Hashem did remain true to His covenant with Israel and initiated a plan/event that would remove the idolaters from the Land – the Assyrian Exile. As the Assyrian forces swept over the Northern Kingdom, leaving destruction and ruin in its wake, refugees desperately made their way south to Jerusalem, the fortified stronghold.

The ruling King of Yehuda, *Chizkiyahu* (Hezekiah), had to think on his feet how to keep the influx of refugees safe, as well as prepare the city against the approaching Assyrian war machine. Archaeology testifies to two major feats: the enlargement of the city and the rerouting of the water system. Recent archaeological findings further verified the absorption of the refugee influx.

Ortal Chalaf and Dr. Joe Uziel, who led excavations in the City of David, discovered dozens of seals, dated to the days of the Judean kingdom prior to the Babylonian destruction. These seals testify to the names which are familiar to us from the Bible during the Kingdom of Israel, and which appear in Judea during the period following the destruction of the Kingdom of Israel.

"These names are part of the evidence of the fact that after the exile of the Tribes of Israel, refugees arrived in Jerusalem from the northern kingdom, and they were assimilated into senior positions in Jerusalem's administration," according to Uziel.

It is true that the Jews who were exiled to Babylon held within them traces of all the tribes. And this has been the main justification of those shunning the idea that the rest of the Lost Tribes will ever be found again, like water that seeped through the sands of time, unrecoverable. However, this stands against the Talmudic concept of *HaTinok sheNishbah*[26]. Every child of Israel is a universe in itself and, though we might have lost the ability to trace and track these souls, nothing is impossible for the Almighty. In fact, He made a promise regarding their re-identification. He made quite a few actually.

> *"Then the LORD your God will turn your captivity, and have compassion on you, and will return and gather you from all the peoples, from where the LORD your God has scattered you. If any of you that have been driven as far the uttermost parts of heaven, from there will the LORD your God gather you, and from there He will take you."*
> (Deuteronomy 30:3-4)

Where Are The Lost Tribes Now?

The question is, if these sparks exist, where are they currently? Israel-based author Yair Davidy has done tremendous work in this field, tracing the tribes from their initial dispersal and their subsequent journeys. True to tribal character, it appears that they kept together, and certain behavioral patterns are found in these respective groups.

Though they are spread amongst all Nations and religions, the biggest bulk seems to exist within the confines of Christianity and, more specifically, the Protestant and Evangelical movements. These individuals usually associate with Yosef and Ephraim. It is noteworthy to mention that there is a small but significant number within the Arab Nations too.

If the tribes stick to their ancestral character, it is then also easy to connect the dots that Yosef can be found in most of the

---

[26] *Tinok shenishba bein hanochrim*, translates as, "An infant captured among the gentiles." This happens when an individual is not responsible for his actions and sins due to his being raised in a place or situation where Jewish law is unknown to him. The concept originated from the time of the exiles. The child however stays Jewish through the maternal line.

world-governing countries in the West, most predominantly the UK and the US. If so, Yosef has provided for his brothers over millennia. It further does not come as a surprise that Zionist Christians have always felt the obligation, and played a key role, helping their Jewish brothers to return to Israel, with tremendous efforts since the 18th century. Studying their motives proves this obligation stretching beyond a missionary agenda, although such an agenda cannot be excluded.

In a most profound study, Israeli mathematician Shaul Kullook[27] discovered that major changes within Christianity correlate and act in the same behavioral pattern that deals with the exits and entrances into Eretz Israel and other major historical events of the Jewish people.

If Yosef and the rest of the brothers are indeed out there, and these studies and behavioral patterns not only support that thesis but indicate where they are located, **then we have an obligation to investigate and reach out**, and for those doing this, it might even be their very *tikkun* (spiritual correction) in furthering the geula.

This has been the sole purpose in my working with the Nations: to identify my lost brothers and sisters, and to at least put a strong narrative out there of who the Jewish People actually are, negating the anti-Semitic narrative ascribed to us over two millennia.

A bloody history of Christian antisemitism that has now evolved into deceptive missionizing in a more Hebraic disguise makes it very hard for proud, God-fearing Jews who never gave up or in, to engage, never mind navigate, this new minefield.

---

[27] www.facebook.com/Saul-Kullok-Science-and-Torah-108513253869729/

What Happens Now?

This is where things get complicated. Just as the Biblical narrative is often a prototype of a future event that needs to reoccur, usually on a grander scale, the time is coming soon for Yosef to not only give the reigns and the current seat of power it holds in the world over to Yehuda, but also to again submit under the *mechokek* (lawgiver). This inherently means that Yehuda has faithfully kept the Torah in all its facets, and the Ten Tribes, when rejoining, will have to realign, ridding themselves from all idolatrous notions.

Chazal describe, in impressive detail, the powerful face-off between Yosef and Yehuda in Egypt and what really went down[28]. The prophets reiterate this in copious accounts, which means we are inevitably going to face a challenging transition. A merger is never easy to negotiate. Everyone is bringing something noteworthy to the table. The prophets gave us the outlines, but we are stuck with figuring out the logistics and the goal to not throw the baby out with the bath water.

In my nine years in Israel, I have spent the majority of it working with those souls braving this no man's land. What I've seen is a very complex dynamic with tremendous potential, but also riddled with pitfalls. I have seen the very dubious, initially hidden, but lately openly flaunted messianic missionary agenda here in Eretz Israel, proudly prancing that they have "arrived" at the pinnacle of all knowledge, being upgraded from what they now call idolatrous Christianity but also knowing just that much more than the blind Jew regarding the Jew's own faith – leaving poisonous pamphlets in their wake.

I have also seen sincere souls shunning these actions from their fellow Christians, trying their best to build bridges over this gaping chasm, with a hands-off policy regarding missionary

---

[28] See Midrash 3 in Appendix A

work. I have seen the majority of them sincerely challenging the bulk of their own theology.

I have seen fellow Jews dangerously and sometimes shamelessly overstepping red lines in the name of bridge-building. I have even witnessed some losing their direction due to this irresponsible approach. On the other side of this dangerous feat, I have stood, embarrassed, witnessing the purposeful extortion of facts by Jews, blaming, even framing those few Christians who are making a sincere effort to work together, by the unethical tweaking of their social messages to fit their narrative.

I have also seen Jews proudly representing the Jewish people with no compromise or moving an inch on who we are and what we believe, bringing the truth and beauty of the *Am Segula* (treasured people) to a very ignorant, unchallenged and distorted picture that persists among the Nations. These colleagues might just be the best frontline defense for the Jewish people, by steadily and patiently changing the current landscape regarding the world's tainted opinion of the Jews.

If I can put this process into my own words, it is that of loving Father, knowing, and celebrating His sons' unique strengths and personalities, but also suffering their weaknesses. Remember, God did not choose a man, He chose a nation rooted in twelve brothers. That's twelve. Not two.

Knowing that this nation was set for a long, winding journey of tikkun, He set unique safety measures in place to make sure all the *nitzotzot* (divine sparks) will safely make it to the other side. In His unfathomable wisdom, He harnessed both their resilience, as well as their weaknesses that had to be perfected, into a quintessential algorithm, if you may, and built vessels accordingly that will deliver them on the doorstep of the geula. According to this wisdom and the necessary tikkun they had to make, He placed them in these vessels respectively.

Reunion

Note to the non-Jewish reader: I am describing this from a Jewish perspective, to help explain to a very wary Jewish audience why we engage with the Nations.

The split of the Kingdom was preparation for the transition of the Twelve Tribes, ultimately to unite them in the end as the whole House of Israel.[29] They were placed into two Time Pods, if you may. The Northern Kingdom went first, primarily because of the idolatry that was running rampant in their midst. The Ten Tribe Time Pod took on the character of the cause of their exile. The sages speak of this as the *klippah*[30] (impure spiritual force). We already mentioned those dynamics, including the replacement of and/or a medium to God, Jerusalem and the festivals.

At this juncture, it is important to understand that both Houses suffered idolatry, ultimately falling to the lowest spiritual point respectively BUT also that most of the time, both Houses were only caught up in a deviant form of worship.[31]

Why is this important? Because many sincere souls seek a genuine relationship with God but fall prey to deviant worship due to a lack of knowledge.

The tables of blissful ignorance are turning. Take, for instance, the awareness explosion amongst the Nations regarding the persecution of the Jews, so much so that they have called global gatherings, collecting accounts, researching them and ultimately apologizing and genuinely seeking forgiveness from the Jewish People for the atrocities done during the last two millennia.[32] Is

---

[29] See Ezekiel 37: 15-28
[30] The concept of the klippah is a very high Kabbalistic concept that I touch on here in a very crude and basic way. A simple translation would be a husk or peel, such as can be found around fruit.
[31] See Rabbi Chaim Klein's book *God versus gods*
[32] Nations' 9th of Av https://9-av.com/

it enough? Not even close, but it is a worthy start. And shame on those who want to stifle such efforts.

Regarding the concept of a klippah: as much as the klippah is the place where the negative forces reside, keeping its content "captive", it simultaneously provides the necessary protection as the content develops, ultimately allowing it to reach its potential[33]. At the auspicious time, the klippah must be removed in order not to stunt its content's growth. This is the concept of threshing, where the very thing that carried you, assisting in your development, can kill you if not removed in a timely fashion. The same goes for the umbilical cord. At the time of birth, the very life force that sustained you now has to be removed. It is of this that Rabbi Hirsh comments in the Haftara of Vayishlach (Genesis 32:4-36:43)[34]:

"The condition of a child before birth is regarded by our sages as a condition of bliss. The unborn child thinks it will last forever, but when the birth-throes start, out it must come into the raw world. Just so Ephraim believes its present state, ... would last forever, and does not see that chevlei yoldah (birth pangs) are coming, coming inevitably, reckoned on in advance in accordance with God's Rule regulating the world, just like the natural pains that come when the fruit has reached its maturity. But when these hours of pangs come..., no moment can he remain in the happy condition he had hitherto enjoyed, out he must come unwillingly, into the cold raw world."

The klippah, womb or Time Pod that the Ten Tribes are in now *is* their reality and they respond to it with sincere commitment, reaching out to God. They were placed there by Divine decree; it is part of their tikkun. But a birth is inevitable and imminent.

---

[33] This paradoxical dynamic can be found throughout Judaism, for example the Yetzer Harah which is our biggest challenge to overcome, but without it we can't survive in this world.

[34] "The Pentateuch" - Rabbi S.R. Hirsch Translation and commentary on the weekly and festival Haftarot, p. 77

In fact, we have seen the redemption of many of these precious sparks already.

There is another side to this coin. Yehuda was also set into its own Time Pod, one that had been buffered with ample halacha pertaining to the galut. These very halachot are now bringing strain within the transitioning into the geulah. You don't have to look further than the kitniyot quibbles during Pesach[35]. When these halachot that were vital to the survival of the Jewish people in galut are not correctly understood within their meticulous context, they become grossly misinterpreted by those outside of Judaism, and let's face it, have driven many of our own into assimilation due to the lack of Jewish education. Moreover, it has become a favorite tool in the hands of those self-hating Jews who have set up shop in Israel, painting their fellow brothers as blind fools, stirring the Messianic missionary agenda amongst the Nations.

Specific protocol was built into both Time Pods in order to keep them from interfering with one another. Yehuda, being commissioned as the mechokek was the guardian of the full Torah, Written and Oral. It had to cultivate and keep it for more than 2,000 years at a great personal cost.

Yosef, or the Ten Tribe counterpart, had to be kept at arm's length, as it naturally gravitates to alter the holy writings according to its current deviant state. Having a diluted form of the Written Torah in Greek and subsequent translations into almost all other languages around the globe allowed Yosef to keep the essence of the Torah alive in their consciousness and enable it to reach the four corners of the world, but did not allow them to touch the multi-dimensional universes that are only to be found in Hebrew.

They were even told that the Oral Torah is detrimental and should be avoided at all costs – which has proven very effective,

---

[35] The raging debate every Passover about the kosher for Passover status of beans, seeds, rice and other foods

but again, at a very high cost on Yehuda's side. The way that the sages "programmed" these protocols within both these Time Pods was masterfully done, but that is beyond the scope of this article. It is worth mentioning that even an exit strategy exists with markers embedded within this protocol[36].

So when the auspicious time comes, nothing can stop the extraction of the sparks from their Time Pod. **A sure sign is the sudden, unstoppable urge amongst a chosen few in the Nations to start learning Hebrew, to study the significance of the chagim, to get back to the root – their roots, to dig deeper.**

Of course, things will be mixed up and messy in the beginning. Show me a birth that isn't. But where the sages bemoaned the inevitable descent into darkness in the beginning of this process, this time the same words come as a comfort. If this is from God, you cannot stop it.

Rabbi Hirsh beautifully describes this in his commentary on the Rosh Hashana Haftara[37]:

"The reason why just this chapter has been chosen for the Haftora for Rosh Hashana lies deeper. The choice was fixed out of an extremely delicate consideration, out of the deepest feeling of brotherhood. We, who are assembled as members of the House of Jacob before our Father, yes all of us whom we know for over two thousand years as our Jewish brethren, the bearers of the tradition, the teachers of our people, the arrangers of our prayers, we all

---

[36] A well-known mashal within the Christian writings is that of the (younger) prodigal son who shuns his inheritance and end up with the pigs (idolatry) but ultimately realising his mistake and returning to his father's household. A very often skipped over character in this mashal is the elder brother who never deviated or left his Father's house. Ultimately the younger will return, but the older brother will retain the heritage. Zechariah 2:12 and many other psukim speak of Yehuda being God's portion.

[37] "The Pentateuch" - Rabbi S.R. Hirsch Translation and commentary on the weekly and festival Haftarot, pp. 638-639

descend from the exiles of the Kingdom of Judah. The ten brother-tribes, who earlier had already set aside the bond of the Torah, really had never been very tightly bound by it, they had forsaken the Father's house early, they have been missing for thousands of years. As the first to renounce God's Laws, the first to secede from Zion, to sink back into the night of idolatry, but also as the first to be overtaken by the doom they had brought on themselves, do they live in our memory. Is it not then a stroke of touching tenderness that the wise arrangers of our Divine Service should have taken care that the sons of Judah as assembled before their God on Rosh Hashana - after the figures of their great ancestors Abraham and Isaac on Mount Moriah have been called up before their eyes as everlasting shining examples, should also remember in love their missing brethren? For that, they chose this word of the Prophet which, as no other, announces just the future also of these children of the House of Jacob who have been estranged so long. It sees them, how they "come up" to Zion, to God, to "our God from the mountains of Samaria memories of Ahab! It shows us Ephraim, from whom the defection started, as God's "firstborn", and Israel (the kingdom of Israel L.L) coming back to God as one of His children; shows us Rachel weeping for her children alas, just the tribe of Joseph, coming from her were the first in the defection; - Although withdrawn from our sight, from the mother's eye looking down from heaven they are not hidden, she sees her children, but the mother misses the Father, she misses God in the homes, the lives, the hearts of her children, therefore "she weeps bitterly", and therefore "she refuses to be consoled". Rachel is also Our mother, her children are also our brethren, **on Rosh Hashona we remember them and long for the time of reunion to arrive.** But it must be a reunion as God has promised here. Not that we come to a compromise with them in the defection. But rather, on the day when we examine ourselves before God, and work seriously on ourselves to become more and more in truth sons and daughters of Zion, we look forward to the time when they too will come back, "as children, to their original home" back to the ground of God's Torah. That is the thought of reunion and peace which, at the beginning of every New Year, makes the sons of Judah who have *remained faithful and who are working on fortifying themselves, at making themselves grow ever stronger and firmer in their faith - hope and pray for the time of their reunion with all their brethren of the House of Israel.*

It is evident that Judah cannot shy away from this task. And perhaps by studying the plethora of commentaries[38] by the sages on this very subject, we can carefully and responsibly work towards this inevitable and ultimate union.

Behold, how good and how pleasant it is for brethren to dwell together in unity...

for there the L-RD commanded the blessing, even life forever.
(Psalm 133:1 and 3 paraphrased)

AnaRina Bat Tzion Kreisman worked successfully in the Broadcast and Marketing industry in South Africa, before throwing her weight in with the Jewish Agency for Israel in Johannesburg. There she was Head of Marketing, mainly promoting aliyah (Jewish immigration to Israel). She decided to put word to deed and made aliyah to Israel at the beginning of 2012. In Israel she continued working in Special Projects of the Jewish Agency's Aliyah Department. She joined the City of David in 2014 and started the Jerusalem Watch Project. In November 2018, she launched a new Biblical Advocacy program called Align With Zion. The project aims to assist pro-Israel supporters in understanding the eternal covenant and dynamic between God and His people (Am Israel), how it plays out in modern history, and to ultimately empower them in their support of Israel by aligning them with the true essence of Zion. Through mutual friends recognizing their shared love for God, His People, Eretz Israel and teaching the Nations, AnaRina was introduced to Tamir Kreisman (Tent of Abraham). The couple got married Erev Shavuot 2020, in a small wedding ceremony overlooking the Temple Mount and ancient Biblical Jerusalem.

---

[38] See Appendix A for a few Midrashim touching on this topic.

Ger Toshav - What Jews Need To Know

RABBI DAVID KATZ

The Bible has over 50 mentions of *ger*, often translated as stranger, alien, sojourner, foreigner or convert. Countless times, nearly every week, you will encounter this term/concept in the parsha. Often, one reading an English translation of the parsha will not realize this foreigner, alien, etc. is ger in the Hebrew. Very rarely in the Bible is ger translated as convert.

Yet, ask any semi-learned Jew what a ger is, and nearly unanimously, they will answer "a convert". But wait a minute! Didn't we just say that, more often than not, ger is translated as stranger, alien, sojourner or foreigner?

Ger is an extremely nuanced term, both Biblically and rabbinically. Like with many matters of wisdom, the more nuanced a concept is, the more frequently it is reduced to a simple concept and term. 'Common' is the art of blocking nuance, and unfortunately, religion often defaults to common context. Nuance, is left for scholars and obscure dialogue.

The irony is, the world is nuanced, religion is nuanced, language is nuanced... EVERYTHING has nuance, but society somehow manages to willingly sacrifice nuance in favor of common meaning and understanding.

Ger in the Bible is a preservation of nuance, a remnant of Godly wisdom. In many, if not most instances of ger in the Bible, the word has no connection to the modern construct of ger as a convert who has undergone a halachic conversion. The prevailing Jewish attitude is that conversion is unnuanced; you are either a full convert or you aren't. There is no such thing as kind-of converted.

In fact, the halachot of nuance in conversion are largely ignored and/or omitted from a general discussion on the topic. This means that if ger is being used in this context, it is either describing a halachic sequence leading to conversion, or it isn't. In this case, there are no shades of gray.

However, ger is *only* gray, hence, it is highly nuanced. Is this ger a stranger, alien, sojourner, foreigner or a convert? Thank God we have a Torah and rabbinic tradition that identifies every term of the Bible in the Oral Torah. In this regard, we are not orphaned. We have inherited thousands of years of wisdom and nuance. Stranger, alien, sojourner and foreigner each have a different, subtle context; this is why the translations vary slightly. One fact that is abundantly clear is that, almost exclusively, we are *not* referring to a halachic convert to Judaism.

This is why ger is ultra-important to Judaism. The nuanced term ger is a preservation of unadulterated Torah wisdom. Once we realize that ger in the Bible is meant to describe something other than a convert, it should serve as a wakeup call. One's conscious thought after grasping this realization ought to be, "I was told that ger means convert, but it just doesn't. It doesn't mean any one thing; it is nuanced."

Once this expanded understanding of ger opens up in our minds, it serves as a key. What else in the Bible is ripe for renewed meaning? The answer is - all of it! And it doesn't just end there. All of our reality needs reexamined, because we have adopted common, inferior meanings for many important concepts. Ger is a reminder of the Oral Torah, urging us to slow down, think, research and reclaim nuance.

If it's not referring to a halachic convert, what is a ger by today's standards? Does it even exist?

A non-Jew is commanded in the Seven Laws of Noah. A non-Jew who does not keep them is called a *goy* (non-Jew), *akum* (worshiper of stars and constellations), *nochri* (foreigner), etc. These are all nuanced terms. And if he keeps the Seven Laws of Noah, he is called a *ger toshav*. Were you taught that a ger toshav is a resident alien that doesn't exist today? One word will resolve this misunderstanding. That word is nuance.

Ger and ger toshav are not the same thing; ger in the Bible as a ger toshav is hinted at, but not explicitly mentioned, and is described as a non-Jew who keeps the Seven Laws of Noah either as a slave, a captive, a worker or a pious individual. Keeping the Seven Laws of Noah makes them acceptable to be in proximity to the Jew.

Ger toshav, on the other hand, is purely Talmudic, and is the halachic parallel to the Noahide ger. The Talmud often mulls over what quality defines the ger toshav.

The word Noahide, as you might have guessed, is a common term, stripped of nuance. It belongs in the family of stranger, alien, foreigner and convert. We prefer the term Noahide over aliens and strangers because it implies a direct association to the Seven Laws of Noah and their observance. But remember, by definition, if we lump these terms together, they have one common root, and that is the word ger.

Ger toshav actually serves to distinguish one kind of ger from closely associated terms. The nuance of adding toshav to the unadorned term ger implies keeping the Seven Laws of Noah. The problem with this is that the term toshav is as nuanced as the term ger. It can mean a resident, dwelling, sitting, or rabbinically as observant of the Seven Laws of Noah. The consequence is that the term ger toshav is also nuanced and subject to the same tendency to oversimplify it. As a result, the term Noahide was born out of necessity.

It's crucial to remember that Noahide is a common term, born from disassociation from nuance. It's an oversimplified term that masks nuance. Beneath every instance of Noahide, if we refer back to the original Hebrew source, we will find a nuanced ger term.

In short, both the Noahide and the ger toshav are righteous non-Jews who keep the Seven Laws of Noah. The path of the Noahide in Torah begins and ends there. But with the ger toshav, the journey of nuance is only beginning. Ger represents the eternal opportunity to rediscover God's great wisdom, revealed at Sinai, that we inherit in each generation.

Today we do not have a full-fledged ger toshav, but on a very practical level, there is a subtle benefit to recognizing ger toshav, as opposed to Noahide. A Noahide keeps the Seven Laws of Noah without any clarification of these laws. A ger toshav goes further and personally rejects idolatry by taking an oath before three Jews. Oddly, this halachic component, as mandated by the Oral Torah, is omitted by those rabbis working with the Noahide community today.

Without a *Sanhedrin* (supreme religious and legal court in the Land of Israel), recognition of the full status of ger toshav today is limited. It carries no significant practical weight for the Jew, but to the non-Jew, it carries spiritual liberation from idolatry.

Where a Jew can benefit from learning more about the ger toshav concept lies in being introduced to a Torah realization that would otherwise remain concealed. Presently, while we await the appearance of *Moshiach ben David* (the final Messianic redeemer), we have time to discover an ancient Torah that has been largely hidden all of this time.

The ger toshav will eventually return to the world in its full sense. A Jew today can prepare for that eventuality, and many other new realities, by connecting to the depths of Torah that are kept closed until relevant. Imagine if we found a red heifer, a nazirite, a prophet or any other Torah concept that has been largely theoretical for thousands of years. Truthfully, it would force us to look more deeply into the Torah. The ger toshav of today provides this opportunity now.

Our perception of Jew, gentile, ger, convert, Noahide and other central Torah concepts needs a return to nuance. One day, as geula dawns, there will be a difference between an Israelite Jew and a Kohen, between a goy and a ger, between a ger toshav and a Noahide. With these nuances come profound distinctions. For example, a goy may not learn Torah at all according to some opinions, whereas the Noahide can. It is the ger tradition in halacha that sheds light on the permissibility of a non-Jew learning Torah.

In an overly simplified fashion, most Jews today think of a non-Jew as a Christian. Yet, if we look at Tanach, there were many different kinds of non-Jews. Those nuances have, in the main, been lost to most Jews.

In the future, this overly simplified form of Jewish understanding I call Sunday School Judaism will cease to exist altogether. When Moshiach ben David reveals his Torah, the deeper nuances that have been with us since Sinai will be revealed anew.

Ironically, studying about the non-Jew in Torah can open the eyes of Jews to the nuances in our own tradition in more profound ways than we can dare to imagine.

Rabbi David Katz is an international lecturer and author for Noahides, specializing in Ger Toshav. He is the author of Laws of Ger Toshav: Pious of the Nations. *Rabbi Katz lives in Jerusalem with his family.*

The Third Temple
and The Nations

RABBI AVRAHAM GREENBAUM

The Third Temple, destined to stand eternally on Mount Moriah, the Temple Mount, as prophesied by all the Hebrew prophets, is The House of Prayer for all the Nations. In the words of Isaiah:

> *"For so says the LORD... As for the **foreigners** who attach themselves to the LORD, to minister to Him and to love the Name of the LORD, to be His servants—all who keep the Sabbath and do not profane it, and who hold fast to My Covenant*
>
> *I will bring them to My sacred Mount and let them rejoice in My House of Prayer. Their burnt offerings and sacrifices shall be welcome on My altar; For My House shall be called A House of Prayer **for all the Nations**"* (Isaiah 56:4-7)

The commentator Rashi (ad loc.) underlines the point: "And not for Israel alone, but also 'for all the Nations.'"

Indeed, when King Solomon inaugurated the original Temple on this spot, he specifically included the non-Israelites in his prayer:

> *"Or if a **foreigner** who is not of Your people Israel comes from a distant land for the sake of Your Name—for they shall hear about Your great Name and Your mighty hand and Your outstretched arm--when he comes to pray toward this House, Oh, hear in Your heavenly abode and grant all that the foreigner requests of You. Thus, all the peoples of the earth will know Your Name and revere*

You, as does Your people Israel; and they will recognize that Your Name is attached to this House that I have built." (I Kings 8:41-43)

The Temple in Jerusalem is the source of blessing for all the people of the world. In the words of a well-known midrash: *"If the Nations of the world had known how much blessing the Holy Temple brings them, they would have set guard-posts all around it to protect it and would not have destroyed it."* (Bamidbar Rabba, 1:3) The Talmud states: *"Said Rabbi Yochanan: 'Woe to the pagans who have lost and they do not know what they have lost. At the time when the Holy Temple stood, the Altar atoned for them. But now who will atone for them?"* (Talmud Bavli, Succah 55b).

Towering 18th c. Kabbalist Rabbi Moshe Chayim Luzzatto, the Ramchal, in his *Mishk'ney Elyon*, expounding on the mystical, spiritual meaning of the Third Temple and its services as prophesied by Ezekiel (chapters 40-48), explains that the Temple is the center point of the world, where all the branches of the Tree of Life, human, animal, vegetable and inanimate, connect with their spiritual roots, drawing a flow of sustenance and blessing to the entire world.

Exile

It is but a sign of Israel's continuing exile and the concealment of the Torah from the wider world that the meaning and purpose of the Temple as a practical proposition are almost completely unknown among the Nations of the world, and apparently to a large proportion of Torah-observant Jews as well, let alone the non-observant and those alienated from their Judaism.

The overwhelming majority of the member-states of the United Nations clearly agree that even the slightest change to the status quo on the Temple Mount in Jerusalem (except in favor of the Muslims) would spark a terrible conflagration. Nowhere on the table in any of the successive Middle East peace plans is there any practical proposal to actually build the Temple as prophesied by all the Hebrew prophets, or even to relate to the idea. Indeed,

UNESCO, the international body charged with preservation of the world's cultural heritage, routinely ignores any Jewish link to the Temple Mount, while denial of the historicity of the First and Second Temples is rampant among revisionist historians.

The law of the State of Israel supposedly gives Jews religious rights on the Temple Mount, yet those charged with state security routinely prevent Jews from even opening their mouths in prayer on the Mount, let alone prostrating or performing any other act of devotion, lest this might spark the feared conflagration.

Every single day of the year, on weekdays, Sabbaths and festivals, observant Jews offer prayers for the rebuilding of the Holy Temple and the restoration of its services, themes that feature prominently in the blessings after meals and the thrice-daily Amidah prayer.

Yet while Jewish people of many different kinds and persuasions surely yearn for the Messianic redemption and the return of the Temple, the passive majority quite clearly do not see it as an immediate challenge to get up and build it. Except for a courageous few, many of us only sigh in near-despair at the seeming impossibility of actually succeeding in changing anything under the current international strategic stranglehold.

With the Enlightenment and the inroads of the *Haskalah* (Jewish Enlightenment) movement into the minds and hearts of many Jews, the bloody Temple sacrificial system came to be seen as primitive and retrogressive. Prayers for its restoration were completely erased from the Reform liturgy together with any kind of Temple consciousness in the minds of most of the wider Jewish population.

Among the observant, study of the Talmudic tractates dealing with Temple law has a central place in certain Lithuanian yeshivot, such as Brisk, yet few, if any, of their students would ever become Temple activists. In the wider Haredi world, both in Israel and the Diaspora, those Jews who do take an active stand for the Temple, such as the Temple Mount Faithful, Temple

Institute, Nascent Sanhedrin and others, are widely perceived as wild dreamers and fringe elements, if not as dangerous extremists, and they are certainly portrayed as the latter such across the mainstream Jewish and secular media in Israel and internationally.

Despite so much antagonism, there has, in fact, been a great awakening of Temple consciousness among many Jews and also among many non-Jewish people across the world, even if unreported and unacknowledged in most of the media. With the reclamation of the Temple Mount by Israel in the 1967 Six Day War, many believed that the ancient prophecies about the restoration of the Temple were being realized, though they were to be sadly disappointed.

Nevertheless, the importance of Jews studying subjects related to the redemption as well as the Temple and its services was emphasized by the late Lubavitcher Rebbe zt"l, probably the single most widely influential leader of post-Holocaust Jewry. Among much else, he instituted cycles of daily study at different levels for men, women and children of Maimonides' comprehensive Torah law code, the Mishne Torah, about one third of which deals with the laws of the Temple and the associated requisite ritual purity.

The Lubavitcher Rebbe urged us to "want Moshiach NOW", and he was personally interested in all Temple-related projects, encouraging Jews to ascend to permitted areas of the Temple Mount. He also gave his blessing to the Hebrew printing of Rabbi Moshe Chayim Luzzatto's *Mishk'ney Elyon* on the Third Temple. However, while the Rebbe strongly advocated promoting the Seven Noahide Commandments among non-Jews, he did not seemingly encourage the building of the Temple as a practical project at the present time or the promotion of the Temple idea among people of the Nations of the world.

In the past three decades, the work of the Temple Institute and others has brought increasing awareness of the Temple to many Jews across the spectrum, observant and non-observant, to many

Noahides (as the Noahide movement has rapidly expanded), also to great numbers of non-Jewish religious pilgrims and other tourists visiting Israel. Christians in particular are often deeply interested in the idea of the restoration of the Temple, being more aware of the Temple idea since it figures prominently in their scriptures. Among Muslims in Israel and around the world, there are also those who understand the Jewish right and the global need to build the Third Temple, including prominent leaders such as Adnan Oktar in Turkey, Imam Abdul Hadi Palazzi in Italy and others.

The Great Reset

Everyone can now see that the entire world is in complete turmoil in the wake of the corona pandemic. International, and even domestic travel within countries, has largely come to a standstill. National economies have ground to a halt, livelihoods have been destroyed, the education of children and students has been disrupted, and the long-term emotional cost of wearing face masks, social distancing, endless lockdowns and other restrictions on people of all ages everywhere is incalculable.

Well before the outbreak of the COVID-19 pandemic, major international organizations and leading think tanks were incessantly warning about impending global doom on account of climate change. Now, the disruption of lives and whole economies because of corona is encouraging even stronger calls for an urgent Great Reset, intended to break earlier, ingrained lifestyle habits of people across the world now deemed unsustainable.

Viable? Acceptable?

Believers in the word of the LORD as revealed in the Hebrew prophets can only wonder about the viability and desirability of this grandiose agenda, which omits any mention of faith in God or obedience to His Law, let alone the Holy Temple prophesied by all the Hebrew prophets as the key to blessing, prosperity and harmony for the entire world. This is nothing but yet another symptom of the depth of the exile of Israel and the concealment of the Torah and its teachings from all the Nations and from many Jews – the final subjugation under the empires. Enormous, powerful vested interests keep their iron grip on the status quo, preventing even the slightest adjustments to the very delicate Middle East balance, lest it spark the feared, or threatened, conflagration.

To Torah-observant Jews, the small print of the proposed Great Reset presents serious challenges, if not dire threats, to traditional Jewish family life and education (as, for example, the emphasis on sex education and gender fluidity from early childhood) – the likes of which are already being felt in Jewish communities in Britain, Europe and other First World countries. In many ways, the Jewish people may be seen as being faced with a growing wave of a new form of Hellenism that threatens to engulf us.

The restoration of the Temple services and the miracle of the menorah oil was at the very center of the redemption of the Jews in the time of the Maccabees. The clear message to today's rabbis, Torah students, Charedim, religious Zionists, Israeli nationalists and others of all shades across the spectrum, is that our only hope of surviving this menacing cultural tsunami is through stoking the fires of our passion for our ancestral Torah dream of the redemption and the restoration of the Holy Temple as a physical reality in this world, through massive campaigns of promotion and education in every possible way, through every possible medium.

Rabbi Nachman of Breslov said that if many people focus intently together on one idea, they can make it happen.

Dreaming the Dream

In the light of over 25 years of contacts I have had in personal meetings or through internet correspondence with innumerable non-Jews across the world from every kind of background and belief matrix, I have no doubt that our greatest challenge at this time is to unashamedly take these campaigns way beyond the boundaries of our observant Jewish communities and networks to the wider world of non-observant Jews and, even more importantly, to the many, many non-Jews who are waiting, yearning and calling out precisely for this.

Thirty years of internet usage has revealed that **there are untold millions across the globe who are true lovers of Israel, our people and our land, who have no secret ulterior motive to convert us, but who simply crave a connection with the God of Israel and knowledge of His Torah.**

Since its inception in 2004, some of the leading rabbis of the Nascent Sanhedrin have played a prominent part in organizing and executing colorful spectacles of priests performing "as-if Temple-time" rituals as close as possible to the walls of the Temple Mount in Jerusalem. These are executed as a graphic educational tool, presenting the Temple services as a reality, with priests clad in white, blowing shofars and trumpets, carrying live lambs and kid goats and baskets of fruits, stoking the fire on a mock altar, and the like. These have touched and aroused the hearts of many, including numerous Noahides and Righteous Gentiles, some of whom are now actively organizing under the banner of "Seventy Nations" under the guidance of the Sanhedrin.

With the power of the internet as the principle, swift and most effective medium of international communication, promotion and networking, to create the infrastructure for a strong, unified internet presence of a redemption-Third Temple networking movement, reaching out to all people, complete with website, database, chatting and blogging etc. would be relatively inexpensive, most certainly in comparison with the very heavy expenses involved in building or even renting and maintaining a physical facility that would, in any case, be practically inaccessible to most people across the world.

Do Jewish rabbis, teachers and leaders have the courage to join hands across our various affiliations and differing perceptions in order to respond to the desire and yearning among these millions across the world for Torah light, guidance and clear, authoritative leadership in the situation of growing darkness they feel they is facing in the world of the corona pandemic and its aftermath? These people are to be found at all levels in countries, different social and cultural groups or as individuals across the world. **We need to understand that these people are our greatest allies, and that, as Jews, we are responsible for them as part of our mission as God's chosen people.**

> *"Hillel says: Be of the disciples of Aaron, loving peace and pursuing peace, loving the creations and drawing them to the Torah."* (Avot 1:12)

As Jews, we do not own the Torah or the Temple idea. Our role is to be their guardians. This means our role is not limited to keeping and observing the Torah ourselves and praying for our own redemption and the rebuilding of the Temple for Israel. **The redemption and the Temple are of vital, urgent importance, not only to us but to the entire world.** We are to be a light to *all* the Nations, and as such we must do all we can to shine the Torah light to the Nations, as has begun to be done by many uncoordinated or only loosely-coordinated Torah/Jewish outreach organizations.

Let all who yearn and pray for the redemption and the restoration of the Temple begin by talking one with another (Malachi 3:16) and seriously plan and implement a joint project of education, promotion and outreach to people everywhere, including governments, international agencies and every other possible target, to bring the Temple idea down from Heaven to this very earth.

Perhaps it is through starting to spread the dream and planting the idea in people's minds everywhere that we may reconcile the seemingly opposed views as to how the restoration of the Temple will come about. On the one hand, Rashi holds that: "The future Temple for which we are waiting will be revealed and come down from heaven fully built and complete, as it is written (Exodus 15:17): 'The Sanctuary, God, that Your hands established'" (Rashi on Succah 41a and see Tosafot there; see also Rashi on Rosh Hashanah 30a and Tosafot on Shavuot 15b).

On the other hand, Maimonides, the Rambam, states that the main identifying sign of the Moshiach is that he will physically build the Third Temple in its proper place (Hilchot Melachim 11:4).

Through the words of Ramchal, we may perhaps begin to understand how both opinions express different aspects of the process by which the Third Temple will come into this world. He writes:

"In time to come, not only will the Heavenly and earthly Temples be similar. The Upper House will extend until it reaches the lower world. This is the meaning of the saying of our Rabbis that the Third Temple will be the work of the hands of God. For the Heavenly Temple will not be uprooted from its place. Rather it will extend until it reaches the lower world. Around it a physical structure will then be built as befits this material world, and the two structures will be joined and become one and will never again separate. God's glory will be fully revealed there, as it is said: 'And the glory of God will be revealed, and all flesh will see' (Isaiah 40:5). Then there will be complete peace and happiness forever" (*Mishk'ney Elyon*).

In other words, a spiritual emanation of the Temple will come down into this world from the Upper World – into people's minds and hearts – and around this dream and vision, the physical reality of the Third Temple will be built.

The more Jews and non-Jews alike study, grasp, dream and envision the Temple idea, the sooner, with God's help, humanity will come to its senses, cease its futile cycles of waste, pollution, environmental abuse, governmental and bureaucratic mismanagement, corruption, rivalry, conflict, warfare and destruction, and join together with one accord to worship the One God in the Third Temple, the "House of Prayer for all Nations".

Rabbi Avraham ben Yaakov Greenbaum is an internationally-known Torah teacher, author of over thirty books, and one of today's foremost English-speaking expositors of Chassidut and Kabbalah and their practical contemporary relevance in personal growth and wellbeing, preventive healthcare, healing and other vital areas. Born in Britain in 1949, Rabbi Greenbaum gained his MA in classics and social sciences at Cambridge University. As a Harkness Fellow in the U.S.A. he studied at Harvard and Columbia, after which he worked as a BBC World Service current events commentator and producer. A lifelong yearning for spirituality led to his return to the Torah. In 1980 Rabbi Greenbaum moved to Israel with his wife and family and settled in Jerusalem, where he was ordained in 1988. He maintains the Azamra website, and teaches at the Tiferet Study Center in Jerusalem. Rabbi Greenbaum can be reached at rebavraham@azamra.org.

Editor's Conclusion

DR. RIVKAH LAMBERT ADLER

As part of the process of geula, the world needs to undergo a dramatic change of consciousness. Since the destruction of the Second Temple, we have been living in a time of constricted spirituality. The potent pull of the physical, material world has limited our ability to connect to the eternal, spiritual, mystical and metaphysical aspects of human life.

Now, as we are perched on the precipice of geula, we are being called upon to actively shift our consciousness. For Jews, among other things, that means that the time has come to expand our understanding that the Torah does not belong exclusively to us. There are untold millions of individuals who want to be our students, just as Zechariah foresaw.

> *So said the Lord of Hosts: In those days, when ten men of all the languages of the Nations shall take hold of the corner of the garment of a Jewish man, saying, "Let us go with you, for we have heard that God is with you."* (Zechariah 8:23)

Higiah ha'zman – the time has come for us to step up to our role as Ohr LaGoyim.

To the non-Jewish reader, please understand that this paradigm shift is very difficult and controversial. The Jewish people have spent the past 2,000 years guarding and protecting the Torah from hostile Nations, and Christians have been the most hostile of all[39].

---

[39] For details, read *The List: Persecution of Jews by Christians Throughout History* by Ray Montgomery and Bob O'Dell available at root-source.com/product/the-list-persecution-of-jews/

Nevertheless, as redemption draws ever closer, more and more Jews are prepared to share the universal messages of God's Torah with you. May this book contribute to that goal. And may we meet very soon in Jerusalem, to worship the Master of the Universe in unity!

Request For Reviews

Thanks for reading *Lighting Up The Nations: Jewish Responsibility Towards the Nations Today and in the Messianic Era*.

If you enjoyed the book and/or recognize the value of its core message, please leave a review on Amazon or Goodreads. Every review, no matter how brief, helps the book be seen by more potential readers.

If you'd like to be in touch to share your thoughts or ask questions, you can reach me at rivkah@kotevet.com or on Facebook.

ADDENDUM

Editor's Note: Just as this modest work was nearing completion, one of its contributors, Rabbi Avraham Greenbaum published a monograph in which he explores two questions that rabbis today are being asked with increasing frequency. The questions concern who among the non-Jews may study the Torah and observe Shabbat. In responding to these questions, Rabbi Greenbaum delves into the different categories of non-Jews that Jewish law recognizes.

Since these questions arise naturally from the ideas presented in this book, Rabbi Greenbaum agreed to allow his monograph to be republished as an addendum to Lighting Up The Nations. *While the material presented here is a bit more technical than the rest of the essays, the theme of Rabbi Greenbaum's work is so closely connected to the rest of the book that it serves to support the book's central theme - that the Jewish people are being asked to respond to spiritual seekers of all kinds in ways we haven't seen since the advent of Christianity.*

For a PDF of the complete text, including Hebrew, go to

www.azamra.org/nations/who-goy-download.php

Any errors in formatting between this text and the original PDF are mine.

WHO IS THAT GOY?
Who may study Torah?
Keep Shabbat?

BY RABBI AVRAHAM GREENBAUM

Preface

My purpose in this work has been to seek answers to two questions repeatedly posed to many rabbis these days:

1. May a Goy study the Torah?
2. May a Goy observe the Shabbat?

To this end, I have sought to clarify a number of different halakhic statuses that might apply in different cases of people who would be considered by Jews, and also by those people themselves, as "non-Jews" or "Goyim". To do so, I have examined sources in the Hebrew Bible (*TaNaKh*), Talmud, the later halakhic authorities with particular reference to the comprehensive *Mishneh Torah* law code of Rabbi Moshe ben Maimon, "RaMBaM", Rabbi Moses Maimonides, and the teachings of Rabbi Nachman of Breslov.

Information on all the rabbinical sages cited and sources quoted is given in the Index of Sages and Sources.

I have largely provided my own translations of the Biblical, Talmudic, Halakhic and Chassidic sources quoted with the intent of highlighting what I believe may fairly be deduced from them. For the convenience of those with a knowledge of Hebrew, I have included the original Hebrew texts of most of the sources quoted, with acknowledgement and thanks to the outstanding **Sefaria Digital Library of Jewish Texts**. Where one of the Hebrew names of God appears in quoted sources, I have followed the convention of replacing the Hebrew letter *heh* with the letter *kuf* to avoid possible desecration of the names of God. In my English transliterations of Hebrew words, I have used the contemporary Sefardic pronunciation and rendered the Hebrew letter *cheit* as "ch" (not as in "lun*ch*" but as in the Scottish "lo*ch*" or German i*ch*) and the Hebrew letter *khof*, as "kh" (pronounced as a more guttural version of the *ch* in "lo*ch*").

It is not my intention to offer rulings on any questions of practical Halakhah as I am unqualified to do so. My hope is that, with God's help, these discussions and conclusions will stimulate further examination of the issues and facilitate the return of all the scattered souls of Israel quickly in our time.

Avraham Yehoshua ben Yaakov Greenbaum

Jerusalem, Eve of the Festival of Shavuot 5781

WHO IS THAT GOY?

WHO MAY STUDY TORAH?
KEEP SHABBAT?
by Rabbi Avraham Greenbaum

It is a time to act for the LORD, for they have violated Your Torah.(Psalm 119:126)

The Hebrew may also be rendered: There is a time when to act for the sake of the LORD, you must breach His Torah!

He who is wise will consider these words, He who is prudent will take note of them. For straight are the paths of the LORD, and the righteous shall walk in them, while sinners shall stumble in them.(Hosea 14:10)

Introduction

WHAT IS A GOY?

Most Jews well know that the term "Goy" is used of any person who is not considered "Jewish" by some criteria or other, and many non-Jews are also fully aware that this is how Jews may refer to them.

The use of this term by Jews when speaking of non-Jews perpetuates the distinction between "us" and "them", which has historically been one of the main keys to Jewish survival as a unique nation. Yet, excluding "them" can and often has been quite offensive to non-Jewish people. Moreover, as I hope to show in this discussion, in some cases excluding "them" may be quite unjustified, because the supposed "non-Jew" may indeed turn out to have a "Jewish" or "Israelite" soul. Being aware of the possible offense which use of the term "Goy" may cause, some Jews prefer at least in public to use the term "gentile", which they feel to be "softer".

In its root Biblical sense, the Hebrew word *Goy* simply means a "people" or "nation", and is used of the Children of Israel themselves as well as of the other Nations. God told Abraham: "I will make you into a great **nation**", **goy** gadol (Genesis 12:2). He told Moses that He chose Israel as "a kingdom of priests and a holy **nation**", **goy** kadosh (Exodus 19:7 and see also Deuteronomy 4:7). The central blessing of the Shabbat afternoon Amidah prayer says: "And who is like Your people Israel, one **nation, goy** echad, on the earth?" However, in rabbinical literature and in widespread Jewish parlance until today, the word "Goy" usually refers to a member of the supposedly "non-Jewish" people of the world.

Most Jews understand that a Goy may become a fully-fledged Jew through conversion, and the traditional pathway to becoming a full or "righteous" convert – *Ger Tzeddek* – is spelled out in detail in the Halakhah, practical Torah law. Today, Jewish sectarian movements such as the Reform and Conservative offer various alternatives to the traditional halakhic path, though their conversions are not recognized as valid by the "Orthodox" who adhere to the Halakhah.

At the same time, many if not most Jews today remain quite unaware that in countries all around the world there are growing numbers of individuals, families and in many cases entire communities of people, whom they would not consider to be "Jewish" or to have any connection with the Jewish people, yet who are seemingly quite spontaneously seeking to learn more about the Torah, to practice its commandments as they understand them, and to connect with Jewish rabbis and established Jewish communities.

With the worldwide proliferation of the Internet over the past decades, and particularly with the ever-expanding use of social networking platforms, numerous Jewish rabbis and others engaged in "Torah outreach" are increasingly discovering how widespread and persistent are such seekers. Yet their appeals for recognition as legitimate Torah seekers are met with different responses from rabbis of differing perspectives.

For most of Jewish history (though not always) outreach to non-Jews inviting them to convert was strictly discouraged. Indeed, in many places in different periods until today, conversion of non-Jews by Jews was strictly forbidden by the non-Jewish governing authorities on pain of death. The Halakhah itself requires that rabbinical courts must initially rebuff applicants for conversion as a way of testing their seriousness, and it often happens that the conversion process is drawn out over lengthy periods of time.

Some present-day rabbis view these "non-Jewish" Torah seekers who are today appearing all over the world as nothing but

"Goyim" like any others, who should not be encouraged to study or practice Torah but who should be taught that they are required only to accept and observe the Seven Commandments of the Children of Noah. Some rabbis fear, not without cause, that some of these seemingly "would-be" Jews may in fact be non-Jewish infiltrators, missionaries or "Messianics" of some kind seeking an entrée into Jewish communities through adopting an outward pose.

Yet in many cases these non-Jewish Torah seekers have totally rejected the religious beliefs and practices with which they grew up, and they find that their spiritual aspirations are far from satisfied with a narrow range of permitted Torah study and no more than the Seven Noahide Commandments, six of which are merely prohibitions which do not constitute a proactive spiritual pathway as such.

These people seek deeper Torah wisdom and understanding, long to practice many more of the Torah commandments, and in some cases seek to embrace fully the lifestyle and Torah practice of observant Jews. Yet the majority of these seekers are located in places far from any orthodox community let alone an orthodox rabbinical court, and thus have no way to fulfill the usual conversion requirements, such as residence in an existing orthodox community for at least a year if not longer prior to conversion.

The acute dilemmas experienced by such people in seeking to express their spiritual aspirations in authentic and permissible ways are encapsulated in two burning questions put repeatedly to rabbis today:

1. **May a Goy study the Torah?**
2. **May a Goy observe the Shabbat?**

In recent times, answers to these questions have been hotly contested among a number of prominent rabbis. Some say that on no account may a person who is not recognized as "Jewish" by heredity or through conversion under the Halakhah be allowed to study Torah or observe the Shabbat in the manner of orthodox Jews. In the view of these rabbis, this would include even candidates for full conversion to Judaism as a *Ger Tzeddek*, "righteous convert", and it would certainly apply to "Noahides". By the same token, the Noahides should not observe other Torah commandments that in the view of these rabbis apply only to "Jews".

On the other side, a number of distinguished contemporary rabbinical scholars have publicly declared that all the people of the world not only may but **must** study the Seven Noahide Commandments and – more radically – that all people of all Nations **must** recognize and honor the Sabbath, even though as non-Jews they are not required to abstain from any of the kinds of labor which the Torah forbids to Israel on the Shabbat (Rabbi Joel Schwartz).

Other well-known orthodox Jewish rabbis are teaching that any "non-Jew" in our time who observes the Seven Commandments in the proper manner may be considered a *Ger Toshav* (literally a "resident stranger"), a non-Israelite who has a privileged status under Torah law and who may observe the Shabbat as well as voluntarily practice other Torah commandments (Rabbi Chaim Clorfene). Some leading rabbis are urging that the time has now come for people of all the Nations to study the Torah and for Jewish Torah scholars to reach out accordingly (Rabbi Yitzchak Ginsburgh).

Such disputes – some quite fierce – between rabbis, can be most confusing and discouraging to many "non-Jews" across the whole world who have emerged disillusioned and skeptical from other cultural and religious matrices to discover in the Torah pathway a whole new universe of truth, wisdom and inspiration. With Torah educational materials freely available through the Internet almost anywhere on earth, they feel slapped in the face as they meet a wall of exclusion erected by certain rabbis whom they would want to respect and whose recognition they crave. These "non-Jewish" seekers include highly serious academics, teachers, doctors, nurses, scientists, engineers, technicians, businessmen and -women, mothers of children and many others of all ages and occupations, who have often spent a life-time of pain and frustration in search of the truth.

Since the lives and soul-journeys of so many people depend on the answers to these questions, they must be considered with the utmost sobriety and without the mutual slogan-tossing and mud-slinging that characterize so much contemporary discussion in many present-day forums.

As we shall see, one of the main keys to unraveling the truth will be to identify important distinctions between various different Halakhic statuses that may apply to different people who come under vague umbrella terms such as "Goy", "Gentile" or "non-Jewish", which turn out to be of little use without further definition.

Hillel and Shammai

Divisions of opinion between different rabbis have been an integral part of what has come to be known as "rabbinical Judaism" since the closing period of the Second Temple in Jerusalem two thousand years ago. The then head of the Great Sanhedrin, the *Nasi*, was Hillel, scion of the House of David, while his deputy, the *Av Beit Din*, was Shammai (Pirkey Avot 1:12).

By their time the Romans were advancing in transforming Judaea into one of the provinces of their empire, and people of many different Nations, Samaritans, Greeks, Romans and many others, either lived permanently or were regularly stationed there or passing through. This gave increasing urgency to issues of how Torah-observant Jews, both in the Holy Land and in the widening Jewish Diaspora beyond its borders, were to relate to their non-Jewish neighbors and visitors. In the same period there were also growing internal divisions between the *Perushim* ("Pharisees") and *Tzedokim* ("Sadducees") on the one hand, and on the other hand between the *Talmidey Chakhamim*, Torah-scholars in general, as opposed to the relatively ignorant and less religiously scrupulous *Am Ha'aratzim* (singular: Am Ha'aretz), "people of the land" (cf. Genesis 23:7 & Leviticus 20:4), and the *Kutim* ("Samaritans" see II Kings 17:24).

The Talmud relates:

> A certain Goy came to Shammai and said: "How many Torahs do you have?" "Two," answered Shammai, "the Written Torah and the Oral Torah". The Goy said to him: "I believe you about the Written Torah, but with regard to the Oral Torah, I don't believe you. Convert me on condition that you will teach me only the Written Torah." Shammai scolded him and threw him out.
>
> The same Goy came before Hillel, who converted him and began teaching him Torah. On the first day, he showed him the letters of the alphabet and said to him: "Alef, Beit, Gimmel, Dalet". The following day Hillel reversed the order of the letters starting with the last letter: Tav. The convert said to him: "But that's not what you told me yesterday". Hillel said to him: "Didn't you rely on me? [You cannot learn without relying on an oral tradition.] Therefore, you should also rely on me with regard to the Oral Torah."
> *Talmud Bavli*, Shabbat 31a

While Shammai justifiably drove out the insolent Goy, the infinitely-patient Hillel acted in full accord with his famous maxim: "Be of the disciples of Aaron, loving peace and pursuing peace, loving humanity [*ha-briyot*, literally, "the creations"] and drawing them close to the Torah" (Pirkey Avot 1:12). With artful wisdom, Hillel immediately gave this Goy a lesson in the first foundation of the pursuit of Torah: Self-nullification (*bittul*) and submission to the higher wisdom. This has come down to us from our ancestors and teachers and is the essence of Emunah, faith in the God of Israel, His Torah and His true sages, just as Israel accepted His Kingship and His Torah at Sinai with the words: "We shall do and we shall hear", *na'aseh v'nishma* (Exodus

24:7). First, we submit to practicing the tradition as received without demanding reasons and explanations. We do so in full trust that in God's good time we will be granted to "hear" and understand the truth and discover endless levels of deeper meaning in the Torah.

It makes no difference if the Goy who wanted to convert was a Greek, Roman or of some other nation. We are not told if he was an idolater, one of the epicurean non-believers of the time, or other. He clearly had an interest in converting according to his level of understanding, and it is surely noteworthy that Hillel did not send him to register for a protracted official rabbinical *Beit Din* conversion program that might take many years and endless challenges to complete. Hillel was actually willing to convert him on the spot and to start teaching him despite his stubborn resistance to the Oral Torah.

The difference between Shammai's high-wall-closed-doors policy and Hillel's open-armed welcome is deeply embedded in the souls of Israel, and may be seen in the conflict between King Saul and King David (see *Likutey Moharan* Part I, Lesson 283) and in more recent times in the division between the *Mitnagdim* ("Opponents") and those whom they opposed, the Chassidim, followers in the path of Rabbi Israel the "Baal Shem Tov" (see *Shevachey Ha-Baal Shem Tov* #228, notes).

The Talmudic Sources

The Talmudic source for the prohibition against the study of the Torah by a gentile is found in the Babylonian Talmud, Tractate *Sanhedrin* in the name of Rabbi Yochanan.

> Rabbi Yochanan said: An idol-worshipper who engages in Torah study is liable to the punishment of death, as it is stated: "Moses commanded us Torah, an inheritance of the congregation of Jacob" (Deuteronomy 33:4). This indicates that it is an inheritance for *us*, and *not for them*.
> *Talmud Bavli, Sanhedrin* 59a

The Talmudic source for prohibition of the observance of Shabbat by a gentile comes in an earlier section of the same tractate, towards the end of a lengthy discussion about the Seven Commandments of the Children of Noah, their Biblical sources and detailed laws. (The discussion begins at the bottom of *Daf 56b* with the words: "Our rabbis taught: The Children of Noah were commanded seven commandments".)

The Talmud states in the name of Rabbi Shimon ben Lakish:

> An idol-worshipper who observed Shabbat is liable to the punishment of death, as it says: "And day and night shall not cease" (Genesis 8:23).
> *Talmud Bavli, Sanhedrin 58b*

The Hebrew word rendered here as "observed Shabbat" is the verb *shaavath*, literally "rested". It should be noted, as will be discussed at greater length later, that in rabbinical writings this word specifically denotes resting in the sense of abstaining from the labors that are forbidden to Israelites on Shabbat. However, this does not necessarily preclude even the gentile idolater from giving some kind of recognition and honor to the Shabbat of Israel even while performing any labor he may choose.

The commentator Rashi explains (ad loc.) that if the idolater were to rest a full day from his labor, the reason he would be liable to the punishment of death is because the verse literally means: "Day and night *they shall not rest*", which is interpreted homiletically to apply also to humans.

Who is an idolater?

It is quite shocking to hear that a person might be liable to be punished by death for the seemingly harmless acts of studying Torah teachings or resting on the Shabbat. Is the death penalty to be understood literally? Is it conceivable that we could be talking about any and every Goy? It would surely be reckless to take such statements at face value without careful examination. To interpret them correctly, we must first understand to whom exactly they apply. We will then quickly see that blanket terms like "idol-worshipper", "gentile" or "goy" will no longer be of use because they are simply imprecise.

The Hebrew term used in both of the above Talmudic texts is *Oveid Kokhavim*, literally: "one who worships stars". This is an abbreviated form of the full expression *Oveid Kokhavim U'Mazalot*, "one who worships planets and constellations". [Technically the word *kokhavim*, should be translated as "planets", which in rabbinic thought include the sun and the moon, while *mazalot*, are "constellations", such as those of the Zodiac.] This phrase is usually printed in rabbinical texts using the acronym AKUM. The Hebrew terms for idolatrous worship used throughout the Talmud and rabbinical literature are *Avodah Zarah*, literally "strange" or "alien service" or "worship", or *Avodat Elilim* or *Avodat Gilulim*, "worship of idols".

In the comprehensive *Mishneh Torah* law code of Rabbi Moshe ben Maimon ("RaMBaM", Rabbi Moses Maimonides), he explains in the opening sections of the Laws of Idolatry that originally idolatry involved literal worship of the stars and planets based on elaborate rationalizations developed in very early times (*Mishneh Torah, Hilkhot Avodat Kokhaim, Laws of Idolatry, chapters 1-2*). However, he states that the Torah prohibition of idolatry extends beyond the worship of stars and planets:

> The essence of the commandment against idolatry is not to serve any one of all the created beings, not any angel or sphere or star or planet, and not any of the four elements [fire, air, water and earth] nor any of all that are created from them, even if the worshipper knows that the LORD is the [Supreme] God.
> (*Mishneh Torah, Hilkhot Avodat Kokhaim, Laws of Idolatry 2:1*)

Understood in this way, it is readily understandable why any actual, practicing *Oveid Kokhavim* or "idolater" should be forbidden to study the Torah and observe the Shabbat, both of which are the very opposite of idolatry, for he will surely pervert both and turn them into service of his god or gods. This will be discussed in greater detail below. [Yet despite this, even a practicing AKUM is permitted to bring a burnt offering for sacrifice by the priests in the Holy Temple in Jerusalem (*Mishneh Torah, Maaseh Hakorbanot, Laws of Sacrificial Procedure 3:2-5*).]

But could the Talmud possibly be including **all** the Goyim throughout the entire world at all times under the term *Oveid Kokhavim*, regardless of their actual beliefs and practices, merely because they are not halakhically recognized as Jews? Is every Goy considered an idolater?

The answer must obviously be a definitive, resounding "No!" as can be proven from many sources in rabbinical literature.

Talmudic terms for non-Israelites

It should be noted that the Hebrew term for Jew, *Yehudi*, is found less frequently than might be expected in Talmudical and rabbinical literature. This is because Torah law recognizes no distinction between "Jews" (technically, descendants of the tribes of Judah and Benjamin), and other members of the people of Israel, including genuine descendants of the supposedly "lost" Ten Tribes, as well as full converts (the *Geirey Tzeddek*) and their descendants. For: "There is one Law for the homeborn and for the convert who dwells among you" (Exodus 12:49; cf. Numbers 15:15).

Rather, throughout most of rabbinical literature in Hebrew, the generic term for all people who are subject, whether by heredity or conversion, to the Six Hundred and Thirteen Commandments of the Torah is *Yisra'el*, an "Israelite". For this reason, in this work I generally use the term Israelite in that sense. Many translations routinely render the Hebrew *Yisrael* as "Jew", but this is imprecise and misleading.

When it comes to the status of those who are not Israelite, by no means everyone can simply be considered an AKUM. When working with the very Talmud texts themselves and numerous later rabbinical works, hand-written or printed, it is essential

Introduction

to understand that Jews in exile often lived under the strictest restrictions, and their books were subject to rigorous censorship by the dominant non-Jewish religious authorities. Rabbis had to take precautions to ensure that their statements relating to Torah laws about idolatry and kindred subjects would not be construed by the censors as assaults on the dominant religion.

For this reason, different Talmud manuscripts and printed texts from various different times and places use a variety of different terms referring to non-Jews. These may include: *Goy*, a "member of the Nations", *Nokhri*, a "stranger" or "alien", AKUM, as defined above, *K'naani*, a "Canaanite", *Mitzri*, an "Egyptian", *Kuti*, a "Samaritan" (see II Kings 17:24), *Tzeddoki*, a "Sadducee" or "heretic", *Acherim*, "others", and more.

The term *Nokhri* signifying a "stranger" or "alien" is specifically defined by Rambam as an idolater: "Wherever the term *Nokhri* is used without further definition, it refers to one who practices the worship of planets and stars" (*Mishneh Torah, Hilkhot Maakhalot Assurot,* Laws of Forbidden Foods 11:18). Rashi commenting on Exodus 12:43, which forbids every "son of a *Neikhar*", to eat from the Passover offering, explains that this term refers to "any person whose deeds have become *strange* to his Father that is in Heaven, and it may refer either to a Goy or to an Israelite apostate". Thus, we see that even a born-Jew could turn into an AKUM, so that to be an idolater in the literal sense of the term is a matter of belief and practice and not dependent upon an accident of birth.

Although the Talmud states that the sages of the Second Temple prayed to nullify the evil desire for idolatry (*Talmud Bavli, Sanhedrin 64a*), they apparently did so mainly for the Jews in order to wean them from the idolatry of the likes of Jeroboam, Ahab and all who went in their footsteps in earlier times. However, as regards the other Nations, the perception of the Talmudic and later rabbis was that idolatry was still rife though by no means universal.

Thus, the commentator RaDaK writes on Zechariah 11:14:

To annul the brotherhood between Judah and Israel"
(Zechariah 11:14): The brotherhood that existed
between Judah and Israel – the Ten Tribes – in idol-
worship was broken then, when Judah went into exile
and no idolaters were left in the Land of Israel. For prior
to the exile of Israel, they did not leave aside the service
of any kind of idolatry despite all the troubles that
came upon them, and when they went into exile and
saw that the words of the prophets were true inasmuch
as the land was devastated, they did not worship idols
afterwards. Judah also worshiped idols until they went
into exile, and when they went into exile idolatry ceased
among them, for the brotherhood that previously existed
between them and the idol worshippers was broken.
(RaDaK on Zechariah 11:14)

Some consider that ancient sun worship was incorporated
into the institutionalized Roman version of Christianity,
and Rambam states that the "Edomites [or in some editions,
Canaanites] are idolaters and Sunday is their festival..." (*Mishneh
Torah, Hilkhot Avodah Zarah,* Laws of Idolatry 9:4). However
later authorities, particularly after the Reformation, considered
some denominations of Christians to be monotheistic. There
were some rabbis who viewed certain Islamic rituals as being
rooted in ancient idolatry (see Ibn Ezra on Daniel 11:30).
However, Rambam viewed the "Ishmaelites" as not coming
under the category of idolaters as such, since the law prohibiting
all benefit, including financial, from the wine of an idolater
does not apply to their wine (although it may not be consumed)
and they are seen as having the same status as the *Ger Toshav*,
"resident stranger", who observes the Seven Noahide Laws:

It is forbidden to drink the wine of a *Ger Toshav*, one
who has accepted the Seven Mitzvot of the sons of
Noah... but it is permitted to derive benefit from it [e.g.,
financially] ... And so too the wine of any Gentile who
does not worship idols, **such as the Ishmaelites**, may
not be drunk, but one may derive benefit from it, and so

ruled all the Ge'onim. However, one may not derive any benefit from even the regular (i.e., non-sacramental) wine of those who worship idols.

(*Mishneh Torah, Hilkhot Maakhalot Assurot*, Laws of Forbidden Foods 11:7)

The latter-day halakhic authority, Rabbi Yechiel Michel Epstein, writes as follows on the laws of a Torah scroll that was written by a Jewish apostate, which must be burned, as opposed to a Torah scroll written by a non-Jew, which is not burned but put away in an honorable manner (*Genizah*):

> And why in the case of scrolls written by the above categories of gentile did they say only that they should be put away, while in the case of a scroll written by a Jewish apostate it must be burned? The reason is because in the case of gentiles who wrote a Torah scroll, it is only the Torah that disqualified them, **but their intention is not for the sake of idolatry.** And even in the case of a *Mitzri* (lit. Egyptian) **we do not say that without further specification his thought is to idolatry.** However, the Israelite apostates are tightly attached to idolatry and will have written the scroll for the sake of their idol, and for that reason such scrolls must be burned.

> And this applies to the apostates in the times of our sages of blessed memory, but this does not apply now, for they do not believe in the stars but they have simply thrown off the yoke of the Kingdom of Heaven, and they come under the category of sinners, but their scrolls require only putting aside but not burning. And it is necessary to understand that the Rambam, the *Tur* and the *Shulchan Arukh* and all the Halakhic authorities who wrote that scrolls of an apostate (*Min*) and a heretic (*Apikoros*) should be burned were referring to those in the time of the Talmud, but today they are not found."
> (*Arukh HaShulchan, Yoreh De'ah #281*)

Part I

WHO IS THAT GOY?

Different statuses, different laws

Despite the exclusion of the "idolater" from Torah study and Shabbat observance, Elijah the Prophet strikingly declares:

> I call the Heavens and the Earth to testify for me: Be it an Israelite or an Idolater, whether a man or a woman, whether a bondsman or a bondswoman, everything is according to the deeds which the person does, so holy spirit dwells upon them.
> (*Tanna d'vei Eliahu Rabba #9:1*)

If even the literal idolater may change, repent, and through work and effort attain holy spirit, then surely the many people across the world who have repudiated idolatry cannot simply be pushed into the category of idolaters, even though they may not be considered halakhically "Jewish".

In fact, Talmudic, Halakhic and other rabbinical sources discuss a variety of different categories of non-Israelites, each of whom has a distinct halakhic status. In addition, there are various levels of "captured" or "assimilated" Israelite souls who may currently have little or no connection with their authentic Torah heritage. It is essential to clarify the distinctions between these different statuses before we can address the questions about the eligibility of those who occupy them to study the Torah and observe the Shabbat.

With God's help we shall discuss in turn the following different statuses:

1. **Ger Tzeddek**: The "full convert" to Torah
2. **Ben Noah**: "Son of Noah" or "Noahide" (plural *Bney Noah*, "Noahides"): These are the "Righteous of the Nations", members of the Nations who have undertaken the Seven Commandments of the Children of Noah, which apply to all humanity.
3. **Ger Toshav**: A "resident stranger", a particular category of Noahide who enjoys certain privileges, including the right to reside with the Tribes of Israel in the Holy Land
4. **Tinok Shenishbah**: A "captured child", an Israelite who from early childhood was captured and held in captivity, either physically or culturally and spiritually, by people of other Nations and thus grew up with little or no knowledge of his or her connection with the people of Israel and the Torah
5. **Hamitbolelim**: "Assimilated" Jews who may have little or no awareness of their Jewish identity or Torah heritage
6. **Ger hamitgayer le-vein ha-goyim**: "A convert who converted among the nations"
7. **Ger hamitgayer beino le-vein atzmo**: "A convert who converted on his own" or "privately"
8. **Aseret Ha-sh'vatim**: The Ten Tribes.

1. Ger Tzeddek

Ger Tzeddek, "The Righteous Dweller", is the term Jews give to a gentile who has converted to Judaism before a rabbinical court and has undertaken to observe all of the 613 commandments of the Torah. From being a complete Goy, the *Ger Tzeddek* has become a fully-fledged Jew or Israelite, with all the associated obligations, responsibilities and privileges. The *Ger Tzeddek* is permitted to marry within the *Kahal*, the "Assembly" of recognized members of the Children of Israel, and obviously is not only permitted but *obliged* to study the Torah and observe the Shabbat in all its details as well as all the other commandments.

The term Ger is defined by the biblical commentator Rashi as "a person who was not born in a particular state but came from a different state to reside there" (*Rashi* on Exodus 22:20.) Since Ger is a generic term that also includes the halakhic status of *Ger Toshav*, the full convert is termed a *Ger Tzeddek*, where the term *Tzeddek*, is an epithet meaning "righteousness".

The Canaanite Slave

Another case of a non-Israelite "idolater" who may become a member of the Covenant, though ineligible to marry into the *Kahal*, is the "Canaanite slave" or "bondsman", *Eved K'na'ani*, though not necessarily from one of the seven ancient Canaanite peoples (Leviticus 25:44-46, *Mishneh Torah, Hilkhot Avadim*, Laws of Slaves chapters 5-9). He or she may be a member of any nation who had been sold (or sold him/herself) into servitude to an Israelite and formally undertakes this status at the time of being immersed in a mikveh under the hand of the new master.

The Canaanite slave is subject to all the three hundred and sixty-five prohibitions of the Torah but is obliged to observe only those of the two hundred and forty-eight positive commandments that apply to Israelite women (i.e., excluding "mitzvot occasioned by time", *mitzvot sh'ha-z'man geraman*). While the Canaanite slave may not study Torah, he or she is obliged to abstain from all the labors that are forbidden to Israel on the Shabbat. If the Canaanite slave is formally freed by his master, he becomes a full member of the *Kahal*, the Assembly of Israel, liable to all of the 613 commandments and permitted to intermarry within the community.

With the formal abolition of slavery in modern times (though de facto slavery continues in many parts of the world), the halakhic status of the Canaanite Slave is not relevant and will therefore not be discussed further here.

2. Ben Noah or "Noahide"

A "Noahide" is a person who has explicitly disavowed idolatry and has formally embraced the Seven Noahide Commandments before a panel of three Torah-observant, learned Israelites (*Mishneh Torah, Hilkhot Melakhim*, Laws of Kings 8:10). In the words of Rambam:

> Anyone who accepts upon himself and carefully observes the Seven Commandments is of the Righteous of the Nations of the World and has a portion in the World to Come. This is as long as he accepts and performs them because he truly believes that it was the Holy One, Blessed Be He, Who commanded them in the Torah, and that it was through Moses our Teacher that we were informed that the Sons of Noah had already been commanded to observe them. But if he observes them because he convinced himself logically through his own intellect and conscience, but he does not agree that they were commanded by God, then he is not considered a Ger Toshav and is not of the Righteous of the Nations of the World, but merely one of their wise."
>
> (*Mishneh Torah, Hilkhot Melakhim*, Laws of Kings and their Wars 8:11)

3. Ger Toshav, "Resident Stranger"

Included in the general category of the Noahide is that of the Ger Toshav or "Resident Stranger". He is required to make a formal declaration before three Torah-observant, learned Israelites undertaking to observe the Seven Noahide Commandments (*Mishneh Torah, Hilchot Melachim*, Laws of Kings 8:10). The *Ger Toshav* has the right to dwell in the Holy Land (unlike idolaters). In addition, the Torah commands the Children of Israel to protect the Ger Toshav against danger and to "vitalize" him, i.e., sustain him economically where necessary (Leviticus 25:35; *Talmud Bavli, Pesachim 21b*).

In the words of Rambam:

> The *Ger Toshav* is a gentile who took upon himself not to worship idols together with the other commandments given to the Children of Noah but has not circumcised

nor immersed. We accept him, and he is of the Righteous of the Nations of the World. And why is he called by the name of 'resident'? Because we are permitted to let him dwell among us in the Land of Israel."
(*Mishneh Torah, Hilkhot Issurey Biyah*, Laws of Forbidden Unions 14:7)

Rambam proceeds to state that the full status of *Ger Toshav* (as opposed to Noahide) applies only in times when the law of the Jubilee year (Leviticus 25:8ff) is observed, i.e., when a duly-constituted Sanhedrin sits in the Temple in Jerusalem:

> The *Ger Toshav* is not accepted except at a time when the Jubilee Year is observed, but at this time even if he undertook upon himself the entire Torah with the exception of one detail, he is not accepted."
> (*Mishneh Torah, Hilkhot Issurey Biyah*, Laws of Forbidden Unions 14:8)

An important annotation by Rabbi Avraham ben David, ("Raavad"), in his *Hasagot* (critical glosses) on Rambam's *Mishneh Torah* clarifies what this statement implies:

> **Except at a time when the Jubilee Year is observed**: The Raavad of blessed memory wrote: The opinion of this writer [i.e., Rambam] is closed and sealed and he does not explain what it means that "the *Ger Toshav* is accepted only at a time when the Jubilee year is observed" and what are the commandments incumbent upon Israel in connection with the *Ger Toshav*? Namely, he is not permitted to dwell within the city, as taught in *Sifrei* on Deuteronomy 23:17: "'with you he may dwell' – but not in the city itself". And it is a mitzvah to sustain him, as it is written: "And your brother shall *live* with you" (Leviticus 25:35). And he may purchase a Hebrew slave just as may an idolater.

The following are the laws that apply to him only at a time when the Jubilee is observed, some being more lenient upon him while others are more stringent. For at a time when the Jubilee is not observed, he may dwell even in the city itself, because the holiness of the Land is not upon it as it was formerly. In addition, he may purchase a Hebrew slave for whatever period of time he wants, because there is no specified time for the slave to serve, and these are leniencies. However, we are not commanded to sustain him, and this is a stringency, and it would seem that the reason is because in the time of the Jubilee the fields were deemed ownerless and he could sustain himself without being a burden on the community, but now he is unable to do so. As regards a gentile servant who stipulated that he will not circumcise and not immerse for as long as he wants, we may keep such a servant at all times. (Raavad, *Hasagot on Mishneh Torah, Hilkhot Issurey Biyah*, Laws of Forbidden Unions 14:8)

4 & 5: The Captive Child and the Assimilated

Many of the "non-Jews" who are today reaching out to rabbis may fit neatly into the categories of potential *Ger Tzeddek* or *Bney Noach*. At the same time, we are also witnessing an extraordinary arousal to Torah among people in all parts of the world who cannot be so readily classified. They manifest a compelling drive to connect with the God of Israel, His Torah and its precepts, the people of Israel and their land. In many cases they say they have always, even from earliest childhood, experienced deep feelings of alienation from their own cultural matrix together with profound cravings for a true and authentic spiritual pathway. Many feel highly frustrated when told that, as non-Jews, they are eligible only to observe the Seven Noahide Laws, for they feel that from the very roots of their souls they are being called to higher levels of observance and connection.

With the advent of the Internet, which facilitates instant global communication on a scale unimaginable in any past age, those active in the field of Torah outreach have in recent times had unparalleled opportunities to discover ever-growing streams of such people, because they are regularly using Torah websites, listening to rabbis' podcasts, watching and commenting on their videos, corresponding via email and messaging applications, posting and discussing on social networking platforms, purchasing Judaica online, donating to Torah causes and other worthy projects in Israel and elsewhere, etc. They are located quite literally on every continent – Europe, Africa, Asia, Australasia, North and South America – sometimes in the remotest outposts. In many cases they live far away from any Torah-observant community, let alone a rabbinical *Beit Din* that is qualified to give a recognized conversion, and for most, the possibilities of their moving to such a community are practically non-existent.

How are Torah-observant Jews to relate to such people? If we are commanded to vitalize and encourage the *Bney Noah*, are we not to open ourselves to those who claim to seek a path of Torah observance that will truly fulfill their spiritual cravings? Are we permitted to offer them teaching and guidance, and encourage them in their quest? Or are they to be given the cold shoulder and told to wait until all the "known Jews" have returned, or until the prophet Elijah will come with Mashiach to determine their status?

Rabbi Nachman on the Sparks of the Souls of Israel

Rabbi Nachman teaches that great glory comes to the Almighty when those who were farthest away come to recognize Him:

> For the essence of God's greatness is that the idol-worshippers too should know there is an Almighty who rules and governs the world. As stated in the *Zohar* (II, 69a): "When Jethro came and said, 'Now I know that God is great' (Exodus 18:11), with this His Name was greatly magnified and exalted above and below." But the idol-worshippers can only know of the greatness of the Holy One through the aspect of Jacob, as it is written (Isaiah 2:5): "O House of Jacob, come let us go in God's light." This is because Jacob revealed the greatness of the Holy One even more than the other patriarchs...

(*Likutey Moharan* Part 1, Lesson 10:2-3)

If it is only Jacob – the nation that faithfully observes the Torah – that can show the gentiles the way of God, are we to rebuff these people knocking at our gates, who have disavowed idolatry, often at great personal cost and pain, and who crave for connection with the Torah?

Where indeed lie the roots of these souls?

The answer to this question may be gleaned from a unique rabbinical teaching contained in another lesson of Rabbi Nachman given on Shabbat Chanukah 1805 and printed in *Likutey Moharan* Part I, Lesson 17:

> How is it possible to win converts when they are so very distant from the holiness of Israel? And what is it that prompts them to even think of converting? ... How is it possible to talk to them so that they listen and come to convert?
>
> But just as when one is very far away from one's friend and cannot talk to him directly so that he will hear, one must write him a letter, likewise it is necessary to send the gentiles a written script so they may hear, even though they are distant.
>
> Now, when the air is tranquil and pure, and one who is capable of speaking the language of Israel – holy speech – talks, then these words are inscribed and engraved in the air, as in: "My tongue is like the pen of a skillful scribe" (Psalms 45:2). And then his holy words go out and are heard from afar, as in: "His fame went out to all the provinces" (Esther 9:4) – for when the air is calm and clear, it is possible to hear from afar.
>
> These words then come to be written in the literature of the Nations, "every province according to its writing" (Esther. 8:9). And so, the gentiles discover in their own

books ideas which are contradictory to their received religious beliefs...

But how is it that these individuals in particular find contradictions to their religion in their books and come to acknowledge the faith of Israel, while the others find nothing and remain with their traditional beliefs?

But know! This is because of the good that is suppressed under the control of the Nations – namely, the parts of the souls of Israel which they hold in captivity. For all true goodness is with the souls of Israel.

In other words, this occurs when the Nations hold sway and prevent Israel from practicing the commandments – such as when they issued decrees forbidding circumcision and compelling Shabbat desecration (*Rosh HaShanah 19a; Me'ilah 17a; cf. Bava Batra 60b*). The good which Israel was supposed to perform then becomes caught captive under their control. This is also the case even when they inadvertently prevent the Jews from serving God, by exacting from them levies and taxes, as well as denying them benefits. Through all of this, the good – the souls of Israel – is held captive under their power.

Initially, this good which they hold captive remembers that it comes from a very holy and exalted place. But afterwards, the good under their control is overpowered and dominated to the point where it becomes trapped and bound to them. Eventually, the good itself forgets its exaltedness.

But when the words of Israel go forth and come to be inscribed in their books, as explained, this good held captive there then finds them in their books. That is, the good finds contradictions to their religion there and thereby is reminded of its exaltedness. It remembers that it came from a very exalted place,

that it is a part of the souls of Israel, for whom all the worlds were created.

Then this good begins to grieve and pine over its having come from such an exalted level and is now held captive under the control of the impure, evil forces and could, God forbid, come to be eradicated and lost, and it longs and desires to drag itself back and return to its place...

And know! There are times when the evil realizes that this good is pining with desire to get away and return to its place. They then suppress the good even more powerfully and bring it into an even greater concealment, into the inner recesses of their thought. That is to say, they start thinking maliciously about this good, and by so doing, bring it into even greater concealment and obscurity in the inner recesses of their mind.

As a result, this good then emerges through the offspring that these gentiles bear. This is because the good is hidden and concealed in the inner recesses of their thought and mind, from which the seed issues forth. Therefore, the good emerges in the seed that produces their offspring, and the evil in these offspring is then incapable of overpowering the good which they have within them. In this way, the good emerges through the offspring, resulting in converts. As our sages said (*Gittin 57b*): "The grandchildren of Sennacherib studied Torah." And the Talmud also mentions other wicked people whose very offspring became converts, as explained.
(*Likutey Moharan* Part I, Lesson 17:5-7)

Potential and Actual Converts

Rabbi Nachman added to this discussion in a teaching given a few years later on Rosh Hashanah, New Year 1809:

The elevation of the fallen faith of idolaters makes converts, for by restoring and refining fallen faith, which is the sustaining force of [idolatrous] belief, their old belief is weakened, and they then come over to our holy faith and so become converts.

Sometimes they become only potential converts, while sometimes they become actual converts. That is to say, either idol worshipers actually come and convert; or this may happen only potentially, when their fallen faith is elevated and their original belief is weakened so that holy faith is revealed to them *in their place.* There, in their place, they believe that there is the One Primordial God, as in the words of the prophet: "In every place offerings are burned and presented to My Name" (Malachi 1:11).

This depends on the strength of the original false belief. If it was initially strong, then afterwards – when it is broken and the fallen, holy faith is lifted up from there – they become actual converts. But if their false faith was not so strong initially, then when it is broken and turned toward holiness, it produces only potential converts.
(*Likutey Moharan* Part II, Lesson 5:4)

Assimilation and Return

God has promised in the Torah:

Then the LORD your God will restore your fortunes and take you back in love. He will bring you together again from all the peoples where the LORD your God has scattered you.

Even if your outcasts are at the ends of the world, from there the LORD your God will gather you, from there He will fetch you. - Deuteronomy 30:3-4

Every true lover of Israel who yearns for the final redemption with the ingathering of all the exiles and the ultimate Restoration will surely want to know: Who are these souls? How did they get there? And for our part, what are we do to assist them in coming home and rejoining their people? Even if there is no iron-cast certainty that these are our brothers and sisters, if there is even a shadow of a doubt that they might indeed be so, are we permitted simply to ignore them? Do family ignore even the faintest clue in searching for a lost son, daughter, brother or sister or cousin...? If one of these souls is a "potential" convert but not a candidate to become an "actual" convert, a *Ger Tzeddek*, should we not at least "send" them Torah teachings to nourish their souls in the place where they are? One of the greatest commandments of the Torah is to redeem captives. Here we are not even required to pay ransom money since we can fulfill the commandment through emails and Internet posts.

Captive Israelite slaves and their offspring

The mysteries of Divine providence over the souls of Israel, their incarnations and repair over many generations, are discussed in the *Zohar* (*Mishpatim 95a* ff) and other kabbalistic sources (*Shaar Hagilgulim* etc.). Yet even without reference to these teachings, we can easily recognize how highly plausible it is that at least some of these seeking souls may well be descended from members of the Children of Israel who were at some time or other either literally or figuratively taken captive, raised and assimilated among the Nations to the point where they lost all awareness of their true identity and soul roots.

From the earliest times Israel's oppressors would capture their children and sell them into slavery, as we find in the prophecy of Joel:

> And you have sold the children of Judah and the children of Jerusalem to the Greeks, in order to distance them far away from their homeland.

> Behold, I will rouse them from the place where you sold them, and I will repay your deserts on your heads.
> Joel 4:6-7

In the first major exile of Israel from their land, the Assyrian king Sennacherib transplanted the Ten Tribes far away in central

Asia (II Kings 17:7), where according to tradition, the great majority of them became assimilated and never returned, to the point that they seemingly disappeared completely.

Later oppressors took great numbers of Jews into slavery, as in the case of the Romans, who transported innumerable captive slaves from Israel to Greece, Italy, France, Spain, Germany, Britain, North Africa and other locations across their empire. In Arabia, Mohammed's armies would routinely slaughter the entire male populations of Jewish settlements while capturing and forcibly converting all their women and children in order to breed slaves.

Even a cursory glance at later Jewish history shows a repeating pattern of separation from Jewish tradition and assimilation into the surrounding non-Jewish population. This happened on an enormous scale at the time of the Spanish and Portuguese Inquisitions, when many sought safety through outwardly acting as Christians while striving to practice Judaism secretly at home. Great numbers were absorbed into the populations of Spain and Portugal and their colonies in North and South America and elsewhere across the world. Today many of their descendants – the *Bney Anousim*, "Children of the Forced [Converts]" – are becoming newly aware of their roots and identity and returning to Torah observance with great fervor.

During the last five hundred years, oppression and discrimination against Jews across Europe pressured many into converting to Christianity or abandoning religious faith entirely in favor of philosophical skepticism and moral relativism. During the Bolshevik, Communist and Nazi persecutions, some Jews sought to survive by blending in or intermarrying with the surrounding gentiles, while others entrusted their children to foster-parents, nunneries etc. to be brought up as Christians. Since the Second World War, untold numbers of Jews in countries across the world, facing the challenges of rampant secular materialism, have lapsed either partially or completely from Jewish self-identification and observance. Particularly in cases of intermarriage between a

Jew and a gentile, it often takes only a generation or two for all connection with Judaism to be lost.

Matrilineal Descent

Obviously, any child born of an Israelite mother, even where the mother had been taken into literal or spiritual captivity and separated from her native cultural matrix, not only has "Jewish" genes but is also considered as being fully Jewish under the Torah law of matrilineal descent. Under this law, one born of an Israelite mother is accounted a native-born Israelite even where the father is from one of the other Nations (Rambam, *Mishneh Torah Hilchot Issureyi Biyah*, Laws of Forbidden Unions 12:1-2). Indeed, even in cases where the mother has lost all Jewish identity, her children are in certain respects still considered halakhically Jewish, as exemplified in the following law in *Shulchan Arukh, Yoreh De'ah*, Laws of Interest:

> The Samaritans come under the legal category of an apostate to idolatry [and it is permitted to lend and borrow from them with interest], but the Karaites do not come under the category of apostates, and it is forbidden to make them loans with interest [just as it is forbidden to give a loan to a fellow-Jew with interest], and no need to add that it is forbidden to take loans from them with interest.

> A child who was taken into captivity among the idolaters and knows nothing of the Torah of Israel has the same law as the Karaites and it is forbidden to make him a loan with interest. For this reason, in the case of a woman who became an apostate to idolatry and who has a son from an idol-worshipper – in which case the son has the same status as she does and is called an apostate – it is forbidden to make a loan to him with interest because he is like a child that was taken captive among the idolaters.
> (*Shulchan Arukh, Yoreh De'ah* 159:3)

How should we treat the captive children?

Clearly the category of the "Captive Child" may include more than literal physical captivity and enslavement and also encompasses the social and cultural captivity of Israelite souls within the worldviews, belief systems, lifestyles and behaviors of the Nations as a result of upbringing, education and social conditioning. It was in this wider sense that the term "Captive Child" has been widely used in recent generations by outstanding Torah leaders, most notably Rabbi Menachem Mendel Schneerson, the Lubavitcher Rebbe, of blessed memory, in seeking to connect with the alienated and assimilated Jews of our times in a manner of kindness and understanding rather than one of condemnation and rejection.

This approach is set forth clearly by Rambam in *Hilkhot Mamrim*, Laws of Rebels:

> A person who denies the validity of the Oral Law is one of the heretics and should be put to death.

> To whom does this apply? To a person who knowingly denied the Oral Law in accordance with his perception of things, who went after his superficial understanding and his stubborn heart and denied the Oral Torah as originally [in Second Temple times] did the heretics Tzaddok and Baithos... But in the case of the children of these errant people and their children's children, whose parents led them astray and who were born among these Karaites and raised according to their ideas, they are considered as a child captured among them whom they raised.

> Such a child may not be eager to take grasp of the pathways of the commandments, for it is as if he were under compulsion. Even if he later hears that he is Jewish and saw Jews and their religious practice, he is still considered as one who was under compulsion, for he was raised according to their mistaken path. This

applies to those whom we mentioned who follow the erroneous Karaite path of their ancestors. **Therefore, it is appropriate to motivate them to repent and draw them with words of peace until they return to the eternal Torah.**
(*Mishneh Torah, Hilkhot Mamrim*, Laws of Rebels 3:1 & 3)

Liability of the Captive Child to Torah and Mitzvot

When the Captive Child becomes aware of his true spiritual roots, is he or she liable to study the Torah and observe the Shabbat and all the other commandments?

The answer is of course: "Yes!" In the eyes of the Halakhah, the Captive Child is considered a fully-fledged Israelite. This is the foundation of the law requiring a Captive Child who returned to the fold in Temple times to bring a sacrifice to atone for unwitting transgressions committed even at a time when he was unaware of his true identity:

> In all situations where a person is obligated to bring a fixed sin-offering for his inadvertent transgression and he transgressed inadvertently and he becomes aware of the transgression after violating it, he is liable for a sin-offering, even though he was not aware initially that this act was a transgression.

> Thus, if a child had been captured by gentiles and raised by them without knowing either about Israel or their faith, then if he performed labor on the Sabbath, ate forbidden fat or blood and the like, when he discovers that he is an Israelite and is commanded to renounce all the above, he is obligated to bring a sin-offering for each category of transgression, and the same applies in all similar situations.
> (Rambam, *Mishneh Torah, Hilkhot Shegagot*, Laws of Unintentional Sins 2:6.)

See also *ibid.* 7:2 on the same law with respect specifically to violations of the Shabbat prohibitions.

Since the Captive Child is liable to bring a sin-offering to atone for his unwitting transgressions, it is clear that in the eyes of the Halakhah he is considered a fully-fledged Israelite and not in need of "conversion". Without clear evidence of Jewish matrilineal descent, a *Beit Din* may not wish to give a license to a self-declared Captive Child to marry into the Jewish community without at least a symbolic conversion, but his liability to bring sin-offerings for earlier transgressions indicates that such an individual is and always was fully bound by the laws of the Torah.

Rabbi Nachman imagines being a captive

... Even after overcoming these threats, the Rebbe and his attendant were still in indescribable danger. They were two Jews, alone on a warship filled with Turkish troops. These Turks would think nothing of selling two Jews as slaves in some faraway place. The very thought filled the Rebbe's heart with terror.

He began to think about it. What would he do if he were sold as a slave in a faraway place where there were no Jews? What if nobody knew about it? How would he keep the mitzvot of the Torah? This particular worry bothered him the most. The Rebbe pondered the possibilities again and again. Finally, he was worthy of realizing that he could serve God even if he were unable to actually keep the mitzvot. He comprehended the devotion of the Patriarchs, who lived before God even gave the Torah. They also kept all the mitzvot, even though they often did so only in a symbolic manner. Thus, Jacob fulfilled the mitzvah of tefillin through the sticks he peeled while watching Laban's sheep (Genesis 30:37).

The Rebbe thought along these lines until he understood how he could keep all the mitzvot in this manner. He could continue to serve God even if he were sold as a slave in the most distant land.

From *Shevachay HaRan*, The Praise of Rebbe Nachman, Part II: "Rebbe Nachman's Pilgrimage to the Land of Israel". Printed in "Rabbi Nachman's Wisdom" (Breslov Research Institute)

6 & 7: One Who Converted Among the Nations & One Who Converted on His Own

The Talmud in *Shabbat* 68a-b discusses dissenting opinions among the Amora'im on the above-quoted law of the liability of the Captive Child to bring a sin-offering for unwitting desecration of the Shabbat. It is in the context of this discussion that mention is made of two other categories: **a convert who converted among the gentiles,** and **a convert who converted on his own.**

The Mishnah under discussion by these Amora'im (*Mishnah Shabbat* chapter 7 Mishnah 1) speaks of the liability of different individuals to bring a sin-offering for unwitting desecration of the Shabbat, depending on whether they were entirely ignorant of the Shabbat according to Torah law or had once known but forgot. The Amora'im dispute which cases of Shabbat desecration by individuals of different halakhic statuses would properly come under the category of "unwitting" such as to carry the liability to bring a sin-offering:

> It was **Rav and Shmuel who both said: Our mishnah** is referring to both **a child who was taken captive among the gentiles** and was never educated *and a convert who converted among the gentiles* and never learned the halakhot of Shabbat. **However,** one who once **knew** of the essence of Shabbat and **ultimately forgot is liable for each and every Shabbat,** as we learned in the Mishnah with regard to one who knows the essence of Shabbat...

Shabbat 68a interleaved with the commentary of Rabbi Adin Steinsaltz

And it was **Rabbi Yochanan and Rabbi Shimon ben Lakish who both said:** He is liable to bring a sin-offering **specifically** if **he knew** of the essence of Shabbat **and ultimately forgot. However, a child who *was taken captive among the gentiles and a* convert who converted among the gentiles** are **exempt** from bringing a sin-offering. They have the legal status of one who performed the prohibited labor due to circumstances beyond his control.

Shabbat 68b

We have cited above Rambam's halakhic ruling that the captive child and one who converted among the gentiles are indeed liable to bring a sin-offering for their past unwitting transgressions, in accordance with the opinion of the Amora'im Rav and Shmuel. However, our focus here is on clarifying two other categories involved in this discussion in the Talmud. The first is mentioned explicitly: **a convert who converted among the gentiles**. The second is a related category which is mentioned by the commentators on the above discussion, that of **a convert who converted on his own.**

With regard to the **convert who converted among the gentiles,** the Tosafot in their commentary (*loc. cit.*) define this as a case of a person who converted before three regular Jews (as opposed to competent, knowledgeable rabbis) but they failed to inform him fully about the commandment of Shabbat (such as the severe penalties for its infringement). Similarly, Rabbi Moshe ben Nachman, "RaMBaN" (*loc. cit.*) defines him as "one who converted before three and they informed him about some of the other commandments but not about the commandment of Shabbat, or they erred and failed to inform him properly".

Both the Tosafot and Ramban in their commentaries here make reference to that other category of Ger: **one who converted on his own,** or "privately", i.e., a person who voluntarily embraced Torah practice but never submitted to a formal halakhic conversion under the supervision of a duly constituted rabbinical court (*Beit Din*). The Tosafot and Ramban state unequivocally that such an individual **is not considered a Ger** (i.e., a *Ger Tzeddek*), and reference the Talmudic source for this law in the Babylonian Talmud, Tractate *Yevamot* in the name of the Tanna, Rabbi Yehudah: "One who converted on his own is not a convert" (*Yevamot 47a*). Rashi in his comment (*ad loc.*) explains that this is because the Torah requires that a conversion must be performed before a rabbinical court, *Beit Din*, as derived from Deuteronomy 1:16, where the Torah includes the Ger in the commandment to the judges of Israel to "judge righteously", which implies that the Ger must be "judged" before a court of law at the time of conversion.

There is no dispute in the Talmud or among the commentators about the halakhic status of **the convert who converts among the nations** (i.e., before three Jews) with respect to his liability to the commandments. His conversion process may have been defective because the three Jews who made up the *Beit Din* that performed his conversion failed to conform to all the halakhic norms and did not caution him properly about the gravity of Shabbat infringement. Yet it is still considered a conversion, carrying with it full liability to observe all the commandments. [It is a point of contention whether for practical purposes some of the many "moonlight" conversions performed by various different groups of possibly well-meaning yet halakhically unversed Jews in many parts of the world can be seen in this category.]

However, **a convert who converted on his own**, i.e., a gentile who converted privately without any supervision on the part of a *Beit Din* or even three ordinary Jews, **is not considered a Ger**. And this would most certainly apply to the halakhic status of the many self-styled "Jews by choice" in our times who have in some way embraced the Torah and at least some of its commandments but have not undergone a halakhic conversion – and in many cases are unlikely to be able to do so.

The respective statuses of "a convert who converted among the gentiles" and of "a convert who converted on his own" are defined in the Halakhah as follows.

With regard to **one who converted among the gentiles**:

> When a court did not check a [potential] convert's background and did not inform him of the mitzvot and the punishment for [the failure to observe] the mitzvot and he circumcised himself and immersed in the presence of three ordinary [Israelites], he is a convert. Even if it is discovered that he converted for an ulterior motive, since he circumcised himself and converted, he has left the category of gentiles and we view him with skepticism until his righteousness is revealed. Even if he afterwards worships false deities, he is like an apostate Israelite. If he consecrates a woman as his wife, the consecration is valid, and it is a mitzvah to return his lost object. For since he immersed himself, he became like any Israelite...
> Rambam, *Issurey Biyah*, Laws of Forbidden Unions 13:17

However, with regard to the status of the **convert who converted on his own**, Rambam states:

> When [a convert] immerses himself alone and converts alone – or even if he does this in the presence of two persons – his conversion is not valid. If he comes and says: "I converted in the court of so-and-so and they had me immerse," his word is not accepted with regard to license to marry within the Assembly unless he brings witnesses to testify to the truth of his statements.
> Rambam, *Issurey Biyah*, Laws of Forbidden Unions 13:7

Rambam writes further:

> [The following laws apply with regard to] a female convert whom we observe conducting herself at all times according to the ways of Israel, for example, she

immerses herself after menstruation and she separates the priestly tithe from dough or the like, and likewise to a male convert who follows the paths of Israel, for example, he immerses himself after a seminal emission and performs all the mitzvot. These are considered as righteous converts even though there are no witnesses to testify before whom they converted. Nevertheless, if they come to intermix within Israel, we do not permit them to marry within the Assembly until they bring witnesses or until they immerse themselves in our presence since the presumption was that they were gentiles.

Ibid 13:9

In the light of these laws, it is perfectly understandable why Jewish people in our times who seek to follow the Halakhah assiduously will not agree to intermarry with anyone who is a self-styled, uncertified *Ger* – "Jewish by choice" – without their undergoing a rabbinically supervised conversion.

Yet while we may not without this conversion accept this *Ger* into the Assembly, we clearly have no authority or ability to judge or determine his or her status in the eyes of God Almighty. Rambam's words are: **"These are considered as righteous converts** even though there are no witnesses to testify before whom they converted."

If the "Jew by choice" is sincere in Torah observance, then should not those who are sure of their own Jewish identity accord them at the very least the same respect that should be accorded to *Bney Noah*, whom the Jews are commanded to sustain and teach?

Are Jews permitted to teach Torah to such "Jews by choice" and to encourage them in their chosen pathway? We cannot know the true soul-roots and history of any given person. But what if in some of these cases of doubt, *safek*, there is a possibility that the person does indeed have an Israelite soul?

He or she is not considered a *Ger Tzeddek*, and we may not fully accept them into our communities as such. But are we not to show them some respect, basic human decency and good manners? Can we not acknowledge their spiritual pathway as one that brings glory to the Almighty, as in the case of Jethro? Can we not give them encouragement in their efforts to follow the ways of prayer and devotion to God and the study of Torah, and where appropriate provide them with reliable information about how to do so? If we are commanded to support and sustain the *Ben Noah*, surely all the more so must we do so in the case of those who may possibly have Israelite souls. If we are permitted to greet even idolaters as one of the pathways of peace (*Mishneh Torah, Avodah Zarah*, Laws of Idolatry 10:5) and to wish them success in their labors (ibid., *Shemittah VeYovel*, Laws of the Sabbatical and Jubilee Years 8:8), are we at liberty to ignore sincere souls in search of Torah truth?

Let us remember that the very first and original convert who "converted on his own" was none other than the patriarch Abraham, father of all the converts, who established the Torah pathway yet sought no license from any rabbinical court or other earthly authority in order to follow the Way of the LORD (Genesis 18:19).

8. The Ten Lost Tribes

Countless numbers of people from all kinds of backgrounds and locations are today awakening to the Torah, seeking contact with rabbis and pleading for some kind of recognition. Among them are very large numbers who consider themselves to be rooted in one way or another in the Ten Tribes of Israel.

Most Jews with even a vague notion of the history and destiny of our people are familiar with the idea that ten out of the Twelve Tribes of Israel were taken into exile some generations prior to the destruction of the First Temple and subsequently disappeared into oblivion. However, with the exception of a tiny number of Jews who set off at different times until the present in search of their lost brethren (such as the prophet Jeremiah,

Benjamin of Tudela and Menasseh ben Israel in the past, and today the Shavei Israel organization, Rabbi Yitzchak Tchenagel, Rabbi Avraham Fried and others), most Jewish people seem to show little practical interest in looking for the Lost Ten Tribes, if they even give them a single thought.

The Mishnah records a dispute between Rabbi Eliezer the Great and his outstanding disciple and study-partner, Rabbi Akiva, as to whether the Ten Tribes will return:

> The Ten Tribes are not destined to return, as it is stated: "And He cast them into another land, as it is this day" (Deuteronomy 29:27). Just as this day passes, never to return, so too, the Ten Tribes go but do not return. These are the words of Rabbi Akiva. Rabbi Eliezer says: "As it is this day," meaning: Just as the day darkens and then the sky brightens the next day, so too with regard to the Ten Tribes as well, although it is dark for them now, so it is destined to brighten for them.
> *Mishnah Sanhedrin* 10:3

The Jerusalem Talmud commenting on this Mishnah adds:

> Rabbi Shimon son of Judah from the village of Akhus says in the name of Rabbi Shimon: "If their deeds were 'as this day' they will not return, but if not, they will indeed return." Rabbi Hezekiah and Rabbi Abahu say in the name of Rabbi Eliezer: "If they come, they will be righteous converts (Geirei Tzeddek) in time to come."
> Jerusalem Talmud, *Sanhedrin* 53b

No elaboration is provided as to the procedure whereby the returning Ten Tribers will become righteous converts. Are we to believe they will be subjected to protracted conversion procedures of the kind often imposed today by rabbinical conversion courts? Or might we perhaps witness a new level of "conversion" akin to the simultaneous "conversion" of the Children of Israel at Mount Sinai? Time alone will tell.

Among those today claiming to be from the re-emerging Ten Tribes or "Ephraimites", some are overt followers of Jesus, even if they do not consider him to be divine. Some consider him to have been sent primarily to gather in the Ten Tribes. In many cases they consider that Jesus himself was a "Torah-observant Jew" and they seek to emulate his way of life as they see it through some level of practice of the commandments according to their understanding. However, coming from Christian upbringings with all the accompanying misconceptions, suspicions and fears of "The Law", Talmud and Kabbalah etc., many strongly resist accepting the Halakhah as practiced by Torah-observant Jews, which they consider to be "man-made" and non-binding.

Obviously, Torah-observant Jews see this as an affront to the unity of the Written Torah with the Oral Torah, and find it difficult if not impossible to take such "Ten Tribers" seriously, further increasing the gulf between those who consider themselves unquestionably Jewish and those knocking on their doors from the outside.

To all Torah-observant Jews, it is manifestly clear that one and the same Torah, including both the Written and Oral Torah, applies equally to all Israel, whether "Jews", "Judah", "Israelites", genuine "Ten Tribers" and "Ephraimites", homeborn or true converts:

> As for the congregation, there shall be **one law for you and for the stranger** (*Ger*) who dwells; it shall be a law for all time throughout your generations. You and the stranger (*Ger*) shall be alike before the LORD.
> Numbers 15:15; cf. Exodus 12:3

From the perspective of observant students and practitioners of the Torah, the antagonism of such "Ten Tribers" to the Oral Law and the Halakhah is based upon an erroneous perception of how the Written Torah must be understood, and only when they are willing to accept the Torah in its entirety as all Israel accepted it at Mount Sinai will they be considered to have repented and returned to the Children of Israel, as stated in the Jerusalem

Talmud quoted above: "If they come, they will be righteous converts (*Geirei Tzeddek*) in time to come."

The prophet indicates that the first stage of the redemption of the Ten Tribes is when they remember Him from afar:

> I will give victory to the House of Judah, and triumph to the House of Joseph. I will restore them, for I have pardoned them, and they shall be as though I had never disowned them. For I the LORD am their God, and I will answer their prayers.
>
> Ephraim shall be like a warrior, and they shall exult as with wine; their children shall see it and rejoice, they shall exult in the LORD.
>
> I will whistle to them and gather them, for I will redeem them; they shall increase and continue increasing.
>
> For though I sowed them among the Nations, in the distant places they shall remember Me, they shall escape with their children and shall return.
>
> I will bring them back from the land of Egypt and gather them from Assyria; and I will bring them to the lands of Gilead and Lebanon, and even they shall not suffice for them.
>
> Zechariah 10:6-10

In our time, the return of the Ten Tribes cannot be seen as merely a far-off prophetic dream. For example, an estimated 30 million members of the Igbo people living in Nigeria consider themselves to be descended from the Ten Tribes, and have many traditional practices that include strong parallels in Torah law and custom. The same is true in the case of many other people, including entire communities, both elsewhere across Africa and in countries like Afghanistan, Pakistan and Indonesia, as well as many in Europe and America who also consider themselves descended from or spiritually connected to the Ten Tribes.

* * *

Having clarified the different halakhic considerations that may apply to various different kinds of "non-Jew" with different soul-roots, let us now address our original questions:

1. **May these people study Torah, and may Jewish rabbis teach them?**

2. **Are these people permitted to observe Shabbat and if so, in what way?**

Part II

WHO MAY STUDY TORAH? KEEP SHABBAT?

1. May a Goy study Torah?

As discussed earlier, the Talmudic source for the prohibition against an idolater studying Torah is in *Bavli Sanhedrin*:

> Rabbi Yochanan said: An idol-worshipper who engages in Torah study is liable to the death penalty, as it is stated: "Moses commanded us a law [Torah], an inheritance of the congregation of Jacob" (Deuteronomy 33:4), indicating that it is an inheritance for us, and not for them.
>
> *Sanhedrin 59a*

Following this passage – as will be discussed at greater length below – the Talmud goes on to state that it is a positive mitzvah for an idolater to study the Torah laws relating to the Seven Noahide Commandments (*ibid.*). From this we may infer that the Torah teachings that an idolater is forbidden to study are those that relate to the 613 commandments that were given specifically to Israel.

Thus, in Talmudic times it would have been forbidden for Jews to facilitate a pagan idolater entering into depth study of the Hebrew text of the TaNaKh, the foundation of all Torah study (though the entire TaNaKh was then available in Greek translation). Similarly out of bounds would have been study of the Oral Law, then mostly unavailable in writing, and also the rules of Torah hermeneutics and their application. These could only be learned from those in the academies of the great authorities of the time who made a specialty out of memorizing, collating, comparing and analyzing the many oral traditions in all the different areas of Torah law. Those privy to the mystical traditions handed down from the prophets would certainly not have facilitated their study by pagans. In contemporary terms, this would mean that the idolater must not study large areas of Talmudic, Halakhic, Kabbalistic and related literature.

Having stated that the penalty for so doing is death, the Talmud raises the question as to why the prohibition of an idolater studying the Torah of Israel is not numbered among the Seven Commandments of the Children of Noah. According to one answer, the prohibition of Torah study by an idolater is indeed included in the Noahide code under the prohibition of theft, for which the penalty for a Noahide is death (*Mishneh Torah, Melachim*, Laws of Kings 9:9), because the cited verse from Deuteronomy 33:4 calls the Torah "an **inheritance** of the congregation of Jacob" and an idolater who studies Torah has **stolen** this inheritance from the people of Israel.

According to a second opinion, the letters of the Hebrew word in the verse translated as "inheritance" (MoRaShaH) may be read as MeORaSaH, which means "betrothed", and an idolater who studies Torah is like one who has intercourse with a young Israelite woman already **betrothed** to an Israelite man, for which the penalty is death by stoning (*Sanhedrin loc. cit.*).

While the Talmud does not specifically address here the prohibition against an Israelite teaching Torah to an idolater, it is clearly implicit in the prohibition against the idolater studying Torah, for if an Israelite teaches him, then by causing the idolater to sin, the Israelite is violating the prohibition against placing a stumbling block before the blind (Leviticus 19:14).

Indeed, it is forbidden for one Israelite to teach even another Israelite Torah unless that person is upright and of good behavior or at the very least a person who is pure and moral. But if he was on a bad path, it is first necessary to bring him to improve himself and to guide him on the path of righteousness and to examine his progress, and only afterwards may one bring him into the study hall and teach him (*Mishneh Torah, Talmud Torah* Laws of Torah Study 4:1).

The sages said that someone who teaches an unworthy student is like a person who casts a stone in honor of the pagan god "Markulis", as implied in the verse (Proverbs 26:8): "Like tying a stone in a sling is giving honor to a fool" (*ibid.; Talmud Bavli, Hullin 133a*). This would clearly apply to teaching an idolater.

Rabbi Nachman teaches that the Torah teacher must be most careful not to say something unfitted to the soul and mind of the listener, for this is "adultery", casting the drops of the intellect in a place where they are useless and unproductive. It is called "wasting" of the seed because it does not result in anything whatever being "born" in the recipient in the sense of repentance and good deeds. If anything is born, it is flawed and blemished – i.e., the listener comes to do something inappropriate on his level (*Likutey Moharan I:134*).

The "Death Penalty"?

When the Talmud states that an idolater who studies Torah or observes the Shabbat is liable to the death penalty, does that mean that Israel are required to execute him?

In some cases when the Temple stood, pagan offenders were indeed killed, as in the case of a certain pagan in the time of Rabbi Yehudah ben Beteira, who disguised himself as a Jew and succeeded in eating the Passover lamb in violation of the prohibition against its consumption by a pagan (Exodus 12:43), but was later tricked into revealing his identity and killed (*Talmud Bavli, Pesachim 3b*).

However, a non-Israelite who accidentally or unknowingly violates one of the Seven Noahide Laws is not actually punished with the death penalty except in the case of murder, even if unwitting (Mishneh Torah, Melakhim, Laws of Kings 10:1). Furthermore:

> In the case of an idolater who engaged in Torah study or
> observed the Shabbat... we give him lashes and punish
> him and inform him that he is liable to the death penalty
> for doing so, but he is not actually executed.
> Mishneh Torah, Melakhim, Laws of Kings 10:9

The expression "liable to the death penalty" (*chayav meethah*)
may also carry the connotation of "liable to death at the hands
of Heaven", as in the case of certain transgressions which are not
punished by the earthly court but whose penalty may be an early
and untimely death and some level of spiritual "excision". God
alone knows how to deal with the idolater who studies the Torah
of Israel in honor of his idol.

A scriptural allusion to how an offender liable to execution might
die may be seen in the Hebrew text of Proverbs 19:16, "he who
despises his ways shall die", where the written text (*ktiv*) means
"he shall be put to death", whereas according to the oral tradition
it is read (*k'ri*) as "he shall die". Likewise, where the Torah states
that the owner of an animal that killed a person "shall be put
to death" (Exodus 21:29), the traditional interpretation is that
this means death at the hands of Heaven through an act of God
unless the owner pays the mandatory ransom (*Mishneh Torah,
Nizkey Mamon* Laws of Material Damages 10:4).

It becomes understandable why the idolater would be liable
to such a severe punishment for studying the Torah when we
consider that idolatry is itself a flagrant denial of the entire
Torah.

In the words of Rambam:

> The severity of the violation of the mitzvah
> prohibiting idolatry is as great as violating all the other
> commandments put together. For it is said: "And when
> you stray, and do not observe all these commandments..."
> (Numbers 15:22). By oral tradition, this is understood
> as referring to idolatry. From here you may deduce that
> whoever acknowledges idolatry denies the entire Torah,

all the prophets, and everything in which the prophets were instructed from Adam to the end of time, as it is said: "From the day when the LORD commanded and onward throughout your generations" (ibid. 15.23).
Mishneh Torah, Avodat Kokhavim, Laws of Idolatry 2:4

Rambam continues:

Whoever acknowledges idolatry as truth, even though he may not practice idol worship, is abusing and blaspheming the Glorified and Awesome Name. The idolater and the blasphemer are in one and the same category, as it states: "But whether from among the home-born citizens or a stranger (ger), whoever acts defiantly [worshiping idols] blasphemes the LORD..." (Numbers 15:30).
Ibid. 2:6

One may ask: What might be the motive of the idolater who seeks to study Torah, which is the very negation of his idolatry. Does he seek to show the superiority of his idol by proving to himself that the Torah is wrong and that its sages and expounders were willful falsifiers? From early times until this very day, many have arisen to make such claims, shamelessly twisting the meaning of Biblical verses while distorting, ridiculing and discrediting Talmudic teachings. To use the Torah to justify idolatry is the very height of abuse.

Torah study is not like some academic pursuit, because: "It is not the study that is the main thing but the actual practice" (*Pirkey Avot* 1:17). Israel were deemed worthy to receive the Torah because they committed to performing and "doing" the Torah commandments in practice even before "hearing" and understanding their full meaning and implications, as when they said: "All the things that the LORD has spoken **we shall do**" (Exodus 24:3) and: "Everything that the LORD has spoken **we shall do** and **we shall hear**" (*ibid.* v. 7).

Anyone can pick up a regular book and either take it or leave it, but the study of Torah requires complete submission and obedience to the Word of the LORD and to the teachings of His true prophets and sages in all the generations, submission on every level of mind, heart and soul. The Hebrew word for "study", *Limud*, thus derives from the same Hebrew root as the word *Malmad*, signifying the goad which the farmer uses to spur on his oxen and keep them to the furrow without straying.

Torah for the Noahides

As mentioned earlier, the above-quoted Talmudic statement in the name of the Amora, Rabbi Yochanan, that an idolater who studies Torah deserves the death penalty, is followed by a most important qualification. The Talmud raises an objection to his teaching based on the words of the earlier Tanna, Rabbi Meir:

> Rabbi Meir would say: From where is it derived that even a gentile who engages in Torah study is considered like a High Priest? It is derived from that which is stated: "You shall therefore keep My statutes and My ordinances, which, if a man practices them, he shall live by them" (Leviticus 18:5). It does not state that if priests, Levites, and Israelites do them, they shall live by them, but rather: "a man", which indicates any member of humanity in general. You have therefore learned that even a gentile who engages in Torah study is considered like a High Priest.

> *Sanhedrin 59a.* (See *Ben Yehoyada's* important annotation on the correct version of the text as given here and his commentary *ad loc.*)

The Talmud resolves the apparent contradiction as follows:

> There [in the teaching of Rabbi Meir] the reference is to a gentile who engages in the study of their seven commandments.
> *Ibid.*

Thus, we see that it is a positive mitzvah for a gentile to study the laws that pertain to the seven Noahide mitzvot, and when he does so he is highly regarded.

We therefore need to understand which areas of Torah would be included in what Noahides may and should study. Since the first and second Noahide commandments are the prohibitions against idolatry and blasphemy, they would need a full, clear understanding of all their parameters. Moreover, the knowledge that idolatry is prohibited does not in itself satisfy the craving of the Noahide soul to know God and to reach out to Him, and needs to be supplemented with what in Torah literature comes under the heading of *Hashkafah*, general outlook and worldview, *Sifrey Emunah*, works on faith and the ways of prayer, and *Mussar*, spiritual self-improvement. Above all comes the TaNaKh, which in any case is readily available to people across the world in all languages (though many of the translations can be mildly to highly misleading). The book of Job in particular, all of whose protagonists are Noahide prophets, speaks to all mankind.

The third, fourth and fifth Noahide commandments, the prohibitions against murder, incest and theft, can be summarized fairly succinctly, yet their application in actual, day-to-day life requires considerable further elaboration and detail, and many of their ramifications can only be understood in the light of other related Torah commandments as set forth in the halakhic codes. This applies equally to the sixth Noahide commandment prohibiting the consumption of a limb torn from a living animal, the fulfilment of which in our time requires an understanding of how the Halakhah applies to contemporary meat production and marketing. And proper fulfilment of the seventh Noahide commandment enjoining the establishment of courts of Justice clearly requires a proper grasp of the Torah concept of Justice.

As indicated earlier, the Noahide would not be eligible for depth-study of the Hebrew text of the TaNaKh or of the classical hermeneutical rules as applied to display the roots of the Oral Torah in the written text and to derive practical

Halakhah. This would exclude depth study of Talmud and much technical halakhic literature, though not necessarily the study of summaries of practical Halakhah in various areas. While the study of general works on Emunah most certainly applies to the Noahide, the study of kabbalistic texts dealing in depth with the Hebrew names of God and mystical meditations (*kavanot*) would not be included.

The Thirty Future Noahide Commandments

We cannot complete this discussion without referring to the tradition that in time to come the Noahides will have **thirty** commandments. The Babylonian Talmud states in the name of the Amora, Ulla, that originally the Nations accepted thirty commandments upon themselves but later abandoned most of them (*Hullin 92a*). The Jerusalem Talmud also speaks of thirty commandments which the Bney Noah will take upon themselves **in time to come** (*Yerushalmi Avodah Zarah 9a*).

The commentator Rashi on the passage in *Hullin 92a* states that the thirty commandments are not specified, nor do we know from where they are deduced.

According to Rabbi Menachem Azariah of Pano (1548-1620), they are all subcategories of the Noahide Laws. His listing of the thirty commandments in seven groups is as follows:

A: 1. Prohibition of idolatry, 2. Do not pass a child through fire in the worship of the Molech idol, 3. Prohibition of stick divination, 4. Prohibition of divining auspicious times, 5. Do not rely on omens, superstition, 6. Prohibition of witchcraft & sorcery, 7. Prohibition of charms & incantations, 8. Do not consult mediums, 9. Do not consult oracles, 10. Prohibition of necromancy,

B. 11. Forbidden sexual unions, 12. Be fruitful, 13. Multiply seed, 14. Don't draw up marriage contracts between males, 15. Don't crossbreed animals, 16. Don't castrate, 17. Don't graft different species of trees.

C. 18. Prohibition of Murder, 19. Do not strike an Israelite,

D. 20. Prohibition of Blasphemy, 21. Give honor to the Torah and her sages, 22. Study the Noahide code.

E. 23. Theft, 24. Don't study non-relevant parts of the Torah,

F. 25. Establishment of a system of justice, 26. Do not cease from all labor on Shabbat,

G. 27. Do not eat all or part of a living creature, 28. Do not consume blood of a living creature, 29. Do not eat *Neveilah*, carrion, an animal that died without proper slaughter, 30. Do not eat human flesh.

Rabbi Menachem Azariah of Pano, *Asarah Ma'amarot, Ma'amar Chakor Din* Part 3 chapter 21.

A somewhat different list of the thirty commandments is found in the writings of Samuel HaKohen ben Hofni, who was the Gaon of Sura (d. 1034).

1. Prohibition of idolatry; 2. Prohibition of blasphemy; 3. Unification of the Name; 4. Prayer; 5. Not to swear falsely; 6. Prohibition of suicide; 7. Murder of another; 8. Adultery; 9. Marriage by contract; 10. Prohibition of relations with a sister; 11. Prohibition of male homosexual intercourse; 12. Bestiality; 13. Prohibition of Castration; 14. Prohibition of consumption of Neveilah, Carrion; 15. Prohibition of consuming a limb from a living creature; 16. Prohibition of consuming blood from a living creature; 17. Prohibition of interbreeding different animal species; 18. [*Missing from manuscript*]; 19. Sacrifices; 20. Prohibition of robbery and theft; 21. Honoring father and mother; 22. Prohibition of passing one's son or daughter through fire in Molech worship; 23. Prohibition of Sorcery and occult arts; 24. Prohibition of divining through astrology; 25. Prohibition of stick

divination; 26. Prohibition of witchcraft; 27. Prohibition of casting spells; 28. Prohibition of asking a spirit (*Ov*); 29. Prohibition of the *Yid'oni* oracle; 30. Seeking out the dead.

Sinai Vol. 72, p. 205 and "Samuel ben Hophni's Noahide Law"

Rav Saadiah Gaon (882/892-942) adds the commandments of Tithing and Levirate Marriage. Rav Nissim Gaon (990-1062) adds 1. Obedience to God; 2. Knowledge of God; 3. Worship of God. Rabbi Meir ben Todros HaLevi Abulafia (c. 1170-1244) and Rabbi Nissim of Gerona (1320-1376) add Charity.

For further details see "The Thirty Mitzvot of the Bnei Noach" at Noahide.net.

Clearly, in the light of these teachings, the array of Torah laws which Noahides must study, understand and observe is very greatly expanded.

The "Captive Children" and "Jews by Choice"

As we have seen earlier, the discussion in the Talmud (*Sanhedrin 59a*) about the eligibility of the non-Israelite to study the Torah applies primarily to the practicing idolater and in a qualified way to the Noahides. It most certainly does not apply to the *Ger Tzeddek*, who is a full convert and who not only may but *must* study the Torah of Israel.

The same is true of the "Captive Child", *Tinok Shenishbah*, and "one who converts among the Nations" *Ger hamitgayer le-vein ha-goyim*. As we have seen, both have the status of full Israelites, as is clear from the discussion in the Talmud about their liability to bring a sin offering for their transgressions (*Shabbat 68a*, see above). The "captive child" was simply not aware of his Israelite identity and obligations. As for one who "converts among the Nations", i.e., before three Israelites, albeit rabbinically unqualified, his conversion is considered valid and he has the status of a full Israelite.

As soon as the "Captive Child" becomes aware of his Israelite identity and the "Convert among the Nations" recognizes that he was ill-informed, clearly both are not only permitted to study the Torah of Israel but are *obliged* to do so in order to learn about their responsibilities as members of the people of Israel and how to fulfill them. It would follow that rabbis and Torah teachers may and should teach and support them in their pathway.

However, in the case of one who "converts alone by himself", we have seen earlier that he is *not* recognized by Israel as a convert (*Talmud Bavli, Yevamot* 47a-b). Even a person of unknown status who is seen to observe the commandments scrupulously and who *is* regarded as a *Ger Tzeddek* is still not allowed to marry into the Assembly until he brings witnesses to his conversion or performs the conversion immersion in front of a rabbinical court (*Mishneh Torah, Issurey Biyah,* Forbidden Unions chapter 13:7 & 9).

Then would it be fair simply to place "one who converts alone, on his or her own" – the "Jew by choice" – in the same category as an idolater who is forbidden to delve into the Torah of Israel and may study only the Seven Noahide Commandments? Although Jewish rabbinical courts may not accept such a person as a convert, the fact is that he or she has freely chosen to embrace the Torah of Israel. Moreover, even without official recognition by rabbis and Jewish communities, there is in actuality nothing to stop them identifying as Israelites. Not only would this seem to apply to many of today's "Jews by choice" across the world, but it would most certainly apply to those who consider themselves "Ephraimites" or "Ten Tribers", who according to their own self-identification are *obliged* to study and practice the Torah of Israel.

Many such people are located far from any established, recognized Torah community, and in practical terms are simply unable to move in order to undergo a formal conversion. Should they therefore be discouraged from the path they seek to follow if they believe it to be their true soul-path?

Some Orthodox Jewish outreach rabbis today have a policy not to offer any encouragement to people whom they do not consider to be halakhically Jewish yet say they seek to observe the Torah. This attitude is further reinforced by the fact that some such people have indeed proved to be covert missionaries, "Jewish Messianics" or the like, who believe in Jesus but do not adhere to the Halakhah and have no intention of doing so. Yet it may be that rejecting all "non-Jews" across the board unjustly penalizes truly sincere "non-Jewish" seekers who may even be rooted in the souls of Israel even if they do not even know how to express this, like the Fourth Son of the Pesach Seder Haggadah, Who Does Not Know To Ask.

Through the Internet today, practically anyone, anywhere on earth, can find abundant online Torah study resources, including all the classic Hebrew texts, translations and commentaries, all kinds of online audio and video classes and entire courses in many different areas. There is no rabbinical police force that can prevent unworthy individuals from participating in such study. However, the public forum is flooded with so much misinformation about Torah masquerading as "truth", that Torah outreach teachers surely owe it to those who are indeed sincere seekers to clarify what is correct and what is incorrect.

There are many cases where non-Jews desire to identify with Israel in some way and believe that they should convert and become Jewish. However, their understanding of Torah obligations may be so distorted and their ability to fulfill them so limited that they need to be informed that the Noahide pathway in the fullest sense is more appropriate for them. This indeed is for their own good, as it is better that they should not consider themselves Jews because of the severe penalties for failing to live up to Torah law.

Yet in other cases, just as Ruth insisted on clinging to Naomi and her people despite Naomi's rebuffs, so there are "Jews by Choice" and "Ephraimites" who insist, no matter what, in pressing on with their chosen Torah pathway. It may be that at the very roots of their souls they are indeed our lost Israelite brothers and sisters. Even if this is no more than a mere possibility, a *safek*, a "matter of doubt", should we not at the very least, as a gesture of compassion, give them the benefit of the doubt and provide their thirsty souls with clear, reliable information about the options before them and the true obligations of the Torah pathway.

As the prophesied redemption of Israel and the Restoration of the lost Ten Tribes draws ever closer, it will be for the rabbinical authorities of the future to determine how the Halakhah would apply to them in practice. As an example of halakhic questions that can arise, consider the tribes in present-day Africa who believe themselves to be members of the Children of Israel descended from the Ten Tribes, some of whom practice polygamy until today. Since their ancestors never knew of or accepted the *Cherem* ("Ban") against polygamy instituted by Rabbenu Gershom (ben Yehudah, "Light of the Diaspora", 960-1040), and in any case, the original timespan for its application is widely considered to have technically expired, can they simply be told peremptorily that "Jews do not practice polygamy today"? Or are they permitted to practice polygamy in accordance with Talmudic law (*Mishneh Torah, Ishut*, Laws of Marriage 14:3)?

Other questions could be raised about the obligations of returning "Ephraimites" in the area of prayer. The Ten Tribes went into exile prior to the redaction of the order and formulae of the prayers by the Men of the Great Assembly in early Second Temple times, as enshrined in the *Siddur* Prayer Book and accepted today as mandatory for all Jews. Are "Ephraimites" halakhically obliged to adopt the Siddur as we have it today for their prayer life, or may they develop their own forms of prayer based on the fundamental, biblically-derived laws of prayer, the Psalms and sources in TaNaKh, etc.? In general, how would the rabbinical decrees from Ezra onwards, including the decrees and customs of the Babylonian Talmud, considered mandatory for all Jews, apply in practice to the returning Ten Tribes?

At the very least, today's Torah-observant Jews should be aware that with the rapidly approaching Redemption and Restoration, the future practice of the Torah and the commandments by the Twelve Tribes of Israel may be expected to differ radically in style and many other respects from those of Torah practice as seen in orthodox Jewish communities today.

Light to the Nations

> O LORD, my strength and my stronghold, my refuge on a day of trouble, to You Nations shall come from the ends of the earth and say: Only falsehood did our fathers inherit, things that are futile and contain nothing that can avail. Can a man make himself gods, and they are not gods?
> Jeremiah 19-20

> And many peoples shall go and say: "Come, let us go up to the Mount of the LORD, to the House of the God of Jacob; that He may instruct us in His ways, and that we may walk in His paths." For instruction shall come forth from Zion, and the word of the LORD from Jerusalem.
> Isaiah 2:3

Numerous passages in TaNaKh stand in marked contrast to the attitude seen in some Jewish quarters today that Torah is exclusively reserved for the Jews and should be practiced almost privately as it were, behind closed doors, with no involvement on the part of "non-Jews" or any kind of outreach to them.

Israel is indeed "a people that dwells apart and is not reckoned among the Nations" (Numbers 23:9). This is because the people of Israel are uniquely appointed to a life of duty, to be "a kingdom of priests and a holy nation" (Exodus 19:6), whose mission is to minister to the Nations of the world.

> I the LORD have called you in righteousness, and will hold your hand, and will guard you, and give you as a Covenant of the people, a Light of the gentiles.
> Isaiah 42:6

And He said: Is it too little that you should be My servant, in that I raise up the tribes of Jacob and restore the survivors of Israel? I will also make you a light of Nations, that My salvation may reach to the ends of the earth.

Isaiah 49:6

Fierce Anger and its Sweetening

Our sages taught: "As long as there is idolatry in the world, there is fierce anger in the world" (*Sifri* on Deuteronomy 13:18).

Not only is literal idolatry practiced, whether overtly or secretly, in many places on earth, until today. Equally idolatrous is the secular materialist consumption-driven culture and worldview that has now overtaken much of the world, whose gods are self-gratification, pleasure, power, prestige and a multitude of others. With rampant murder, crime, sexual license, legalized homosexual "marriages", transgenderism and much else that is in direct contradiction to the Torah of Israel and the Noahide Code, is it any wonder that in front of our very eyes today we are witnessing a veritable global conflagration of rage and anger, accusations and recrimiNations, hatred, conflict, violence and warfare on every level?

As God's "kingdom of priests and holy nation", the people of Israel cannot remain indifferent and passive, as if we have no role in the wider world. Nor did our founding fathers, the patriarchs Abraham, Isaac and Jacob, remain passive and indifferent. The world in their time was no less dark and benighted than ours. Indeed, there are too many parallels between the culture of the generations of the Tower of Babel, Sodom and Gomorrah and ancient Egypt and the rampant God-denying culture of today.

Rabbi Nachman taught that all three patriarchs busied themselves with preaching to the people of their time and educating them in the ways of God (*Chayey Moharan* #395; *Tzaddik* pp. 328-30). Likewise, Moses sought to mitigate the judgment and fierce anger in the world caused by idolatry through making converts, and thus he attempted to draw close the Mixed Multitude in order to make converts (*Likutey Moharan* Part I, Lesson 215).

The idea that the Torah of Israel is of no relevance to the other nations of the world belies the clear significance of key passages in the Torah itself. Our sages taught that Moses himself explained the Torah in the seventy languages of the Nations, as it says: "On the other side of the Jordan, in the land of Moab, Moses began to expound (*bei-eir*) this Torah..." (Deuteronomy 1:5). In the words of Rashi (*ad loc.*): "He explained it to them in the seventy languages" (see *Sotah* 32a). The Talmud (*ibid.*) adds that when the Children of Israel first entered the Land of Israel, they built an altar and laid plaster over it and wrote on it all the words of the Torah in the seventy languages.

Israel are enjoined to reach out to the Nations: "Tell of His glory among the Nations, His wondrous deeds, among all peoples" (Psalm 96:3). "Praise the LORD; call on His Name; proclaim His deeds among the peoples" (Psalm 105:1).

In time to come, the Nations themselves will turn to Israel for spiritual leadership:

> Behold! Darkness shall cover the earth, and thick clouds the peoples; but upon you the LORD will shine, and His Presence shall be seen over you. And Nations shall walk by your light, kings, by your shining radiance.
> Isaiah 60:2-3

> Many Nations will attach themselves to the LORD on that day and they shall become My people...
> Zechariah 2:15

> And many Nations shall go and shall say: "Come! Let us go up to the Mountain of the LORD, to the House of the God of Jacob, that He may instruct us in His ways, and that we may walk in His paths." For instruction shall come forth from Zion, the word of the LORD from Jerusalem.
> Micah 4:2

So said the LORD of Hosts: The peoples and inhabitants of many cities shall yet come. And the inhabitants of one shall go to the other and say, "Let us go and entreat the favor of the LORD, let us seek the LORD of Hosts; I too shall go!" And many peoples and powerful Nations shall come to seek the LORD of Hosts in Jerusalem and to entreat the favor of the LORD. So said the LORD of Hosts: In those days, ten men from Nations of every tongue will take hold—they will take hold of a Jew by a corner of his cloak and say, "Let us go with you, for we have heard that God is with you."

Zechariah 8:20-23

Many are ever more aware that these days have already begun and are upon us now.

2. May a Goy keep Shabbat?

As discussed earlier, the Talmudic source for the prohibition against Shabbat observance by an idolater is in the Babylonian Talmud Tractate Sanhedrin towards the end of a lengthy discussion about the Seven Commandments of the Children of Noah, their Biblical sources and detailed laws:

> Reish Lakish (Rabbi Shimon ben Lakish) said: An idol-worshipper who observed Shabbat is liable to the death penalty, as it says: "And day and night shall not cease" (Genesis 8:23).
>
> *Talmud Bavli, Sanhedrin 58b*

The Hebrew word rendered here as "observed Shabbat" is the verb *shaavath*, literally "rested", i.e., from the biblically-rooted labors that are prohibited to Israel on Shabbat. The commentator Rashi (*ad loc.*) explains that if the idolater were to rest from his labor for a full day, he would be liable to the death penalty on account of the literal meaning of the verse: "Day and night *they shall not rest*" which is interpreted homiletically to apply also to humans.

The Talmud (*ibid.*) adds in the name of Ravina (a later Amora who died about 420 C.E.): "Even on a Monday."

Rashi (*ad loc.*) explains the significance of Ravina's statement:

> You cannot say that the sabbatical rest (*shevitah*) of which Reish Lakish is speaking is for the sake of fulfilling an obligation, as if to say the idolater should not intend to take a Sabbath rest, for example, on Shabbat, which is the day of rest for Israel, or on Sunday, on which the Notzrim observe their Sabbath. Rather, what is prohibited for them is any kind of rest (*menuchah*) in the sense that they should not cease entirely from labor even on a day that is not designated for Shabbat rest, such as Monday, the first day that is not a day for Sabbath rest, but by the same token he could have taken Tuesday or Wednesday as his example.
> Rashi on *Sanhedrin 58b*

In actual fact, it is practically impossible for even the most learned Torah-observant Jew with a lifetime of experience to refrain entirely from all the labors that are forbidden on Shabbat under the various categories of *Avot*, "fathers", the Thirty-Nine paradigm labors, and each of their many subcategories of *Toldot*, "offspring" or "generations", i.e., their related labors. (See *Likutey Moharan* Part I, Lesson 277:4.) More baffling than ever are the challenges of how and under what circumstances on Shabbat we may or may not use the technological marvels of our time – electric lighting, heating and air conditioning, stoves, refrigerators, phones, computers and other devices, cars, medical equipment, etc. etc.

Even so, the Torah-observant Jew is obliged to do everything possible to avoid performing any forbidden labor on Shabbat, whereas the "Goy" is positively encouraged to perform at least some form of "work" on Shabbat. In orthodox Jewish circles, even serious candidates for full conversion to Judaism as a *Ger Tzeddek* or female *Giyoret*, who after lengthy periods living in an observant Jewish community may be observing the halakhic

Shabbat in every way, must still demonstrate that they are aware they are not yet a full Israelite. They are instructed to do this by performing at least one action each Shabbat that for a fully-fledged Jew would be a transgression, such as lighting a match, swatting a fly or the like. This implies that as a "non-Jew" even such candidates for conversion are not allowed to observe the Shabbat in the manner of Torah-observant Jews until after their full conversion.

It clearly cannot be that the "Goy" is never allowed to take even a momentary rest from activity. What may be inferred from the Talmudic discussion is that he or she is strictly forbidden to practice a complete day of abstinence from all the thirty-nine labors prohibited to Israel on the Shabbat, whether they rest in this sense on the Shabbat itself or any other day of the week. Since abstinence by Israel from these labors is the precondition for their Shabbat "rest" – *Menuchah* – the "Goy" is excluded from this level of experience, which is akin to receiving holy spirit or prophecy (cf. Jeremiah 45:3 and Rashi there).

The "Death Penalty" and its rationale

In our earlier discussion about the prohibition against an idolater studying Torah, we saw that the liability to the death penalty is not to be taken literally, and the same would apply to an idolater who observes a complete Sabbatical abstinence from labor.

In the words of Rambam:

An idolater who "rested" as one would on Shabbat, even on a weekday, is liable to the death penalty, and it is unnecessary to add that this would apply if he invented his own festival. The principle here is that they are not permitted to institute a new religion or to create new commandments for themselves based on their own reasoning. Either they must become righteous converts and take on themselves all the commandments, or they should observe their own Noahide Laws without adding or detracting from them. If an idolater engaged in Torah or practiced the Shabbat rest or instituted something new, he is beaten and punished and is notified that he is liable with the death penalty for this. But he is not executed.

Mishneh Torah, Melakhim, Laws of Kings 10:9

In our time no rabbinical police squads are empowered to go around chastising idolaters who observe the full Shabbat rest. Yet even without a literal death by execution for such a violation, the very idea that it carries a liability to some level of "death" seems extremely severe.

Perhaps it may become somewhat more comprehensible when we bear in mind that the observance of the Shabbat is considered equivalent to the observance of all the 613 Torah commandments (*Talmud Yerushalmi, Nedarim* ch 3), and that the Shabbat with its associated rest testifies to God's creation of the Universe (Genesis 2:1-3). Accordingly, if an idolater observes the Shabbat rest in honor of his idol, he is flagrantly denying and blaspheming the Creator of the Universe and mocking His entire Torah.

God's Special Gift

It is indeed abundantly clear that the Shabbat is God's special gift to Israel. In the words of the Talmud:

> The Holy One, blessed be He, said to Moses: "I have a good gift in My treasure house and Shabbat is its name, and I seek to give it to Israel. Go and inform them about it."
>
> *Talmud Bavli, Shabbat* 10b

The Torah states:

> The Children of Israel shall guard the Shabbat, observing the Shabbat for their generations as an eternal covenant. Between Me and between the Children of Israel, it is a sign for ever that in six days the LORD made the

heavens and the earth and on the seventh He rested and was refreshed.
Exodus 31:16-17

Following the recital of these verses in the central blessing of the Shabbat morning Amidah prayer, the prayer continues:

"... And You did not give it, O LORD our God, to the Nations (goyey, plural of goy) of the lands, and nor did You give it to idol-worshippers, and nor shall the uncircumcised dwell in its repose, for to Israel Your people did You give it in love, to the seed of Jacob whom You chose."
From the Shabbat Morning *Amidah* prayer

Rabbi Shmuel Eidels (*Maharsha*, 1555-1631) commenting on the Talmudic prohibition against the idolater observing the Shabbat rest explains:

The Shabbat is called a "bride" and is thus is for Israel like a bride who has entered the marriage canopy but whose marriage has not yet been consummated. Therefore, if the idolater observes the Shabbat rest, it is as if he violated the bride of an Israelite who has entered the marriage canopy but whose marriage has not yet been consummated, and we say that he is subject to the same Torah penalty of death that would apply to an Israelite who did such a thing. And thus, the Shabbat is called a sign "between Me and the Children of Israel". It is as if the King is sitting face to face with the Queen, and someone who comes in between them is liable to the death penalty.
Chiddushey Aggadot on *Sanhedrin* 58b

The Ger Toshav

It may appear as if the sources quoted here entirely rule out the possibility that anyone who is considered a "Goy" or "non-Jewish" may have any part in the observance of the Shabbat. However, such an inference would be far from accurate. Firstly, in the same way as noted in connection with the prohibition of Torah study by various different categories of "non-Jews", the Talmudic prohibition of Shabbat rest applies specifically to the practicing idolater and cannot necessarily be applied to every category of "Goy" who is not recognized as being "Jewish". Thus, in another Torah passage giving the commandment of Shabbat, it says:

> Six days you shall do your work, but on the seventh day you shall cease from labor, in order that your ox and your ass may rest, and that your bondman and the **stranger** (Hebrew: Ger) may be refreshed.
> Exodus 23:12

We must clarify who exactly is the "stranger" or Ger mentioned in this verse? Since this verse is addressed to all Israel, including the *Ger Tzeddek*, the "full" convert, who must observe all the the Shabbat laws like all other Israelites, we cannot say that the *Ger Tzeddek* is the "Ger" or "stranger" mentioned in the verse who must be allowed to be refreshed on the Shabbat. Indeed, Rashi on this verse states that the Ger here is the *Ger Toshav*, the Noahide who has disavowed idolatry and undertaken the Noahide commandments but is not a full convert (Rashi on Exodus 23:12 and see also Ramban on Exodus 20:10).

This verse in no way implies that the *Ger Toshav* is required to abstain from all the thirty-nine kinds of prohibited labors and to observe the Shabbat with all the stringencies that apply to the Children of Israel. As far as the Israelite Shabbat-observer is concerned, the verse is teaching that he may not give the *Ger Toshav* work that needs to be done on Shabbat, but rather must respect the *Ger Toshav's* day of leisure.

However, when it comes to those with the status of *Ger Toshav* themselves, nothing in the verse suggests that they **may not** mark the Shabbat with some kind of recognition, even if not required to refrain from every kind of labor, activity or speech forbidden to Israel. On the contrary, the verse clearly includes the *Ger Toshav* among those who are encouraged to enjoy and be nourished spiritually on the Shabbat day. The Hebrew word in the phrase in the above-quoted verse in Exodus 23:12: "that... the stranger may **be refreshed**", is vayiNaFaSh, which is from the root NeFeSh, "the soul" and thus has a spiritual connotation.

In fact, the Halakhah specifically permits a Jew to invite a non-Jew to his Shabbat meal (*Shulchan Arukh, Orach Chaim* 325:1). This indicates that the door is **not** closed on a non-Jew participating in the Shabbat experience.]

"Remember" and "Guard"

On the contrary, all the peoples of the world are *obliged* to remember and be aware of the Shabbat. This is explained by Rabbi Shlomo Ephraim ben Aaron Luntschitz (1550-1619) in his classic *Kli Yakar* commentary on the Five Books of Moses. On the Torah commandment: "Remember the Shabbat", as given in the first version of the Ten Commandments (Exodus 20:8-11), he writes:

> The Torah did not want to say Guard the day of Shabbat [as in the second version of the Ten Commandments, Deuteronomy 5:12] in order not to give an opening of the mouth to the Nations to say: "How can He be commanding us to guard against performing any forbidden labor since the Children of Noah have already been told that 'day and night they shall not rest' (Genesis 8:22) and from here the sages learned (Sanhedrin 58b) that a member of the Nations who rested on Shabbat is liable to the death penalty?"

> For that reason, it says here: Remember the day of Shabbat. That is to say, even one who is not bound to guard the Shabbat by abstaining from labor is still included in the commandment of remembering the Shabbat. **For all the Nations are obliged to remember the day of Shabbat in order to fix in their hearts the faith and belief in the renewal of creation which is God's faithful testimony to His existence.**

For included in the Seven Commandments of the Children of Noah is the prohibition against idolatry, and even though the Nations are unable to embrace the negative commandment against performing all labor on the Shabbat, they can nevertheless take upon themselves the commandment of *remembering* the Shabbat, to which they are also obliged, in order that the renewal of the universe may be before their eyes for a memorial.

However, in the second version of the Ten Commandments, which were given only to Israel, the Fourth Commandment uses the expression to *guard* the Shabbat, for Israel are obliged to remember the Shabbat and also to guard against the performance of any forbidden labor. This is why in the second version, the reason given for the observance of Shabbat is: "That you may remember that you were a slave". For this is the reason for abstaining from forbidden labor on Shabbat. *Kli Yakar on Exodus 20:8-11*

Shabbat for All the World

In our time the vital importance of recognition of the Shabbat by all the Nations of the world has been strongly emphasized by Rabbi Joel Schwartz, a distinguished halakhic authority in Jerusalem[40] who heads the Renewed Sanhedrin's Noahide Court. He has called for all the Nations to keep the Sabbath and for the Jews to help them in this mission.

Rabbi Schwartz explains that many of the problems facing the world today are due to not recognizing the Sabbath. Observed on its proper day and in the proper manner, the Sabbath is a weekly affirmation of God's creation of the Universe. The Sabbath is not a random or man-made day; God Himself established it as part of the seven-day process of creation. Every seventh day since

---

[40]   www.israel365news.com/120106/noahide-court-messiah-nations-sabbath/

the world was created has been Sabbath. Changing it is to try to replace God and remove Him from the creation.

Rabbi Schwartz expands on the teaching in *Kli Yakar's* commentary quoted above:

"Two different aspects of the Sabbath are expressed in the two versions of the Ten Commandments. The first is in Exodus 20:8, where it says, "Remember the Shabbat day and keep it holy', while the second is in Deuteronomy 5:12, where it says: "Guard the Shabbat day and keep it holy, as the LORD your God has commanded you".

"The first set of tablets, given at Sinai, were written by God and the commandment to remember the Sabbath was a universal commandment: 'Remember the Sabbath'. Since it was universal, it was followed by an account of creation: 'For in six days God made the heavens and the earth and all that is in them, and He rested on the seventh day; therefore God blessed the Sabbath day and hallowed it' (Exodus 20:11).

"However, the commandment in Deuteronomy on the tablets written by Moses was a message specifically for the Children of Israel to 'guard' or 'observe' the Sabbath," says Rabbi Schwartz, noting that it was followed by a description of God taking them out of Egypt: "'Remember that you were a slave in the land of Egypt and the LORD your God freed you from there with a mighty hand and an outstretched arm; therefore the LORD your God has commanded you to observe the Shabbat day' (Deuteronomy 5:15). 'To remember' refers to the positive commandments of keeping the Sabbath while 'to guard' relates to the negative commandments of refraining from labor or other acts that are restricted on the Sabbath.

"By not instructing the Nations in their requirement to 'remember the Sabbath', by actually preventing them from taking part in the Sabbath, the Jews have prevented the full light of Mashiach from being revealed in the world," says Rabbi Schwartz.

"These two different versions of the Sabbath commandment generate two different aspects of the Sabbath, one for Jews and one for the Nations. The Jews are required to both 'remember' and 'observe', performing all the positive injunctions relating to Shabbat commandments as well as refraining from the 39 kinds of forbidden labor."

Rabbi Schwartz goes on to explain how people of the Nations may mark and honor the Shabbat:

"For people of the Nations, the positive mitzvah of remembering the Sabbath is fulfilled through reciting the *Kiddush* – sanctifying the Sabbath – usually performed over a cup of wine. Non-Jews should light two candles in honor of the Sabbath. This is typically done by women. When the non-Jew lights the Shabbat candles at the proper time before sunset on Friday prior to the commencement of Shabbat, a blessing with the name of God may be recited. The sanctity of the Sabbath should be enhanced by having two festive meals including bread, one on Friday evening and the other on Saturday afternoon, and these meals should be accompanied by joyous singing at the table.

"It is no coincidence in this era when people are not keeping the Sabbath or even err as to which day is the Sabbath, that families are falling apart," says Rabbi Schwartz.

"Moreover, when the Halakhah states that it is forbidden for a non-Jew to keep the Sabbath, it is referring to a non-Jew who does not observe the Noahide laws. But a non-Jew who has taken upon himself to keep the Noahide laws is permitted to keep the Sabbath."

This is in accordance with a halakhic ruling explained by Rabbi Yisrael Meir Kagan, (the *Chafetz Chaim*, 1838-1933):

> If at the time of the Ger Toshav's initial acceptance of his obligations as such, he wanted to undertake more commandments in addition to the Seven Noahide Laws, this undertaking is binding and obliges him to fulfill them thereafter... And you cannot question

how he may observe the Shabbat by abstaining from forbidden labors when the Ger Toshav is also forbidden to observe the Shabbat... For this applies to a regular Ger Toshav who undertook only the Seven Noahide Commandments in the usual way, and if so with respect to other commandments he is like a complete non-Israelite. **But this is not the case when he undertook more commandments at the time of his initial acceptance of the obligations of a Ger Toshav and among them was also the Shabbat, and in this case, he can certainly fulfil them and is obliged to fulfill them.** *Biur Halakhah,* appended to *Mishnah Berurah* on *Shulchan Arukh, Orach Chayim* 304

Rabbi Joel Schwartz concludes: **"It is time for a revolution in the world. Even the secular people who don't believe in God know the world is in danger, though they blame it on things like Global Warming. The Sabbath is a precious gift that Hashem gave to the Jews and it demands respect. But it is time observant Jews showed the Nations how they can relate to their Creator."**

Light of Mashiach

At the End of Days, all mankind will recognize and honor the Shabbat:

> "And it shall come to pass that from one new moon to another, and from one Sabbath to another, all flesh shall come to worship before Me," says the LORD.
> Isaiah 66:23

> Happy is the man who does this, the man who holds fast to it, who keeps the Sabbath and does not profane it, and stays his hand from doing any evil. Let not the foreigner who has attached himself to the LORD say:

"The LORD will keep me apart from His people". And let not the eunuch say, "I am a withered tree."

For thus has the LORD said: "As for the eunuchs who keep My Sabbaths, who have chosen what I desire and hold fast to My Covenant – I will give them, in My House and within My walls, a monument and a name better than sons or daughters. I will give them an everlasting name which shall not perish.

"As for the foreigners who attach themselves to the LORD to minister to Him and to love the Name of the LORD, to be His servants: All who keep the Sabbath and do not profane it and who hold fast to My covenant – I will bring them to My sacred Mount and let them rejoice in My House of Prayer. Their burnt offerings and sacrifices shall be welcome on My altar. For My House shall be called A House of Prayer for All the Peoples." Isaiah 56:2-7

We live in a world that is rapidly changing and moving in directions uncharted. What some hail as the "great global reset" is for others a formidable challenge to values they hold dearest and a call to new levels of devotion to God. Among believers there is much talk everywhere of messianic signs. If so, surely not least among them are the burgeoning throngs of people of all backgrounds from all over the world who are turning to Torah in search of guidance. This can only thrill those who understand that the ultimate goal of Creation is for the light of the Torah to shine to all the world.

Rabbi Nachman of Breslov said: "Mashiach will conquer the entire world without firing a single bullet" (*Siach Sarfey Kodesh* 1-67).

Rather, "He shall judge the poor with equity and decide with justice for the lowly of the land. He shall strike down a land with the rod of his mouth and slay the wicked with the breath of his lips" (Isaiah 11:4).

The defining quality of Mashiach is that he speaks *peace* to the nations:

> Rejoice greatly, daughter of Zion; raise a shout, daughter of Jerusalem! See, your king is coming to you. He is victorious and triumphant, yet humble, riding on an ass, on a donkey foaled by a she-ass. And I shall banish chariots from Ephraim and horses from Jerusalem; the warrior's bow shall be banished. And he shall speak peace to the Nations, and his rule shall extend from sea to sea and from the river to the ends of the earth. Zechariah 9:9-10

The mission of all members of God's nation of priests today is to embrace this messianic spirit and likewise to speak peace to the Nations and to shine the light of Torah everywhere, in every way possible.

Nobody can deny the dire state of the world today, whether because of "climate change", "pandemics", frustration, high tension, rage, hatred, crime, violence, strife, war and the accompanying economic, social and cultural upheavals.

It is all too easy to envisage a scenario in which, "Throughout the land, declares the LORD, two thirds in it shall be cut off and expire and one third in it shall survive" (Zechariah 13:8).

On the "third in it that shall survive", Rashi explains: "They shall convert and they shall live", (*yitgay'ru ve'yichyu*). The term "they shall convert", *yitgay'ru*, can apply equally to the *Ger Tzeddek* and the *Ger Toshav*.

If so, shining Torah to the Nations is a mission of mercy and literal rescue from death.

The "rod" of Mashiach is the "quill" with which he pens his Torah teachings:

> Initially [in the First Redemption from Egypt, Moses split] the physical sea, consisting of that "material" [i.e. the revealed Torah of Asiyah], but in the Final

Redemption, the "Splitting of the Sea is entirely in the Sea of the Torah [namely the revelation of her secrets]. The rod with which he will split the sea in the future is the quill, because upon it is revealed the Arm of the LORD, of which it is said: "Upon whom is the Arm of the LORD revealed?" (Isaiah 53:1).
Tikuney Zohar, Tikun 21, Daf 43a

In the words of Hillel: "Be of the disciples of Aaron, loving peace and pursuing peace, loving humanity (Hebrew: *ha'briyot*, literally, 'the creations') and drawing them close to the Torah" *(Pirkey Avot 1:12).*

Therefore, we put our hope in You, O LORD our God, to see soon the glory of Your strength, to remove all idols from the earth, and to cut off completely all false gods; to repair the world under the sovereignty of the Eternal, and for all living flesh to call upon Your Name, and for all the wicked of the Earth to turn to You. May all the world's inhabitants recognize and know that to You every knee must bend and every tongue must swear loyalty. Before You, O Lord our God, may all bow down, and give honor to Your precious Name, and may all take upon themselves the yoke of Your rule. And may You reign over them soon and forever and always. Because all rule is Yours alone, and You will rule in honor forever and ever, as it is written in Your Torah: "The LORD will reign forever and ever." And it is said: "The LORD will be Ruler over the whole Earth, and on that day, God will be One, and His name will be One.

Last paragraph of the *Aleinu* prayer, recited three times daily at the conclusion of every Jewish prayer service

Rabbi Nathan's prayer for the Captive Souls

From *Likutey Tefilot* Part I, Prayer 17 (translated by Avraham Greenbaum, printed in Volume 2 of "The Fiftieth Gate", Breslov Research Institute)

Charity – the key to unlocking the exiled Godliness

Loving God: Help me give abundant charity to genuinely deserving, needy people, and to the true Tzaddikim, so that I may become unified with a multitude of the souls of Israel and thereby bring the good hidden within me out into the light. You know the great beauty, the holiness and goodness I have inside me. It's just that they've been suppressed and locked away in a long, bitter exile for years and years, from my very first day on earth until today. I've still not been able to take myself in hand and bring this hidden good out of exile and into the light. I find it impossible to keep in mind where I am in the world. I don't know what to do to bring out the good I have inside me.

Please, God, guide me as to what I should do. Show me Your love and give me complete success. Do wonders with me and give me *life*. Don't let me be like a dead person in my own lifetime! Treat me with the unstinting kindness that befits You, not according to my wrongful, shameful behavior and attitudes. Please have pity on my poor, broken soul and stir up Your compassion for the essential goodness within me. Only with this will I be able to fight and conquer the body and its desires, until the good will take command over the bad and all my bodily desires and bad character traits will be removed, and I will always lead my life the way You want me to.

Father in Heaven! Father in Heaven! Kind, truly loving Father, Who takes pity on the poor and hears the cry of the needy; Who sees the disgrace of the wretched, and hears and attends to a cry from the lowest depths of hell and lower. There is no sigh or cry from anywhere that You do not hear. Teach me and guide me as to what I should say to You. Let me know what I should cry out to You.

Please, please have pity on me! I feel so humiliated. My heart is so crushed. I feel so bereft of intelligence and sensitivity. I am so weak, so confused, so driven, so mixed up. The good inside me is literally trapped and imprisoned in a bitter exile. I'm hemmed in by thousands and thousands of fences, barriers and walls of iron. Thousands upon thousands of guards and lurking enemies stand in wait for me the whole time, and they won't give me back my soul!

I find it impossible to do even the slightest thing in the proper way. Even when I feel inspired to do something holy, I feel incapable of taking the smallest step with the beauty and splendor that befit an Israelite, as You know. Woe! It is so bitter! bitter! Woe! It is all so very bitter. Woe for my soul - the soul that acted this way! Woe for the days and years I've wasted on vain emptiness, futility and evil. Master of everything: to You I cry and scream. Compassionate God! Turn Your ear to me and hear! Open Your eyes and see my devastation! See my wretched plight!

Master of the Universe: In Your great love, You gave me the privilege of being a member of the People of Israel. You were kind to me and brought me close to the true Tzaddikim – to believe in them and long for them. In the merit of those holy saints, now at rest in the earth, deal with me kindly and help me experience a true spiritual awakening. Let the good within me be genuinely aroused and let me be aware of it! Let the good in me come to understand its great worth and know from where it was taken – from the Supreme Thought of the Holy One, blessed be He. There I arose in the Primordial Thought, together with all the souls of Israel – and I, the lightest creature in the "sea" – above all the four worlds, *Atzilut, Beriyah, Yetzirah* and *Asiyah*...

In my root I am higher than all of them, for I am a member of the People of Israel, who arose in the Primordial Thought. With us God took counsel in creating all the worlds and everything in them, down to the depths of *Asiyah* – this world, together with everything in it, in the heavens, on earth and in the seas.

And now, after all this, please help me! Strengthen me! Fortify me! Stir me and let me *wake up*! Kind, loving God: Help me realize exactly where I am, where I've been cast down to, and how distanced I've been from You for so long. Would anyone believe that the true goodness rooted inside me could have been cast down to such a dismal, shadowy, lowly place, into such abject darkness, down to such degraded, lowly places – places so remote from holiness that they can't even be called places?

Please, God, have pity on me! Every time I want to speak to You and express my feelings, I have no idea where to start or how to finish. I'm under such extreme pressures and my needs are so many that even tens of thousands of pages wouldn't be enough to explain them all. As a result, I can't open my mouth at all. Even when I do start to talk a little, everything I say is confused, because I have so many different needs that I cannot begin to set them all out and explain everything.

But to You, Master of everything, all secrets are revealed going right back to the very beginnings of creation. You know what is hidden in our hearts and in the depths of our thoughts, and how in my innermost, innermost thoughts, the good in me screams out in the most heart-rending, unbearably bitter voice. The true pity of my condition is beyond all measure. Then why have You closed Your ear to me and hidden Your face for so long? Why have You held back Your love from me?

O LORD our God and God of our fathers: Just as You showed such abundant love and kindness in creating me a member of the People of Israel, so too may it be Your will to arouse Your mercy for me now and help me attend carefully to the words of the true Tzaddikim. Let my eyes be open and my ears hear and my heart understand their message, because their constant labor is to awaken the goodness rooted in the souls of the Jewish People and lift it out of its exile, by bringing people to repent and making converts.

Let me hear the voice of the Tzaddikim of this generation, and the words of the true Tzaddikim now at rest in the earth, as written in their holy works. Let me hear, see and understand their holy words, until the good within me is awakened in its full strength and holy power, so that I will fight against the evil in me, break it, and drive it out of me completely. Let me return to You with all my heart in perfect, genuine Teshuvah – Repentance – and live in the way You want me to live in holiness, purity, joy and good-heartedness.

O God: Please, have pity on me and fulfill my request. And so too, loving God, let the truth be revealed to the whole world, and let the entire People of Israel be aroused so that they come to complete repentance. Let those who are far from You hear and come to recognize the power of Your sovereignty. Show Your love for the People of Israel, and for the good that is imprisoned among the Nations of the world. O God: It is in Your power to work mighty miracles and wonders. Do so now, and send a new awareness to the goodness that is scattered and dispersed amongst the Nations, so far away from holiness. Let those scattered, exiled souls realize where they are in the world, and where they are likely to go, God forbid, if they do not come back to their Source. Arouse them until they take themselves in hand and remember God and repent and convert wholeheartedly.

O God: You alone know the full tragedy of this goodness, imprisoned as it is in such places. You know the truth, that nothing in the world is more pitiful. No pain and suffering on earth can compare with the unbearably bitter torment suffered by this good, which is in such deep exile and so far away from its Father in Heaven. "What does it benefit the Father to have banished His children? And woe to the son who has gone into exile from his Father's table!" Woe! How bitter for this son! Woe! how terribly, terribly bitter for this son, who was once in such an exalted place and has now fallen so low.

If You Yourself will not take pity upon us, who will? Who will stand up for us? We have no-one to depend upon except You, Heavenly Father. The true Tzaddikim, who had the power to arouse the imprisoned good to awareness of the truth, have passed away because of our many sins. What are we to do in this time of trouble, the like of which has never been? We have been left like a solitary mast on top of a mountain, like a lone banner on a hill. We have nothing to lean upon for support. Our strength is gone. We have no-one to lead us and help us. See how impoverished we are. Our hearts are full of pain and sorrow. Help us, because we are relying on You, for You are good to all.

For the sake of Your goodness and glory, do what You will do to bring all this scattered and dispersed goodness out of its exile among the Nations and back to holiness. Keep on bringing more and more true converts and penitents back, until the whole People of Israel and all the people in the world will turn to You with all their hearts. Let us see the splendor of Your power, and let all the idols and false gods be utterly cut off, until the dominion of the eternal God will be revealed over the whole world and all flesh will call on Your Name. Let all the wicked turn to You, and all the inhabitants of the earth will acknowledge You and know that to You every knee must bend and every tongue swear.

Index of Sages and Sources

Amora (plural: Amora'im)
Generic term for a Torah sage in the generations following the Tannaim of the Mishnah who is quoted in the Jerusalem or Babylonian Talmud or Midrashim. The Amora'im reviewed, analyzed, compared and contrasted the many oral formulations of the law and other teachings received by tradition from the different schools of the Tannaim.

Arukh HaShulchan
See **Yechiel Michel Epstein, Rabbi.**

Avraham ben David, Rabbi ("Raavad" c. 1125-1198)
Talmudic commentator and key link in the chain of Torah mysticism; author of the Hasagot, critical glosses on Rambam's Mishneh Torah.

Baal Shem Tov (c. 1698-1760)
Literally "Master of the Good Name". This is the title given to Rabbi Israel son of Eliezer, healer, outstanding mystic, and founder of the Chassidic movement.

Ben Yehoyada
Commentary on the Babylonian Talmud by Rabbi Yosef Chaim, the "Ben Ish Chai" (1835-1909), outstanding sage and halachic authority from Baghdad.

Chayey Moharan, "The Life of Our Master Rabbi Nachman"
Biographical work compiled by Rabbi Nachman's closest disciple, Rabbi Nathan of Breslov, recounting numerous episodes in the Rebbe's life and recording many of his sayings, teachings and parables. Translated into English by Avraham Greenbaum under the title Tzaddik, published by Breslov Research Institute (1986).

David Kimche, Rabbi, ("RaDaK" 1160–1235)
Leading Biblical commentator, philosopher and grammarian.

Epstein, Yechiel Mikhel, Rabbi (*Arukh HaShulchan* 1829-1908)
Halakhic authority known as the Arukh HaShulchan after his magnum opus of that name, explaining and analyzing all the laws in the classic Shulchan Arukh Torah law code.

Gemara
Generic term for the Talmud and its teachings as handed down by oral tradition.

Ge'onim
Plural of Ga'on, literally "luminary", referring to the outstanding spiritual leaders and scholars who headed the Talmudic academies that flourished in Babylon and Israel from the 7th to 13th centuries C.E.

Gershom ben Yehuda, Rabbi (960-1040)
Rabbenu Gershom Me'or HaGolah, "Light of the Diaspora", lived and taught in Germany and is considered the spiritual father of Ashkenazic Jewry. He enacted important prohibitions including that against polygamy.

Halakhah
Practical Torah law as derived by the legal authorities from the Biblical, Talmudic and other rabbinical sources.

Hillel ("The Great" or "The Elder") 110 B.C.E.-10 C.E.
Born in Babylon, Hillel ascended to Jerusalem where he became head of the Sanhedrin in the time of King Herod and Emperor Augustus. He was renowned for his love, piety and endless patience. His disciples are known as Beit Hillel, the "House" or "School" of Hillel.

Ibn Ezra c. 1089-c. 1167
Rabbi Avraham ben Meir Ibn Ezra, leading medieval Jewish Bible commentator and philosopher.

Joel Schwartz, Rabbi, b. 1939
Torah scholar and prolific writer on Noahide law, teacher in Yeshivat Dvar Yerushalayim, Jerusalem, Deputy Chancellor of the Renewed Sanhedrin and Chief Justice of the Court for Noahide Issues.

Karaites
A breakaway sect that originated in Second Temple times and later expanded, with adherents until today, who consider themselves the authentic Israelites but recognize only the authority of the Written Torah while denying the Oral Tradition as codified in the Mishnah, Talmud and Halakhah.

Kli Yakar
Classic commentary on the Five Books of Moses by Rabbi Shlomo Ephraim ben Aaron Luntschitz (1550-1619).

Likutey Moharan
Collected teachings of Rabbi Nachman of Breslov (1772-1810).

Likutey Tefilot
Collection of prayers based on the lessons in Rabbi Nachman of Breslov's master work, *Likutey Moharan*, composed by his leading disciple, Rabbi Nathan (or Nosson) of Breslov and translated into English and published by Breslov Research Institute under the title "The Fiftieth Gate".

Maimonides (RaMBaM 1138-1204)
Rabbi Moses Maimonides, known as RaMBaM from the acronym of the initial letters of his full Hebrew name, Rabbi Moshe Ben Maimon, outstanding physician, scientist, philosopher and Torah scholar, author of the comprehensive *Mishneh Torah* law code.

Meir ben Todros HaLevi Abulafia, Rabbi ("Ramah" c. 1170-1244)
Prominent Spanish Talmudist and Halakhic authority.

Menachem Azariah of Pano, Rabbi (1548–1620)
Italian Talmudist and Kabbalist.

Mishnah
First written codification of the Oral Torah, redacted in Israel in the 3rd century C.E. by Rabbi Yehuda HaNasi (R. Judah the Prince, c. 135-217 C.E.). The teachings in the Mishnah are analyzed and discussed in the Talmud.

Mishnah Berurah
The "Clarified Teaching" by Rabbi Yisrael Meir Kagan (1838–1933), also known as the *Chofetz Chaim* ("He who desires life" Psalms 34:13). *Mishnah Berurah* is a commentary on all of *Orach Chayim*, first of the four parts of the *Shulchan Arukh* dealing with laws of prayer, synagogue, Shabbat and holidays.

Mishneh Torah
Comprehensive Torah Law Code in fourteen volumes covering all of the 613 Commandments in all their details, by Rabbi Moshe ben Maimon (RaMBaM, Moses Maimonides 1138-1204). The *Mishneh Torah* is also called *Yad HaChazakah*, the "Mighty Hand", where the word *Yad*, the sum of the mathematical values of whose Hebrew letters is 14, alludes to the 14 volumes of the work.

Moshe ben Maimon, Rabbi (1138-1204)
Known as RaMBaM or Rabbi Moses Maimonides, outstanding physician, scientist, philosopher and Torah scholar, author of the comprehensive *Mishneh Torah* law code.

Moshe ben Nachman, Rabbi, (RaMBaN or Nachmanides, 1194-1270)
Known as "RaMBaN" from the acronym of the initial Hebrew letters of his full Hebrew name, Rabbi Moshe Ben Nachman, he was a leading medieval rabbi, philosopher, physician, kabbalist and commentator on the Five Books of Moses and Talmud.

Nachman of Breslov, Rabbi (*"Moharan"*, "Our Teacher, Rabbi Nachman" 1772-1810)
Great grandson of Rabbi Israel Baal Shem Tov (c. 1698-1760), founder of the Chassidic movement. Through combining kabbalistic Torah teachings with in-depth scholarship, R. Nachman revived the movement with "a new pathway which

is really the old, old pathway our ancestors followed", the path of Torah study and practice combined with personal prayer and devotion. He attracted thousands of followers during his lifetime, and his influence continues to spread.

Nachmanides
See Moshe ben Nachman, Rabbi.

Nathan (or Nosson) of Breslov, Rabbi (1780-1844)
Leading disciple of Rabbi Nachman, he transcribed and printed all his master's works as well as composing his own prayers, collected in *Likutey Tefilot*, and authoring extensive Torah discourses of his own based on Rabbi Nachman's lessons, collected in *Likutey Halakhot*.

Pirkey Avot
"Chapters of the Fathers", one of the 63 tractates of the Mishnah compiling in six chapters the ethical sayings and maxims of the Mishnaic sages.

Raavad
Rabbi Avraham ben David (c. 1125-1198). Talmudic commentator and key link in the chain of Torah mysticism; author of the *Hasagot*, critical glosses on Rambam's *Mishneh Torah*.

RaDaK
David Kimche, Rabbi (1160–1235), prominent Biblical commentator, philosopher and grammarian.

RaMBaM
Acronym of **R**abbi **M**oshe **B**en **M**aimon, Moses Maimonides (1138-1204), outstanding physician, scientist and Torah scholar, author of the comprehensive *Mishneh Torah* law code.

RaMBaN
Acronym of **R**abbi **M**oshe **B**en **N**achman, also known as Nachmanides. Leading medieval rabbi, philosopher, physician, kabbalist and commentator on the Five Books of Moses and Talmud.

Rabbi Nissim ben Reuven, ("RaN", 1320-1376)
Known also as Rabbi Nissim of Gerona (or Gerondi), he was one
of the last great medieval Spanish Talmudists.

Rashi
Acronym of **Rabbi Shlomo Yitzchaki** (1040-1105). Outstanding
medieval French rabbi, acclaimed for his ability to present the
basic meaning of Torah texts clearly and concisely. He authored
the most celebrated commentary on the Five Books of Moses as
well as commentaries on the other books of the Hebrew Bible
(*NaKh*) and on most of the Babylonian Talmud.

Rav ("Abba Arikha" 175-247 C.E.)
Amora of the first generation after the redaction of the Mishnah,
he was a descendant of a distinguished Babylonian family who
traced their lineage to King David's brother Shimei. He founded
the Academy of Sura for systematic study of the Oral Law and
debated on many issues with Shmuel of Nehardea.

Rav Nissim ben Yaakov Gaon (990-1062)
Head of the Kairouan academy in Tunisia, known for his
Talmudic commentary *HaMafte'ach* ("The Key").

Ravina
An Amora of the later generations, died c. 420 C.E.

Sa'adiah ben Yosef Gaon, Rav (882/892-942)
Prominent rabbi, philosopher and exegete of the post Talmudic
period of the Ge'onim ("luminaries"), known for his works on
Hebrew linguistics, Halakhah and philosophy.

Samuel HaKohen ben Hofni (d. 1034)
Gaon of the Sura Torah Academy in the city of Sura, Babylon
from 998 to 1012. Author of responsa on Torah law and many
lost works including commentaries on Talmud written in Arabic,
of which fragments survive.

Shaar Hagilgulim
"Gate of the Incarnations", one of the *Shmoneh Shaarim*, "Eight
Gates" written by Rabbi Chaim Vital (1542-1620) setting forth

all the teachings in different areas that he received from his master, the kabbalistic giant Rabbi Yitzchak Luria, "ARI" (1534-72).

Shammai (50 B.C.E.-30 C.E.)
Leading contemporary of Hillel and *Av Beit Din*, deputy president of the Sanhedrin. Though very different in personality from Hillel, Shammai disagreed with him only on three issues. However, his disciples, the "House" or "School" of Shammai, disputed many halakhic questions with the disciples of the "House" or "School" of Hillel.

Shevachey Ha-Baal Shem Tov
"Praises of the Baal Shem Tov", the earliest collection of biographical information and stories about Rabbi Israel Baal Shem Tov (1698-1760), founder of the Chassidic movement.

Shevachay HaRan
"The Praise of Rebbe Nachman", by his leading disciple, Rabbi Nathan (or Nosson) of Breslov, giving details of Rabbi Nachman's personal devotions and a full account of his pilgrimage to the Holy Land in 1798-9. Published in "Rabbi Nachman's Wisdom" (Breslov Research Institute).

Shimon ben Lakish, Rabbi (*Reish Lakish*, c.200-c.275)
Leading Amora. According to the Babylonian Talmud, circumstances forced him to give up Torah study in his early youth and he became a gladiator, until he was brought back to his studies by Rabbi Yochanan, who became his teacher and debating partner. Their discussions are recorded throughout the Talmud.

Shlomo Ephraim ben Aaron Luntschitz, Rabbi (1550-1619)
Author of the *Kli Yakar* classic commentary on the Five Books of Moses.

Shmuel (c. 165-254 C.E.)
Shmuel of Nehardea or Shmuel bar Abba, often simply called **Shmuel**, was an Amora of the first generation after the redaction of the Mishnah, a judge, physician and astronomer and head

of the Yeshivah of Nehardea in Babylon. He debated on many issues with "Rav", Abba Arikha.

Shmuel Eidels, Rabbi (*Maharsha*, 1555-1631)
Renowned Polish scholar, famous for his Talmudic commentaries *Chiddushei Halachot*, on legal questions, and *Chiddushei Aggadot* on rabbinic lore, anecdotes, moral exhortations and practical advice.

Shulchan Arukh, "The Set Table"
The standard code of Torah law as applicable in non-Temple times, written in Safed, Israel in 1563 by Rabbi Joseph Karo (1488-1575). Its four major parts cover (1) the laws of prayer, blessings, Shabbat and festivals; (2) Kashrut, family purity, charity, circumcision, conversion, death and mourning; (3) business life and damages; (4) marriage and divorce.

Siach Sarfey Kodesh
Collection of sayings of Rabbi Nachman of Breslov and his followers in the ensuing generations of the Breslover Chassidim.

Sifrei
Midrash Halakhah, classical rabbinic legal biblical exegesis on the books of Numbers and Deuteronomy.

Steinsaltz, Rabbi Adin (1937-2020)
Rabbi, teacher, philosopher, author and publisher. Pioneered a new edition of the Talmud with modern Hebrew translation and running commentary, now translated into English and other languages. In 2004 he was appointed as Nasi, President of the Renewed Sanhedrin.

Talmud
The central text of rabbinic Judaism and primary source of Torah law and tradition. The term *Talmud* is usually used to refer to the collection of volumes or "tractates" making up the "Babylonian" Talmud, (*Talmud Bavli*), completed in Babylon in the 6th century C.E., but it may also refer to the "Jerusalem" Talmud (*Talmud Yerushalmi*), which was completed earlier in Israel during the 4th century C.E. In both cases, each Talmudic tractate follows its

corresponding tractate in the Mishnah, quoting each individual paragraph of Mishnah, and then analyzing and elucidating it in relation to other teachings, as well as venturing into many other subjects and extensive Biblical exegesis.

Talmud Bavli see **Talmud**

Talmud Yerushalmi see **Talmud**

TaNaKh
The Hebrew Bible. *TaNaKh* is an acronym of the initial Hebrew letters of Torah (Five Books of Moses), Nevi'im (Prophets) and Ketuvim (Holy Writings).

Tanna (plural: Tanna'im)
Generic term for one of the sages of the Mishnah or one of their disciples, who memorized and constantly repeated and reviewed the traditional formulations of the Oral Law as received from their teachers.

Tanna d'vei Eliyahu
Collection of Midrashic teachings revealed by Elijah the Prophet to Rabbi Anan, a Babylonian teacher of the 3rd century C.E.

Tikuney Zohar
A collection of 70 kabbalistic discourses on the first Hebrew word of the Torah attributed to the outstanding Tanna of the 2nd century C.E., Rabbi Shimon bar Yochai ("RaShBY"), foremost disciple of Rabbi Akiva and author of the *Zohar*.

Tosafot
Critical and explanatory glosses on the Babylonian Talmud by leading rabbis in medieval France and Germany, printed in most Talmud editions on the outer margin of each page opposite Rashi's notes.

Tur
Short for *Arba'ah Turim*, "The Four Rows" (alluding to the gems in the High Priest's breast plate, Exodus 27:17), a Halakhic code composed by Rabbi Yaakov ben Asher (Cologne, 1270-Toledo, Spain c. 1340), also known as *Ba'al Ha-Turim*. The four-part

structure of the *Tur* and its division into chapters (simanim) were adopted by the later mandatory *Shulchan Arukh* law code.

Tzaddik
Title of the English translation of *Chayey Moharan* ("The Life of Our Master Rabbi Nachman") by his closest disciple, Rabbi Nathan (or Nosson) of Breslov, recounting numerous episodes in the Rebbe's life and recording many of his sayings, teachings and parables. Translated by Avraham Greenbaum (Breslov Research Institute 1986).

Yisrael Meir Kagan, Rabbi ("*Chafetz Chayim*", 1838-1933)
Known as the *Chafetz Chayim*, "He who desires life" (Psalms 34:13) from the title of his book on purity of speech, he is renowned as the author of the *Mishnah Berurah* commentary on *Orach Chayim*, "The Path of Life", the first part of the *Shulchan Arukh* Torah law code dealing with laws of prayer, synagogue, Shabbat and holidays.

Yechiel Michel Epstein, Rabbi (1829-1908)
Halakhic authority known as the *Arukh HaShulchan* after his magnum opus explaining in depth and with great clarity all the laws in the four sections of the *Shulchan Arukh* Torah law code.

Yehudah ben Beteira
Eminent Mishnaic Tanna in late Second Temple times, credited with holy spirit.

Yochanan, Rabbi (180-279 C.E.)

Rabbi Yochanan bar Nappaha (180-279 C.E.)
leading rabbi in the land of Israel in the second generation of the Amoraim, the teachers who expounded the Mishnah. His opinions are quoted thousands of times throughout the Jerusalem and Babylonian Talmuds, and he is generally considered to be the compiler of the Jerusalem Talmud. Not to be confused with Rabban Yochanan ben Zakkai (1st century C.E.) who was a student of Hillel and head of the Sanhedrin at the time of the destruction of the Second Temple and thereafter.

Yosef Karo, Rabbi (1488-1575)
Author of the *Shulchan Arukh* ("The Set Table"), standard code of Torah law as applicable in non-Temple times, written in Safed, Israel in 1563.

Zohar
Discourses of the 2nd Century Tanna, Rabbi Shimon bar Yochai (RaShBY) and his disciples, woven into an extensive Kabbalistic commentary on the Five Books of Moses.

Appendix A

MIDRASHIC SOURCES ON THE UNIFICATION OF JUDAH AND ISRAEL
Prepared by AnaRina Bat Tzion Kreisman

Yalkut Shimoni, Song of Solomon 905
"Behold thou art fair, my love, yea pleasant, also our bed is green" - Song of Solomon 1:16.

"Israel says: Behold thou art fair, my love When you will take retribution from the worshippers of idols. Yea pleasant when you pay the reward of those who fear you. Also our bed...: These are the "Ten Tribes." In Hebrew bed is "eres" while ten is "eser" and uses the same letters, and "our bed" (erseynu) sounds like "our ten" (esereynu). They are those who were exiled beyond the Sambation River. The exiles of Judah and Benyamin [i.e. the present-day "Jews"] are destined to go unto them and bring them back in order to merit with them the Messianic Era and life in the World-To-Come. This is as it says, "In those days the house of Judah shall go unto the house of Israel and they shall come together out of the land of the north unto the land that I have given for an inheritance unto your fathers" (Jeremiah 3:18).

Tanchuma, Nizavim, 4
By way of nature, if a person takes a bunch of reeds and tries to break it in two at one go, he cannot do it. If the reeds are separated one by one even a child can break them. We thus find that Israel and Judah will not be redeemed until they be united in one confederation, as it says, [Jeremiah 3:18] In those days the house of Judah shall walk with the house of Israel, and they shall come together out of the land of the north to the land that I have given for an inheritance unto your fathers.

When they are united, they will be able to receive the presence of God almighty.

Midrash Tanchuma, VaYigash, 4

Isaiah 11:13 - "The envy also of Ephraim shall depart, and the adversaries of Judah shall be cut off, Ephraim shall not envy Judah, and Judah shall not vex Ephraim Concerning who did Isaiah pronounce this prophecy. He was speaking only concerning Judah and Joseph. Said Rabbi Shmuel son of Nachman in the name of Rabbi Yonathan, when Joseph and Judah were arguing (Genesis41:18) the Holy Angels said to each other, Let us go down and see what is happening. Usually when a bull and a lion confront each other the bull retreats before the lion. In this case a bull (Joseph) and a lion (Judah) are arguing and there is a standoff. Jealousy will continue to abide between these two until the Messiah comes, as it says, "the envy also of Ephraim shall depart, and the adversaries of Judah shall be cut off, Ephraim shall not envy Judah, and Judah shall not vex Ephraim" - Isaiah 11:13

Midrash Brayshit Rabati

In the past Jeroboam the son of Nebat who was from Ephraim hated King Rehoboam who was from Judah. There was a controversy between them. In the future there will be peace between these two anointed leaders. They will not be jealous of each other. Concerning them, it says: "the envy also of Ephraim shall depart, and the adversaries of Judah shall be cut off, Ephraim shall not envy Judah, and Judah shall not vex Ephraim" - Isaiah 11:13

Midrash Agadat Brayshit 63

Everywhere you find these two tribes (Judah and Joseph) hating each other and antagonistic to each other, etc. May we infer from this that even the future Anointed Captain of War (who will arise from Joseph) and the Anointed Messiah (who will arise from Judah) will (Heaven forbid) be jealous of each other? No. There will be no antagonism between them, as it says, "the envy also of Ephraim shall depart, and the adversaries of Judah shall be cut off, Ephraim shall not envy Judah, and Judah shall not vex Ephraim" - Isaiah 11:13

Appendix B

SEVEN NOAHIDE LAWS[41]

1. Do not profane G-d's Oneness in any way.

2. Do not curse your Creator.

3. Do not murder.

4. Do not eat a limb of a living animal.

5. Do not steal.

6. Harness and channel the human libido.

7. Establish courts of law and ensure justice in our world.

---

[41] From Chabad.org

Glossary

Aleinu - literally "it is upon us" or "it is our duty", Aleinu is an important Jewish prayer about the obligation to praise God. It is recited in the synagogue three times a day.

Aliyah – immigration to Israel

Amida(h) - the central prayer in Jewish liturgy, also known as the Shemonah Esrei

Am Segula - a beloved or treasured people, generally a Biblical reference to the Nation of Israel

Avraham - Abraham

Ba'al Shem Tov - Rabbi Israel ben Eliezer, 18th century mystic and the founder of Hasidic Judaism

Bamidbar – Book of Numbers

Beit HaMikdash - the Holy Temple in Jerusalem

Bereshit – Book of Genesis

Birkat HaMazon - grace after meals

Bitachon – applied faith

Bracha - blessing

Breslov chassidut – a branch of Chassidic Judaism founded in the 18th c. by Rebbe Nachman of Breslov

Brit Milah - ritual circumcision

Chabad (also Chabad-Lubavitch)– large Chassidic group known for outreach to unaffiliated Jews

Chag (pl. Chagim) - Jewish festival

Challah – braided Shabbat bread

Charedi (also Haredi) - subset of Orthodox Jews characterized by their cloistered lifestyle, often called ultra-Orthodox in the media

Chasidei Umot HaOlam - The pious ones of the nations of the world

Chassidut - the teachings of the Chasidic movement which focuses on spiritual revival and the inner, mystical aspects of Judaism

Chazal - an acronym for the Hebrew *Chachameinu Zikhronam Liv'ravcha* - Our Sages, may their memory be blessed

Chesed - lovingkindness

Chillul Hashem – desecration of God's Name

Chizkiyahu – King Hezekiah

David HaMelech - King David

Derech Eretz – acts of decency and courtesy

Emunah – faith

Eretz Yisrael – the Land of Israel

Galut – exile

Gan Eden - the Garden of Eden

Gehinom - the spiritual realm in which the souls, after the death of the body, are cleansed from the consequences of their sins

Gemara - the Talmud

Geula(h) - the final redemption

Goyim - literally, the Nations, sometimes used pejoratively to refer to non-Jews

Haftara (pl. Haftarot) - a reading from the Books of Prophets that accompanies the weekly Torah portion and is usually connected to it by theme

Halacha (pl. Halachot) - Jewish religious law

Hashem - literally, The Name - a way to refer to God without using one of His holy names

Kabbalah - the mystical tradition in Judaism

Kashrut – Jewish dietary laws

Kavod – honor

Kiddush Hashem – sanctification of God's Name

Kitniyot - literally legumes, a reference to a difference in custom about foods that are permissible to eat on Passover

Klippa(h) (pl. Kipot) - impure or evil spiritual forces that block holiness

Kohen (pl. Kohanim) – member of the priestly lineage

Kohen Gadol - the high priest in the Holy Temple

Korban Pesach - the Passover sacrifice

Koresh – King Cyrus

Maariv – daily evening prayer service

Mashal - a short parable with a moral lesson or religious allegory

Mechokek - Law-giver

Melech HaOlam – King of the World

Menorah - seven-branched lamp that is a symbol of the Holy Temple

Mezuzah - a small scroll with two biblical passages written on it

Midas haDin - God's attribute of strict justice

Midas haRachamim - God's attribute of mercy

Midrash (pl. Midrashim) - biblical exegesis by ancient Judaic authorities

Mishna – central part of the Oral Torah

Mitzvot - Divine commandments

Mikvah - a bath used for ritual immersion in Judaism

Mishne Torah - a code of Jewish law authored by Maimonides

Moshe - Moses

Moshiach - the messianic redeemer

Musaf – additional prayer service on Shabbat and Jewish holidays

Nishmat Kol Chai – literally "the soul of all living" and the name of a prayer of gratitude

Noahide - a follower of a monotheistic Jewish religious movement based upon the Seven Laws of Noah

Olam Haba - the World to Come

Olim (pl) - immigrants to Israel (oleh is a male immigrant, olah is a female immigrant)

Oneg – pleasure

Pasuk (pl. Psukim) - verses, generally referring to Bible verses

Parsha, also Parshat haShavuah - weekly portion of the Five Books of Moses read in synagogue

Perush (pl. Perushim) - Rabbinic commentaries on the Torah

Pesach – Passover

Pesukei d'Zimra - verses of praise, the preliminary part of daily morning prayers

Pinimius of Torah - the hidden, inner dimension of Torah

Pirke Avot - Ethics of the Fathers

Psak Din - ruling in Jewish law

Rabbi Avraham Yitzchak haCohen Kook – first Ashkenazi Chief Rabbi of pre-State Israel

Rabbi Samson Refael Hirsch - 19th c. Jewish Talmudist and philosopher

Rabbi Shimon bar Yochi – 2nd c. sage and author of the Zohar, Kabbalah's foundational text

Rabbi Yehuda Ashlag - early 20th c. Kabbalist known as the Baal HaSulam

Rambam - Maimonides (Rabbi Moshe ben Maimon) very important 12th c. Torah scholar

Rashab - Rabbi Shalom Dov Ber, the fifth Rebbe of Lubavitch

Rashi - preeminent commentator on the Torah and Talmud. Lived 1040-1105.

Rosh Hashana - the holiday that marks the beginning of the new Hebrew year

Ruach HaKodesh - A divine spirit of holiness and a lower form of prophecy

Safed - Tzfat, one of Israel's four holiest cities

Sfas Emes - also known as the Sfat Emet after the name of his most well-known work, Rabbi Yehudah Aryeh Leib Alter served as the Rebbe of the Gerrer Chasidim in 19th c. Poland

Shabbat – Sabbath

Shamor – guard

Shavuot – holiday marking the giving of the Torah on Mt. Sinai

Sheitel - wig

Shema - an important Jewish prayer that declares the Oneness of God

Sheva Mitzvah B'nai Noach - the seven laws of Noah

Shofar – ram's horn

Shituf - the worship of God in a manner which Judaism does not deem to be purely monotheistic

Shlomo Hamelech - King Solomon

Shulchan Aruch - the Code of Jewish Law

Siddur – Jewish prayer book

Spodik - a tall, black fur hat worn by some Chassidic men

Sukkot – Feast of Tabernacles

Tallit – prayer shawl

Tallit katan - four-cornered garment worn under a shirt to which tzitzit are attached

Tanach - Hebrew scriptures

Tashlich - a Jewish atonement ritual performed between Rosh Hashana and Yom Kippur

Tefillah – Jewish prayer

Tehillim – Book of Psalms

Teshuva – repentance

Tikkun (pl. Tikkunim) - spiritual correction/rectification

Tikkun Shavuot - the custom to stay up all night and learn Torah on Shavuot

Tikkunei Zohar – a main text of Kabbalah

Tzadikim - righteous people

Tzedakah – charity

Tzitzit - ritual fringes attached to four-cornered garments

Yaakov - Jacob

Yeshayahu – Isaiah

Yeshiva – school for advanced Torah study

Yigdal - an important Jewish prayer based on the 13 Principles of Faith formulated by Maimonides

Yitzchak - Isaac

Yom HaShoah – Holocaust Remembrance Day

Yom Kippur – Day of Atonement

Yom Tov – Jewish holiday

Yosef – Joseph

Zachor - remember

Zohar - a classic text in Jewish mysticism

Z"l - (also zt"l) of blessed memory; an honorific for a righteous person who passed away

Bibliography

Adler, Rivkah Lambert. *Ten From The Nations: Torah Awakening Among Non-Jews*. Geula Watch Press, 2017.

Bar-Ron, Rabbi Michael Shelomo. *Guide for the Noahide*. Springdale, Arkansas: Lightcatcher Books, 2010.

Bindman, Rabbi Yirmeyahu. *The Seven Colors of the Rainbow: Torah Ethics for Non-Jews*. Resource Publications, Inc., San Jose, California. 1995.

Cherki, Rabbi Oury. *Brit Olam: Prayer Book for Noahides*. Noahide World Center, 2015.

Clorfene, Chaim and David Katz. *The World of the Ger*. 2004.

Clorfene, Chaim and Yakov Rogalsky. *The Path of the Righteous Gentile*. Jerusalem, Israel: Feldheim Books, 1987. Second edition printed by CreateSpace, 2016.

Cowen, Shimon Dovid. *The Theory & Practice of Universal Ethics: The Noahide Laws*. The Institute for Judaism and Civilization, 2015.

Dallen, Michael Ellias. *The Rainbow Covenant*. Springdale, Arkansas:Lightcatcher Books, 2003.

Feld, Rabbi Avraham and OvadYah Avrahami. *Jewish Secrets Hidden in the New Testament: The growing global Torah revolution*. Eldad Publishers, Jerusalem. 2013.

Ginsburgh, Rabbi Yitzchak. *Kabbalah and Meditation for the Nations*. Gal Einai, Jerusalem. 2007.

Greenbaum, Avraham. *Torah for the Nations: Commentary on the weekly Torah readings from the Five Books of Moses with lessons for people of all Nations, backgrounds and beliefs.* Promised Land Publishers, 2019.

Greenbaum, Avraham. *Universal Torah: Lessons for Humanity from the Weekly Torah Readings.* Promised Land Publishers, 2018.

Katz, David. *Laws of Ger Toshav: Pious of the Nations.* Printed by CreateSpace, 2017.

Katz, David. *Soul Mazal: Classic Torah Commentary for Bnei Noach.* Printed by CreateSpace, 2016.

Lichtenstein, Aaron. *The Seven Laws of Noah.* Z Berman Books, 1995 (3rd edition)

Nagen, Yakov. *Be, Become, Bless - Jewish Spirituality between East and West.* Koren Publishers, 2019.

Ophir, Adi and Ishay Rosen-Zvi. *Goy: Israel's Others and the Birth of the Gentile.* Oxford University Press, 2020.

Schwartz, Rabbi Yoel. *A Light Unto the Nations.* Jerusalem, Israel: Yeshivat D'var Yerushalayim, 1988 (out of print)

Weiner, Rabbi Moshe. *The Divine Code.* Ask Noah International, 2018. (3rd edition)

www.ingramcontent.com/pod-product-compliance
Lightning Source LLC
Chambersburg PA
CBHW021138090426
42740CB00008B/829